GATEWAY CITIES
&
OTHER ESSAYS

GATEWAY
CITIES
&
OTHER ESSAYS

Leonard K. Eaton

GREAT PLAINS ENVIRONMENTAL DESIGN SERIES

Iowa State University Press / Ames

Leonard K. Eaton is Professor Emeritus at the University of Michigan, Ann Arbor.

Manufactured in the United States of America

♾ This book is printed on acid-free paper.

First edition, 1989
International Standard Book Number: 0–8138–0346–2

Library of Congress Cataloging-in-Publication Data

Eaton, Leonard K.
    Gateway cities & other essays / Leonard K. Eaton. — 1st ed.
        p. cm.—(Great Plains environmental design series)
    Bibliography: p.
    Includes index.
    ISBN 0–8138–0346–2
    1. Warehouses—Middle West. 2. Commercial buildings—Middle West.
    I. Title. II. Series.
    NA6342.E2   1989
    725′.35′0977—dc19   89–1849

For
ANN

CONTENTS

SERIES EDITOR'S INTRODUCTION

Leonard Eaton is one of architecture's leading social historians. Long involved with questions other than style, Eaton reminds us that architecture is the product of clients, business climates, and socio-political contexts. In this collection, Eaton turns his attention to his native ground, the prairie-plains and their commercial and political iconography.

There is much that binds these essays together. They are cast, for example, within the framework of nineteenth-century transportation history, the big rivers being the basis for settlement, the big railroads the basis for continuous development. The "gateway cities" are the principal issue, along with the economic and social systems that underpin them. The location of these cities is crucial. In an essay written in 1894 Charles Horton Cooley laid down the theoretical framework for gateway-type cities when he suggested that "population and wealth tend to collect wherever there is a break in transportation...an interruption of the movement...to cause a transfer of the goods and their temporary storage." Cooley distinguished between two types of interruption—if a "physical interruption of the movement is all that takes place, we have...a mechanical break; but if...this physical interruption causes a change in the ownership of the transported goods, we have a commercial break." Where the latter occurs arises a commercial city. While Cooley was writing about the emergence of cities at the junction of land and water, the same logic holds true for prairie cities where the railroad car replaced the ship.

Prairie settlement was dynamic, played out with the intensity and scale of opera, but amid the hurly-burly of commerce and politics, there were moments of clarity—the sensitivity of Jens Jensen and the rationality of John Wellborn Root. Taken with George Caleb Bingham's pictures, these are the moments of high art, the *bas relief* of the historic fabric. And, thus, in this second volume of our series, Leonard Eaton contributes greatly to the cultural identity of the region.

Herbert Gottfried,
Series Editor

PREFACE

The sources of this book lie in a career which made me an observer and historian of architecture, city planning, landscape design, and painting in various sections of the American Midwest. Given the disparate nature of the essays which are here offered to the reader, I feel I should explain how the volume came to be done.

I grew up in Minneapolis, a city generally considered to be in the heartland of the region. There was not much in my boyhood or youth which indicated that I was destined for a life connected with the arts. As a matter of fact, I came from a family of attorneys. I went to a country day school, which, in those days (1934–1939) offered no instruction in drawing, painting, or art history. On the contrary, there was a fierce insistence on the traditional subjects of the classical curriculum so that graduates could gain admission to an eastern school. There was not much discussion of the new buildings in the city around the family dinner table. As a matter of fact, there were not many new structures in the central business district during those depression years. I did, however, work two summers as an office boy in my father's law firm, and occasionally he used to send me on an errand into the wholesale district. To this day I can recall being impressed by the huge bulk and stern dignity of the buildings there. I also filed a good many papers in the Hennepin County Courthouse, which I later came to recognize as a version of H. H. Richardson's

great Pittsburgh Courthouse. I still think it is one of the finest buildings in the city. But I did not achieve much consciousness of the visual arts until I went east to college in the fall of 1939.

My family held it as an article of faith that Travel Was Broadening and that an Ivy League Education was a Good Thing. Williams was the family college, and I went there without any argument. In the course of four happy undergraduate years I took two courses under young men who later went on to make a great impact on the profession of art history: S. Lane Faison, Jr., and Whitney Stoddard. Faison and Stoddard have had many tributes. I want to record still another. Unhappily I did not take any work with William Pierson, whom I only came to know later. Under their guidance I learned something of how to look at works of art. My enthusiasm was kindled, and on vacations I began to become acquainted with the great museums of Boston and New York. I can still remember my delight in seeing for the first time Renoir's "Bal au Bougival" in Boston.

On April 1, 1943 (the date has always seemed significant to me), I went into the army, and for the next three years there was not a great deal of opportunity to look at architecture, painting, or sculpture in a serious fashion. Military life affects people in various ways. My own experience made me look back on my years at Williams as a kind of golden period. I could imagine few careers as rewarding as that of a faculty member. After some dalliance with the idea of medical school (I had been a company aid man), I entered Harvard in the fall of 1946 to pursue a doctoral degree in the history of American civilization. At Williams I had been an undergraduate major in American history and literature, so this program was a logical consequence. The years at graduate school were also a golden period for me, though of a different sort. The focus was narrower than it had been at Williams, and the discipline was more intense. As luck would have it, I took only two courses in American art and architecture, one with Professor Benjamin Rowlands and the other with Professor K. J. Conant. Scantily equipped, I began to teach architectural history at the University of Michigan in the fall of 1950. Since most of my architectural education has been on-the-job-training, I want to say a word about my colleagues.

In the 1950s the College of Architecture and Design was an interesting place for a young man to work. Dean Wells I. Bennett, who had taken a chance on me, was engaged in revamping the curriculum to bring it more into line with the developing currents of modern architecture. To this end he had brought in two young men from Chicago who were disciples of Mies Van Der Rohe. Joseph P. Albano and Edward V. Olencki became my close friends and unwitting teachers. From them I absorbed a high regard for the discipline of structure and a continuing preoccupation with its expression in architecture. It is also worth noting that both Ed and Joe had a high regard for Frank Lloyd Wright. Although neither of them was greatly enamored of the direction he was then taking, both were aware of the enormous achievement of Wright, and as native Chicagoans, were very much aware of the quality of the old buildings in the Chicago Loop.

My first chairman, the late Professor Walter B. Sanders, was probably more oriented toward Gropius, particularly as a teacher, but he, too, had a fine sense of the stature of Sullivan and Wright. By good fortune Sanders was a warehouse enthusiast. When I happened to mention my boyhood interest in warehouses, it was he who insisted that I read the chapter on mill construction in Kidder-Parker's *Architects and Builders Handbook* so that I might know something about how these fine old buildings went together. Without knowing it, I had come to a school in which the structural discipline was regarded as of primary importance. Hence, when I came to write about warehouses

many years later, I approached them with a strong sense of the structural and functional considerations inherent in the building type.

I had done my first serious historical research at Harvard under Professor A. M. Schlesinger, Sr. From him, and from Professor Conant, I derived my sense of the importance of the social matrix of architecture and the other visual arts. Professor Conant had two requirements in his course on the history of American architecture. The first was that a student produce a scale model of a building important in American history. The other was that he write a paper showing what the building meant to the people who put it up. On reflection I decided that no building could have more social ramifications than a hospital. I liked the old Bulfinch building, the first unit of the Massachusetts General Hospital, and through the courtesy of Walter Muir Whitehill, then the director of the Boston Atheneum, I was able to consult the Alexander Parris drawings for its completion. After much effort I produced a passable model. The paper led me to ask all kinds of questions about how the building had functioned in its early days, who had paid for it, how it had been administered, and the like.

Ever since I have been asking the same kind of questions about the buildings on which I have written. All of the foregoing is not meant to denigrate the issue of symbolism. Iconography certainly has a place in the analysis of architecture, but it is an approach I have used only to a limited extent. I suppose I have never gotten over the admonition of Professor Conant: "If you are going to talk about symbolism in architecture, you had better have something solid—like a written document." Iconography seems to me to be more applicable in the history of painting, and I have certainly used it in the essay on the political pictures of George Caleb Bingham.

Family responsibilities took me back to the Twin Cities at least once a year for more than three decades, and gradually I became convinced that the warehouses I had noticed in my youth were the most distinguished body of architecture that Minneapolis and St. Paul had to offer. My friends and relatives played a peculiar role in this development. All of them were deeply involved in the Minnesota business community. Knowing that I taught in a department of architecture at a rival state university, they invariably asked me what I thought of the new business buildings going up in the city. In fact, I did not think highly of them, and I worked out numerous ways of getting around the subject. On the other hand, my father-in-law worked at the St. Paul Post Office, which is situated close to the warehouse district, and when I met him there, I noticed that the buildings were of as high a quality as those in Minneapolis. In short, the roots of this work go back a long way, and I can scarcely lay claim to the traditional scholarly objectivity.

The event which unquestionably set me to asking deeper questions about the commercial architecture of the Midwest was my reading of the Gateway City novels by the Omaha writer Carl Jonas. These books, to which I make reference later on, presented to me a world so like the one I knew that I was not surprised when, in 1974, Jonas told me that he had received numerous letters from readers in Minneapolis and St. Paul claiming that he had actually written about their cities and their families.

Gateway City, then, is a metaphor for a large number of cities in the Midwest, as Faulkner's Yoknapatawpha County is representative of a great many counties in the rural South. Some of the details of the topography of Gateway City come from Omaha, but they are common to a large number of other places. Particularly important are the river valley, the railroad network, and for this book, the warehouse district. It was the railroad which called large-scale wholesaling into being, and the connection between yard, spur, and warehouse was intimate. The warehouses and the men who built them demand investigation.

I should add that the warehouse problem is no new issue in architectural history. The form has a long association with seaports. The Romans built magnificent vaulted warehouses at Ostia to house the goods which poured in from all over the empire to satisfy the needs of the people of Rome. In the Middle Ages, on the other hand, warehouses were generally small in scale because overseas trade was uncertain and hazardous. Such trade usually involved luxury goods, which were shipped in small quantities, rather than bulk commodities. Surviving examples of medieval warehouses can be seen in Bruges, Lubeck, Visby, and various other European cities with surviving medieval quarters. In the nineteenth century, however, overseas trade expanded enormously, and large warehouses became features of seaports on both sides of the Atlantic. In England those built by Jesse Hartley for Liverpool are among the most notable. In Boston the ex-

cellent warehouses of the 1840s and 1850s may well have given H. H. Richardson his fondness for quarry-faced ashlar. Warehouses are, in fact, not at all an unrecognized building type for American architectural historians. The great Montgomery Ward warehouse in Chicago by Schmidt, Garden, and Martin (1906) is particularly familiar. Those of the gateway cities of the Midwest are, however, relatively little known. The essays in this volume are an attempt to demonstrate the richness of this portion of our heritage.

Coming to maturity in the late thirties and early forties, I was brought up to believe that business was essentially a necessary, if sometimes exploitive, activity. Carl Jonas's businessmen, particularly Jefferson Selleck, were far more complex beings than the much misunderstood creations of Sinclair Lewis, whom I had studied avidly as an undergraduate. They were also much closer to the men I had known in my youth. Since I was committed to a career in architectural history, I was naturally driven to ask questions about the kind of structures these men put up when they were confronted with the problem of building. Year after year, as I studied the office buildings of downtown Minneapolis and St. Paul, I could not feel that these cities had generally achieved anything of much distinction. They were, in fact, a far cry from Chicago. Like most men of my generation, I had come to know and love the masterworks of John Root and Louis Sullivan in that city, and I was also immensely excited by what Carl Condit has called "The Second Chicago School" of the 1960s. There were simply no equivalents in the provinces. Nonetheless, when I retraced my boyhood steps along First Avenue North in Minneapolis, or stopped for a libation at a tavern on Sixth Street in St. Paul in company with my father-in-law, I had the feeling that I was surrounded by a body of architecture which would compare favorably with any that the nineteenth century had produced anywhere. There seemed to be an extraordinary dichotomy between the warehouses and the office buildings.

By the early 1970s my feelings about this dichotomy had intensified enough that I was moved to undertake a closer investigation of the problem. In the spring of 1972 I did a consulting job for the Ann Arbor firm of Johnson, Johnson and Roy, and one of the partners, knowing of my interest in warehouses, remarked that if I were really interested in these buildings, I ought to go down to St. Joseph, Missouri. He had noticed a great many fine warehouses there. I took his suggestion to heart, secured a grant from the American Philosophical Society, and in the following year, made my first field trip to that city.

It was immediately apparent to me that I had hit upon an important body of unexplored work. For the curious reader, I will add that I also visited Kansas City but found that so much had been torn down that any real study was impossible. I went on to Omaha, which, so far as I knew, had not been investigated, and found there the first of the great farm machinery warehouses of Deere & Company to utilize the concrete flat slab system of construction. This innovation introduced an entirely new factor into the work; from this time onward, I became much more concerned with structure and with the possibilities of recycling buildings. It was also clear that the warehouses of St. Joseph and Omaha were superior in design to the office buildings in these cities. The architectural situation was the same as in Minneapolis and St. Paul, and the generalization also held true for smaller places such as Sioux City, Iowa. The problem became one of explaining the generally high quality of warehouse design.

Following Carl Jonas, I termed these places "Gateway City." I was led to investigate the wholesaling industry and the part it played in the urbanization of the Middle West, and I discovered that it was much more important than I had supposed. The economic historian Thomas Cochran wrote me that the wholesaler was the single most important type of American businessman in the period 1850–1890. As late as 1970 wholesaling was still a growth sector of the American economy; the proliferation of items in certain fields, such as hardware and drugs, has made the wholesaler more necessary than ever. The warehouse and the warehouse district, then, become important determinants of the urban form of Gateway City. They were not the only determinants, but they were extremely significant. I came to believe that the planners and people of Gateway City had to understand the quality of the jobbing district and the warehouse if they were to appreciate their potentialities.

Hence I decided to write a book which would analyze the development of a selection of these buildings and their settings. I must immediately add that I have shown only a small portion of the buildings of high quality that I encountered. I deliberately chose to show a limited number of buildings in reasonable detail rather than attempt to

survey the entire field. Also I have included a few buildings contemporary with the warehouses and related to them in order to show the kind of economic activity the district encompassed. Because the clients and their programs are always important, I have included descriptions of the wholesale merchants and their careers whenever I could obtain the material. The pattern is clear. I hope that my sense of the hardihood of these people has been conveyed.

As I gathered information on the Gateway City warehouses and studied the available, rather scanty, literature on the development of this building type, I increasingly began to wonder if the large railway-oriented warehouse was an exclusively American phenomenon. Does anything comparable to these buildings exist in Europe (or elsewhere)? was the question I asked myself. For purposes of comparison I needed a large territory that had been opened up to agricultural exploitation by the railroad in the nineteenth century. Eastern Europe was one possibility. Aside from the expense and linguistic difficulty, there was a problem in that no preliminary work had been done, and the available records were extremely scanty. Canada was much closer, and having taught in British Columbia for some months, I already knew the customs of the country fairly well and was convinced that it differed in fundamental respects from the United States.

In February 1975 I read a paper at the Winnipeg meetings of the Society for the Study of Architectural History in Canada and saw just enough of the city to suspect that it might offer a fine comparison. Two years later a grant from the American Council of Learned Societies enabled me to revisit Winnipeg and also to inspect the warehouse districts of Regina, Saskatoon, Edmonton, and Calgary. Among these Canadian cities, Winnipeg is by far the richest in fine warehouses and has the additional attraction of being less cut up by superhighways than its American counterparts. Because it started late and was extremely self-conscious, it provided abundant records and was, therefore, an excellent comparative case. As my chapter title indicates, it is a kind of northern anchor for the distributing system which, with the railroad itself, made the westward advance possible.

For these reasons, the warehouse problem, then, was national and international—not only architectural, but also urbanistic, and even psychological. In North American cities warehouse districts are usually compact and easily comprehensible. They are filled with large buildings, railway spurs, loading platforms, and roughly dressed workers. The pavement is rough, but these districts have very little of the menace usually associated with the ghetto; the architectural visitor risks nothing more than occasionally being panhandled. Eating places are likely to contain memorable bits of Americana. The hardy men and the few women who work in these fine old buildings often display a certain attachment to them without being in any way conscious that they are working in architectural monuments. In a way this attitude is refreshing. So must the laborers on the great medieval estates have felt about the barns and vernacular architecture we today esteem so highly. It should be added that while the jobbing industry has changed profoundly in the twentieth century because of the impact of the refrigerator car, automotive transport, and various other considerations, a surprising number of thriving enterprises are still housed in old warehouses. Jane Jacobs, Ada Louise Huxtable, and various other commentators have pointed out that one should be cautious about the destruction of a going concern.

The problem of illustration was difficult. These days there is frequent and often well-justified discontent with the standard architectural photograph. It too often shows a building in ideal conditions on sunny days, and it does not convey sufficient information on color, temperature, humidity, texture, and so forth. We can add that all too often, architectural historians do not use photographs effectively. Now the warehouses of Gateway City were *not* designed to be photographed. They were certainly intended to be effective containers of goods, to be family or company symbols, and to be experienced as important parts of the townscape. Owners and architects were generally happy with the buildings when completed, but contemporary publication was infrequent. Warehouses were simply not seen as *Architecture* in the same sense as churches and city halls. Contemporary photographs and engravings are, therefore, not common in the archives of historical societies or in the architectural press. Where they are available, I have tended to use them, along with contemporary renderings, since they are important historic documents. Often they show buildings before later generations have altered them, and they contain bits of information which are important parts of the story: handcarts and loading platforms, for example.

As I have indicated, new photographs pose other problems.

The climate in Gateway City is a harsh one, and its warehouses and older business buildings are not always seen on clear, sunny days. On the contrary, for several months of the year they are likely to be surrounded by piles of snow, ice, and slush, and in these months the sky is sometimes overcast. So it may be that the proper photographic representation is somewhat dark and evocative of the climate. It may be noted that the beautifully detailed brick walls of the Gateway City warehouses are actually much more weatherproof than the glass and metal membranes to which we became accustomed in the 1950s and 1960s.

Interiors pose another problem. As I have shown in the text, the structure of these buildings was ordinarily a system of timber framing which was repeated again and again. The variations in the system are slight, usually in the treatment of capitals; in a certain sense, when an observer has seen one warehouse interior, he has seen them all. The architectural interest of the problem lies in the numerous expressions of the structural system and in the solutions which were developed with the introduction of the reinforced concrete flat slab. I have, therefore, eliminated most of the interiors, leaving only enough to convey essential character. On the other hand, it seems to me that a few structural drawings can help substantially in describing mill framing, and I have, therefore, asked Robert Daverman to redraw a small number of plans and sections. The reader should keep in mind that equivalent drawings for most of the buildings shown would resemble these. As there is a general similarity in section, so there is in plan, and Mr. Daverman has also done new plans from the original working drawings. I am deeply indebted to him for his help. Finally there is the question of a graphic representation of the relation of the warehouse district to Gateway City as a whole. In this respect the bird's-eye views, of which the nineteenth century was so fond, are helpful.

The foregoing paragraphs explain, I hope, the origins of the essays on St. Joseph, Omaha, St. Paul, and Winnipeg. The section on "Oscar Eckerman: Architect to Deere & Co.: 1897–1942" is essentially a by-product of this warehouse research. In my mind the problem of the company architect in the United States has been too little studied. Perhaps this piece will throw some light on the situation.

The other essays in this volume have a different origin. Early in my career I became fascinated with the work of Louis Sullivan, Frank Lloyd Wright, and the Prairie School. In the course of more than thirty years of travel between Ann Arbor and the Twin Cities, I took a number of different routes in order to see important buildings in the villages and small towns of the Midwest. I recall that when I stopped in Columbus, Wisconsin, to look at Sullivan's bank in that city I walked around it carefully and was soon accosted by a burly police officer. He wanted to know if I was looking the building over with an eye to robbing it. Once he knew of my architectural interest, he warmed up considerably and took me in to meet one of the officers. On another journey I routed myself through the hamlets of Leroy, Adams, and Grand Meadow, Minnesota, to see the banks of Purcell and Elmslie in those places. Subsequently I have wondered how many villages in France, Germany, or England boast such jewels of twentieth-century architecture. On still another trip I went back to Michigan through the state's Upper Peninsula and stopped off in Marquette. There I found the Julian Case house by Burnham and Root. It was a remarkably well preserved example of their domestic work. In this volume I have coupled it with a treatment of the Morley Brothers hardware store in Saginaw. Sometimes the small towns and cities of the Midwest will offer buildings which illuminate the careers of the Chicago architects. Thus most of Louis Sullivan's buildings from the early 1880s in the city are gone, but the work of this phase of his life may still be studied in Kalamazoo.

In the course of this exploration of the Prairie School I kept running across the name of Jens Jensen, a landscape architect, who, it was said, had worked closely with the Prairie architects and stood for many of the same causes in landscape design which they had espoused in architecture. A small amount of investigation in the late 1950s convinced me that this was indeed true and that Jensen deserved extended treatment. In fact, I had an important artist on my hands.

Nineteen sixty was the centennial year for Jensen, and in that year *Progressive Architecture* published "Jens Jensen and the Chicago School." The favorable reception of this piece encouraged me to continue my research. In 1964 I published *Landscape Artist in America: The Life and Work of Jens Jensen* with the University of Chicago Press. The earlier essay is reprinted here as an introduction to a major

figure in midwestern culture. It is a pleasure to note here that the last two decades have seen quite a bit of Jensen scholarship. There are two excellent graduate theses from the University of Wisconsin: Stephen F. Christy, *The Growth of an Artist: Jens Jensen and Landscape Architecture* and Robert Grese, *A Process for the Interpretation and Management of a Designed Landscape: The Landscape Art of Jens Jensen at Lincoln Memorial Garden, Springfield, Illinois*. There is also a moderate periodical literature and a prospect of reprinting for Jensen's own book, *Siftings*. Chicagoans are becoming conscious of the significance of his work for the West Parks. I venture a prediction that in time Jensen will receive the recognition that is his due, not only with professions in landscape design but with the public at large.

The last essay in the book, on the political pictures of George Caleb Bingham, has a different origin. In 1975 the State Museums of the Netherlands undertook an important series of exhibitions on the Dutch architectural heritage. The Kroller-Muller Museum at Otterlo decided to do a show entitled "Americana: 1880–1930." The subject was the impact of American architecture in the Netherlands, and I was asked to do the foreword to the catalogue. The request was a great honor, and I accepted with alacrity. When the exhibitions were presented, the Dutch government very kindly provided me with a round trip between Detroit and Amsterdam so that I could attend.

I gave lectures at the Universities of Leiden and Utrecht and at the Technological University of Delft, but I had sufficient time to myself to visit other museums, among them the Rijksmuseum in Amsterdam. Long an admirer of Dutch genre painting, I was especially struck by a Jan Steen picture entitled *The Quack Doctor*. It reminded me of certain American works, but I could not then say what they were. On my return to the United States I undertook an examination of the American tradition in genre painting and concluded that Bingham, the greatest American genre painter of the pre–Civil War period, must have known the Dutch tradition of the charlatan picture and that he had given it an essentially political interpretation in his famous series of election paintings. This, at any rate, is the argument set forth in this piece. Missouri, I knew from my experience in St. Joseph, is a partly southern and partly midwestern state; so I think the inclusion of the piece in this volume is justified. It demonstrates, in any case, an essential fact about environmental design in the Midwest: It cannot be understood without constant reference to developments in other parts of the world.

The system of mill construction, about which so much is said in these pages, seems to have been introduced into the textile factories of New England about 1828. Such construction was a response to the fire hazard, which was a continual threat in the processing of cotton and wool. At another level Frank Lloyd Wright's continuing fascination with Japanese art and architecture is one of the most striking aspects of his career. H. H. Richardson, after all, was an Eastern designer, and no one had more influence on the architects of Gateway City than he. And although the documentary evidence is lacking, I am sure that Frederick Law Olmsted had an impact on Jensen. In short, the visual culture of the Midwest is no simple problem. My effort has been to set it in its proper context.

For permission to reprint certain of these writings I am grateful to the editors of several journals. Some of the material on buildings for the wholesale trade appeared as two articles for *Urban History Review*: "Warehouses and Warehouse Districts in Mid-American Cities" (Vol. XI, June, 1982) and "Winnipeg: The Northern Anchor of the Wholesale Trade" (Vol. XII, October, 1982). "Oscar Eckerman: Architect to Deere & Company, 1897–1942" can be found in *RACAR-Canadian Art Review*, III (1977), 89–99. The editors of *Progressive Architecture* accepted "Jens Jensen and the Chicago School" for publication in their December 1960 issue, and William Hasbrouck of the late, lamented *Prairie School Review* published "John Wellborn Root and the Julian M. Case House" in the third quarter of 1972. I thank the editors of all these periodicals for permission to reprint my essays. In several cases the text has been amplified to bring the essays up to date and to work them into a coherent whole. The other essays are here offered to the public for the first time.

As I look back on my travels in the Midwest over a period of almost forty years, it appears to me that I was peculiarly fortunate to study the region from a base in southeastern Michigan. In many respects the state is not midwestern at all. Agriculture does not have the primacy it enjoys in the real heartland. Orchards and perhaps vineyards are as important as wheat and corn. And in the southern half of the state the automobile industry is omnipresent. In its architecture Detroit looks more to the East than to Chicago. In his great survey, *The Buildings of Detroit*, W. Hawkins Ferry could find only a handful of buildings which showed the impact of Louis Sullivan. In my mind it is important that Albert Kahn, the city's greatest architect, was as proud of the extremely polished renaissance revival Clements Library in Ann Arbor as of any building he ever did. While I have come to appreciate the Clements Library more and more over the years, it seems to me to have very little to do with the Midwest as I understand the region. So, starting from Ann Arbor, I was able to study the region from the vantage point of a somewhat displaced native son. It is perhaps inevitable that I tend to overstate its virtues. I have grappled with this problem by letting some of the literary figures of the area speak to it in my first chapter.

In the course of so many years of research and travel, I have incurred innumerable obligations to scholars, architects, and municipal officials. Rather than listing them here, I have tried to acknowledge my debts in footnotes. But there is one person, who, by her love, patience, and fortitude is responsible for my completion of the work. To her this book is dedicated.

GATEWAY CITIES

&

OTHER ESSAYS

1

The Gateway City and Its Warehouses

The urbanization of the Middle West is altogether one of the most amazing phenomena in American history. However one defines this huge region, which is generally considered the heartland of the United States, it had in 1860 only three cities with populations in excess of 100,000. These were St. Louis, Cincinnati, and Chicago. Each of these places had distinctive characteristics. St. Louis was an eighteenth-century French foundation, and did not, in fact, come under the American flag until the Louisiana Purchase of 1803. Today its old families still boast of their French blood. Howard Mumford Jones correctly observed that, despite its connections with the westward movement, which are superbly symbolized in Eero Saarinen's famous arch, "St. Louis is seldom considered a part of the Middle West and occupies, as it were, a cultural principality all its own."[1] During the first half of the nineteenth century Cincinnati was an important place with a vital and independent cultural tradition. An old river town with a strong leadership of conservative but civic-minded New Englanders, it was already sending the sons of its leading families, such as the Tafts, to Yale. Chicago, founded only in 1832, has received more attention from historians, and deservedly so, since its growth and character are unique among modern cities.

Situated at the foot of Lake Michigan, it was, by virtue of geographical location, the most important port on the Great Lakes and the natural center of the railroad network which was beginning to cover the country in the 1850s. Chicago possessed overwhelming advantages for the development of commerce, finance, and industry of every kind. It thus attracted the ambitious businessmen who were to emerge as the industrial titans of the post–Civil War era: the Fields, McCormicks, Armours, and Swifts, to mention only a few. It is not surprising that its growth was explosive, and that, as Lewis Mumford so aptly remarked many years ago, it was at the time of the great fire of 1871, "a brutal network of industrial necessities." With regard to architecture and building, the catastrophe of the fire was, of course, a blessing in disguise. It created an immense demand for office space and industrial facilities, and as has so often happened in the past, there was a general public expectation that the new buildings would be finer than the old. Hence outstanding architectural designers were drawn to Chicago from the entire nation.

It has often been pointed out that of the original Chicago School only one minor figure, S. S. Beman, was a native Chicagoan. Louis Sullivan was a New Englander; John Root came from Lumpkin, Georgia; Daniel Burnham from upstate New York; Dankmar Adler from Detroit; and various minor figures from other places. They were all drawn to Chicago like iron filings to a magnet. When the young Frank Lloyd Wright left Madison, Wisconsin, to descend upon the city in the spring of 1887, he was, in a sense, merely repeating the journey of hundreds of other ambitious young men from all over the Midwest. He came to conquer the metropolis. Wright can be seen, in fact, at this stage of his career as the classic gifted young man from the provinces determined to make a name for himself in the big city, a figure who occurs in countless nineteenth-century novels. He is Julien Sorel in *The Red and the Black*, David Copperfield, or any of the numerous and overwhelmingly greedy heroes of Balzac.

Once arrived in Chicago, the bright young men—Sullivan, Root, Burnham, Adler, and, later, Wright—found it a city devoted almost exclusively to making money. The opportunities for this activity, it may be said, were almost unprecedented in the history of Western civilization. Midwestern farmers were opening up an incredibly rich area for agricultural exploitation. They broke the prairie, changed the pattern of American farming from subsistence to commercial, raised, sold, and exported crops for cash. Thus the Midwest became a great processor of farm products and maker of farm implements: in effect a huge conveyor belt between consumers and producers. Finally it became a vast market, made up of farmers and urban workers.

The center of all this frenzied economic activity was Chicago, and those who rose to the top in the brutal struggle were the business titans of the day. Marshall Field, Philip Armour, Gustavus Swift, and Harold McCormick were names to conjure with. They were men of immense ability—bold, ruthless, tremendously energetic, and for the most part poorly educated; until late in life they gave no thought to the social responsibilities of their enormous accumulations of wealth. The key to the entire period, as Howard Mumford Jones has wisely noted, was energy, and it is no wonder that the energies of Chicago were reflected in the cities of the hinterland.

These cities were a new kind of problem in the history of urbanization. Graham Hutton, an English observer, has written:

> The East had something to build cities on. The Midwest built them from scratch, thrust them up the rivers, scattered them along the railroads, dumped them in the prairie or the forest, and then blew them up like balloons with immigrants. Young men who came as settlers to build their own cabins among earlier cabins, and bought little lots on which to build them, found themselves rich men, running big industrial cities before they were seventy, living from the colossal rents of the little original lots—now huge office buildings in the heart of the commercial section of a brand new city—and forming a social elite of wealthy persons who could buy privileges.[2]

Now thousands of immigrant workers, who supplied the essential personnel for the new warehouses and factories, crowded into the slums, especially during the period 1876–1893, when the American economy recovered from the depression of 1873 and entered upon an era of generally sustained economic expansion. In Eugene Rostow's terms, it was a "take-off" period, in which heavy investment in capital assets, especially railroads, resulted in the formation of a tremendous industrial establishment. The entire process, as in England earlier and Russia later, conferred no particular benefits upon the laboring classes and agricultural workers. For them wages were low, hours were incredibly long, and working conditions often unpleasant and frequently hazardous. It is understandable that these years were filled with strikes and agrarian upheavals. Whatever may be one's feeling about these events, the period did see the foundation of American industrial and agricultural supremacy in the Western world. Further it saw the appearance of two exceedingly important new words in the American economic lexicon: distribution and merchandising. In 1860 there were sixty separate areas of trading and distribution in the Midwest; by 1930 the number had diminished to twenty, and of course there are fewer still today.

In the whole process the businessman became a hero. His rise was the consequence of the overwhelming importance of cities, town life, trade, manufacturing, utilities, and communications—and Chicago was the nexus of it all. Industry, cities, and big business burst upon a midwestern society of small town grocers, hardware merchants, meat packers, real estate lawyers, and forwarding agents of various kinds. The businessman made it a region of miracles, America's fairyland. Hutton remarked that what the Rhine, the Rhineland, and the Niebelungenlied are to Germany, the saga of the midwestern businessman is to the heartland of the United States, and he could have added that, as in the famous German epic, there are heroes and villains aplenty.

There were get-rich-quick promoters anxious to exploit both their fellow citizens and the land, and there were solid men, determined to build soundly and well the foundations of the world's most productive economy. In my boyhood one of the tallest office buildings in Minneapolis was lettered at the very top with the name of one of the town's greatest swindlers—Foshay. It was always a reminder to me of the weakness of the business culture in my native town. On the other hand, certain of the city's streets were lined with a really superb collection of warehouses and industrial structures dating mostly from the 1880s and 1890s. These buildings, I have come to feel are the true monuments to the best in the business enterprise of the age. In this context a figure like James J. Hill acquires mythic proportions. A builder of so much in the northwest, it was characteristic of him that he took a close personal interest in the construction of the Great Northern headquarters in St. Paul and ranked the bridge across the Mississippi, which still bears his name, as among the most difficult of his undertakings.

How did the literary men of the Midwest view the visible results of this tremendous economic expansion? The answer must be that they generally took exception to what they saw.

The gentle Brand Whitlock, who was close to Golden Rule Jones and Tom Johnson, the great reforming mayors of Toledo and Cleveland, interviewed John Peter Altgeld in 1892 when the latter was a judge of the Illinois Circuit Court, and while he admired Altgeld for his sympathy with the laboring classes, remarked, "He was just then building one of those tall and ugly structures called skyscrapers."[3] Similarly the Chicago novelist Henry B. Fuller had very little feeling for the remarkable new architecture going up in the city. In *The Cliff-Dwellers* (1893) one of his leading characters, in answer to an admiring remark about elevators, retorts:

> "That's all a building is nowadays—one mass of pipes, pulleys, wires, tubes, shafts, chutes, and what not, running through an iron cage of from fourteen to twenty stages. Then the artist comes along and is asked to supply the architecture by festooning on a lot of tile, brick, and terra-cotta. And over the whole thing hovers incessantly the demon of nine per cent."[4]

The architect in the book, Atwater, advises a new draftsman coming into his office to go in for mining, dredging, building bridges, or railway sheds, but not to believe that architecture has any great place for the artist.

Fuller's Chicago contemporary, Robert Herrick, evidently had somewhat greater understanding of the problems of the architectural profession. While his architect-hero, Francis Jackson Hart, in *The Common Lot* (1904) is a man of enormously weak character, an older colleague of Hart's remarks apropos of a new Chicago business building:

> "What do you think of this thing? Bold, isn't it? That Peyton's got nerve to put up this spiderweb right here on State Street. Now, I couldn't do that. But I guess he's on the right track. That's what we are coming to."[5]

He might have been talking about Louis Sullivan's Carson Pirie Scott Store, the first unit of which was going up while Herrick was writing.

The writer who had the greatest comprehension of what the new industrialism was doing to the cities of the midland was probably the famous Indiana novelist Booth Tarkington. The peculiar circumstances of Tarkington's career and his own unusual visual acuity combined to make him an exceptionally perceptive observer. Born in 1869, he graduated from Princeton in 1893, and then spent the years 1899–1912 in New York and Europe, writing plays, travelling, and living all too well. After a siege of alcoholism, a divorce, and a successful remarriage, he returned in 1912 to his native Indianapolis where he spent a good part of each year for the remainder of his life.

Long foreign and eastern residence had given him a new point of view about the city. Briefly, he was disenchanted with it. People now worshipped materialism, bigness, and speed. His biographer, James L. Woodress, states: "The sedate, well-mannered, and self-contained society that he remembered in Indianapolis before 1900 had crumbled before the irresistible force of big business and the vast complexities of an industrial democracy."[6] Business life in a once relaxed and friendly city was now a frenetic rat race. In Tarkington's youth central Indiana had had natural gas; now the new industries depended on soft coal, and smoke became perhaps his major symbol of the change. Furthermore, Tarkington was a man of unusual visual sensitivity. He formed a fine collection of paintings, and in 1946 wrote the introduction to Lionello Venturi's *Painting and Pictures*. His taste was the subject of a charming essay by no less an authority than Erwin Panofsky. His novels of the decade 1912–1922 deserve more attention than they have received.

While *The Magnificent Ambersons* has an honored place in American literature as the chronicle of the decline of an American family, *The Turmoil* (1914) is little read. The Sheridans, its protagonists, are rising, as the Ambersons fall. Their leader, James Sheridan, is a business giant; among his enterprises are the Sheridan Automotive Pump Works, the Sheridan Building, and the Sheridan Realty Corp. People speak his name with awe. Sheridan, a powerful man physically, calls the smoke prosperity and breathes its dingy cloud with relish. Tarkington writes:

> And when soot fell upon his cuff, he chuckled, he could have kissed it. "It's good! It's good," he said and smacked his lips in gusto. "Good, clean soot, it's our life-blood, God bless it."[7]

Sheridan laughed at a committee of housewives who called to beg his aid against it and told them that it was what brought the paycheck home on Saturday night. The plot of the novel revolves around Sheridan's attempts to run his family like his industrial empire. His oldest son, destined to take over the firm, dies in an industrial accident, and his second boy cracks under the strain and becomes an alcoholic. The youngest, a frail youth with distinct artistic sensibilities, renounces his ambition to be a writer, shows pronounced business ability, and becomes the obvious heir to the vast Sheridan enterprises. In this renunciation there is something very like tragedy. Few harsher indictments of the American business system have been written, though one has the feeling that the boom, which is so important to our story, may have hit Indianapolis a bit later than the other places with which we are dealing. Tarkington himself finally moved from the old family house at 1100 North Pennsylvania Street to a suburban dwelling in order to escape the smoke.

Later novelists, who did not see the boom period with equal clarity, were just as hard on the nineteenth-century architecture of the cities of the midlands. In the famous first paragraph of *Babbitt* (1922) Sinclair Lewis praised the towers of Zenith, but went on to say:

> The mist took pity on the fretted structures of earlier generations: the Post Office with its shingle-tortured mansard, the red brick minarets of hulking old houses, factories with stingy and sooted windows, wooden tenements colored like mud.[8]

Returning to the city after an absence of several years, he wrote in 1942, "Minneapolis is so ugly. Parking lots like scars. Most buildings are narrow, drab, dirty, flimsy, irregular in relationship to one another—a set of bad teeth."[9] The city actually impressed him as an overgrown Gopher Prairie without either planning or style. I would argue that Lewis, who often had a sharp eye for architectural detail, missed a good deal of quality in the city, possibly because he did not look in the right places. Like so many literary men, he could not believe that warehouses and factories might be distinguished works of architecture and he certainly shared Glenway Wescott's opinion that the Middle West was a state of mind among people born where they do not like to live.

More recently Patricia Hampl has commented on the manner in which St. Paul turns its back on the Mississippi River. She writes:

> This disregard for feature and advantage strikes me as American, but even more so as Midwestern. It is compounded of the usual pioneer arrogance and also, strangely, of diffidence: the swagger of saying we don't need beauty is coupled with the pouty lack of confidence of a wallflower . . . [10]

She goes on to note that the poet John Berryman remarked that Minneapolis was not a real city. He said that it did not have ghostliness or "the rudiments of a soul."[11] With all due respect to an extremely gifted writer, who has understood many fundamental aspects of midwestern culture, Hampl needs to go and look hard at the warehouses on Smith Square.

My own attitude toward the cities of the Midwest is closer to the view of Carl Jonas, who, I believe, is one of the overlooked novelists of our century. In a memorable passage he wrote:

> The beauty of the Middle West isn't the beauty of the great beauty spots of the world, and that's well, for the beauty of the great beauty spots is essentially a beauty for the dullards, for

trippers, for the two-week tourist. The beauty of the Middle West is rather beauty for the connoisseur who has eyes with which to see things, modern art, wine for those who have palates. An acquired taste? Perhaps but so is *pate de foie gras* or caviar or a good pale dry Martini. Here, if you look, is the river, the winter sun glinting on a barge downstream turning it into silver and by it a gold froth turned up by the tugboat. Here are the long lavender ribbons of concrete highway. Here is the red of old brick chimneys well sooted, the orange of rust on old bridges and boilers, the hard green of Farm implements, the brown of mud, the blue of well-washed denim, the red again of barns, and the blue again of coal. Here, too, are the bellowing steers being trucked in to the packing houses of South Gateway and the men in Levis and spike-heeled boots who have come in with them, the streamliners gliding, snake-like into Union Station, the castellated grain elevators like Rhine fortresses of robber barons. And there are whirling wind mills, barking dogs, farm wives hanging out wash, and wind, and the transcontinental buses, the great supermarkets, and man himself, perfectible, but imperfect.[12]

In a series of excellent novels Jonas anatomized the history and physical development of Omaha, which he called "Gateway City." The first settler of the place, he said, was a Frenchman, who came up the river and picked the site as a likely source for carrying on the Indian trade. The river was always to be important to the city as an artery of trade and a source of power. This episode occurred in the 1820s or 1830s, and for some years thereafter the population remained very small. About 1850 two important events occurred when the place was incorporated and platted. By this time a number of perceptive businessmen who saw the commercial possibilities of the place were on hand. These, of course, were the ancestors of those families who in later years were known as "Old Gateway."

For the platting a simple gridiron system was used. This was in accordance with common American practice and later proved greatly to the benefit of real estate speculators. By the outbreak of the Civil War, Gateway City was a thriving town of about 10,000 souls, with a few local industries such as sawmills, but occupied mainly with supplying the farmers who were filling up the territory. These farmers outnumbered the city dwellers in the territorial and state legislatures

and generally saw to it that the state capitol was located elsewhere (St. Paul is the only one of our cities which today boasts the dignity of a state capitol).

During the war Gateway City was generally loyal to the Union, as was the entire Midwest, but it did not advance as rapidly as Chicago. The manufacturing establishment which supported the armies of the Union was, after all, centered mostly in the East. Furthermore, in certain sections of the Midwest, there was the very real fear of the Indian menace. This naturally did not affect the city so much as the surrounding agricultural hinterland, which was still thinly settled.

Undoubtedly the most important event in the nineteenth-century history of Gateway City was the coming of the railroad. This ordinarily occurred during the 1870s, and it transformed the entire economic life and physical appearance of the place. Up to this time communication with the outside world had been by water or overland and had been frequently uncertain and always slow. Shipment of any kind of heavy goods was fraught with difficulty. Now it became possible for the city to develop certain kinds of manufacturing and food processing for which it was well fitted and to get its products to market speedily and efficiently. Equally important, a system of wholesale supply was developed to service the thousands of farmers who continued to pour into the rich lands of the Mississippi and Missouri valleys and the Canadian prairies. A jobbing district arose in close proximity to the railroad terminal and its imposing buildings were an important part of the urban environment.

The growth of these cities and their relation to the hinterland therefore depended on long-range trade, not on local commerce as in medieval Europe. North America lacked the restrictive element of a feudal past, and those who developed its commerce necessarily had to think of transporting goods over distances incomprehensible to the European. The wholesaler was the key to the new patterns, and the important cities of the interior developed at points he selected. He was the real pioneer of mercantile capitalism, and he located his business at a site on a major waterway which drained a rich agricultural district. Around this location Gateway City grew up. It was, first of all, a stopping place for riverboats and subsequently an important railroad center. The patterns of distribution which had evolved by 1900 are shown in the accompanying map (Fig. 1.1).[13]

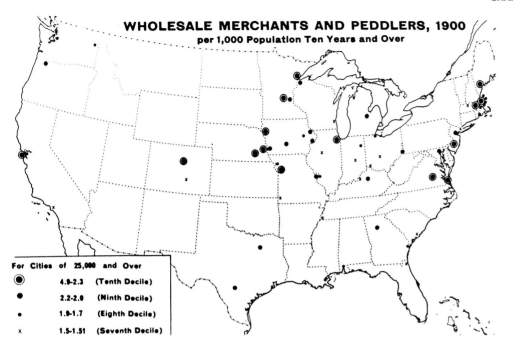

WHOLESALE MERCHANTS AND PEDDLERS, 1900
per 1,000 Population Ten Years and Over

For Cities of 25,000 and Over

◎ 4.9-2.3 (Tenth Decile)
● 2.2-2.0 (Ninth Decile)
• 1.9-1.7 (Eighth Decile)
x 1.5-1.51 (Seventh Decile)

Fig. 1.1. Source: James Vance, The Merchant's World: The Geography of Wholesaling *(Englewood Cliffs, N.J., 1970). Used with the permission of James Vance.*

An analysis of the role of the wholesaler in the economy of nineteenth-century North America is necessary for an understanding of the kind of building he put up. Basically this man supervised the distribution of trade. In an age when overland transportation was confined to the railroad and the horse drawn vehicle, he performed a vital function for the farmer and the small town retailer. His expertise lay in his knowledge of who produced the commodities they required and of the means of bringing buyer and seller together. He was thoroughly conversant with freight rates, forwarding agents, and storage facilities. Thus his services were essential to an economy which was agrarian throughout most of the nineteenth century.

Because of this dependence on the transportation network the wholesalers located their first warehouses near the steamboat landing. When the railroads arrived, they tended to follow the easy grades of the river floodplain and to place their passenger and freight terminals close to the old steamboat docks. As the railroads displaced the steamboats, the jobbers found that goods could be dispatched by carload lots, normally sent by a manufacturer to a wholesaler but sometimes to large retailers as well. This expansion in the size of the shipment was responsible in large measure for the leap in scale which is characteristic of the American warehouse in the 1880s, the period in which it suddenly became a major civic monument. The golden age lasted until about 1910, and during this interval it was usually the best designed public building in the city. The shipments could be moved over sidings built directly to the loading doors of the warehouses. Thus the railroad called the warehouse district into being, and if one examines the area today, one will find it to be a place still intimately connected with the transportation network.

It is also a place which generated a large amount of economic activity other than wholesaling. The jobber of wholesale drygoods, for example, found it easy to move into the manufacturing of overalls. This was a tempting proposition because the farmer had an almost unlimited need for these garments. The same held for work shoes. The jobber himself required banking services, and ordinarily one or two banks in Gateway City would cater to his special requirements. They would be located conveniently on the perimeter of the district. His employees required restaurants and bars; the latter were especially important because they were willing to cash paychecks at hours when the banks were closed. Surviving examples, such as the Hotel Roblin Bar in Winnipeg, always seem to be decorated with stuffed mooseheads. The distribution system could not have worked without hundreds and thousands of travelling salesmen who fanned out from Gateway City into the territories the wholesaler served. When these men came to town, they needed a place to stay. Hence the development of a hotel district and even of specialized "Traveller's Clubs"; one in Winnipeg was even equipped with a Turkish bath where the weary salesman could relax. In short, the wholesale district generated a large range of activities which contributed to the generally sustained population growth of Gateway City. Let us, then, consider the problem of the warehouse.

The Warehouse: Definition and Program

In 1904 the architectural critic Russell Sturgis neatly characterized the problems and program of the warehouse and industrial building:

Without splitting hairs too minutely, we come to the conclusion that anything is either a warehouse or a factory which is devoted to the rougher kind of business enterprise; that is to say, not primarily to offices where professional men sit quietly or clerks pursue their daily task, but one where the goods are piled up, where the unloading and loading, the receiving and the shipping of such goods goes on continually, where the floors are to a great extent left open in great "lofts" and where in consequence the character of the structure within and without is the reverse of elegant.[14]

Sturgis went on to argue that the warehouse or factory might be costly and solidly built. It might be an architectural monument, but it could not be minutely planned with many refinements in interior arrangement. Elaborate exterior decorative treatment was inappropriate, as were extraordinary combinations of masses. The exterior walls would present the appearance of a square-edged, flat-topped box, and the masses would nowhere break into porches or turrets. Delicate stonework was out of the question, nor was sculpture a part of the program. Color, if used, was apt to be applied rather freely.

To this analysis may be added certain considerations which Sturgis omitted. The warehouse or factory had to have a certain amount of office space at the front of the building where managers could carry out their duties, customers could be received, and secretaries and bookkeepers could work. A particularly important section was the sample room where the various products offered by the firm could be shown. Wholesaling was a competitive business, and an attractive display was a necessity.

Symbolism was also a part of the program, and here it is appropriate to observe that a large number of the great western warehousing concerns were family operations. Honor and social position required that the exterior of the building convey a message of stability and enduring strength, which was very much in keeping with the heavy structural system which was employed. The buildings had to signify the status of the owners in the community and the financial soundness of the firms, and they had a major civic importance. Often they appeared in the advertisements and trade circulars of the wholesalers; they were important symbols. The same interpretation could be extended to the branch selling houses of those companies which were essentially family concerns, notably the John Deere Plow Company and Butler Brothers. The branch warehouse of Deere in Omaha, for example, may be considered as much a symbol of the solid worth of the company and the high quality of its products as the much better known corporate headquarters by Eero Saarinen in Moline, Illinois.

The public image projected by the warehouse, then, had to suit the character of the successful wholesaler in Gateway City. About this man too little is known. Obviously he was a man of ability and ambition, and he was able to see the advantages of prime location in carrying on his business. Except in rare cases the records do not reveal much formal education, and certainly no training in architectural discrimination. Personal records—diaries, correspondence with architects, etc.—are equally scarce; the nineteenth-century wholesaler was primarily a man of action, and while he may have paid considerable attention to the buildings he was putting up, he did not discuss them with his family and friends in any extended fashion.

Nonetheless one cannot escape the impression that he was interested in the subject of building. There was probably plenty of talk about the new warehouses within the premises of the Minnesota Club in St. Paul, the Minneapolis Club in Minneapolis, and the Manitoba Club in Winnipeg. Obviously the wholesaler was very much a public figure, and he knew that what he did would have an impact on the physical face of the community. Frequently new wholesale houses were noticed in trade journals such as *The Commercial* in Winnipeg and *Farm Implements* in Minneapolis. Less frequently they were mentioned in the daily newspapers. The exception here is Winnipeg. So fascinated were its citizens with the rapid growth of the town that the *Manitoba Free Press* and the *Winnipeg Tribune* for several years published annual building numbers. These were reviews of progress in construction, and they are a mine of information on trade and building technology.

CHAPTER 1

The Warehouse: Problems of Structure

For centuries the greatest hazard of the wholesaler's business had been fire. With the dramatic growth of trade in the nineteenth century it became an urgent concern, and numerous architects and engineers devoted their best efforts to its solution. The outstanding European contribution was undoubtedly that of Jesse Hartley, the famous Liverpool builder. He was, in fact, so successful that his work was carefully studied by a committee from the American Congress. During the summer of 1846 two of its members investigated the warehousing systems of the major European ports. They were particularly enthusiastic about the work of Hartley, and their report even included some of his signed drawings of the Albert Dock. What especially impressed the congressmen were Hartley's planning, construction, and fireproofing techniques. They recommended similar buildings for the major ports of the United States. While it is impossible to evaluate the circulation of a congressional document, there is no doubt that the Liverpool warehouses were known in the mercantile community which actually used them. American architects probably failed to emulate them not because they were unfamiliar but because they were expensive. Hartley used a system of masonry arches and load-bearing partitions whose cost was prohibitive in the United States.[15]

To solve the requirement of fireproof construction the architects of Gateway City usually turned to mill construction, a system which evolved prior to the Civil War at the behest of the textile manufacturers of New England.[16] Spinning and weaving are, of course, occupations in which there is a substantial hazard of fire because the raw materials are naturally oily and machines require lubrication. The solution for the early New Englanders was a system of deliberate over-design in timber so that wooden structural members would char rather than burn. It was in use by 1827, and it was common knowledge to the mill builders during the following generation in which textile manufacture was at its height. It would certainly have been known, for example, to E. P. Bassford (b. 1837), who received his training in Boston and migrated to St. Paul in the post–Civil War period. A good description of the system was in Frank Kidder's *Architects and Builders Pocketbook* (1885). The system was published earlier by the insurance companies, but the drawings which Kidder used to accompany his text are strikingly clear (see Figs. 1.2 and 1.3). He wrote:

> The desideratum in this mode of construction is to have a building whose outside walls shall be built of masonry (generally of brick) concentrated in piers and buttresses with only a thin wall containing the windows between and the floors and roof of which shall be constructed of large timber, covered with a plank of suitable thickness; the girders being supported between the walls by wooden posts.[17]

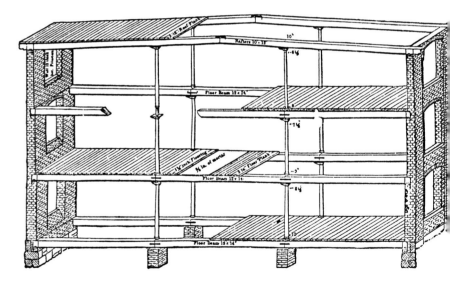

Fig. 1.2. Diagram from Frank E. Kidder, Architects and Builders Pocketbook *(1885). The drawing shows a building framed partly in metal and partly in timber.*

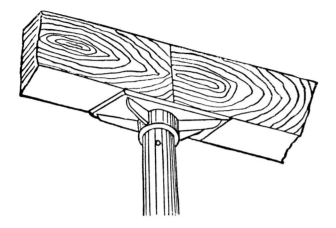

Fig. 1.3. Detail from Kidder showing capital.

Kidder went on to stipulate that there be no furring or concealed spaces, that beams be solid, or double and bolted together, that the posts have ½″ holes near the top for ventilation, that no polish or varnish be used, and that floor planking be not less than 3″ thick. The best construction was laid over 3″ of mortar. Columns, he said, were usually round, 9″ in the first story, 8″ in the second, and 7″ in the third. This was the minimum, and he suggested well-seasoned hard pine or oak. The system and a typical structural detail are shown in Figures 1.4 and 1.5. This, he said, was the most approved construction for factories, mills, and storehouses. These dimensions were adequate for bays in which the columns were not more than 8′ on center. Where bays were larger or floor loads greater, plans and timbers should be proportioned accordingly. When the automatic sprinkler (invented 1879) is added, the system is remarkably fire resistant. Cast iron, unhappily, will deflect under heat, and by using heavy timber, this disadvantage was avoided.

Kidder's book was, of course, simply a handy compilation of all the scientific structural knowledge then available, and significantly, it was dedicated to O. W. Norcross, H. H. Richardson's gifted builder.

For the architects of Gateway City it provided a most useful source of ideas and a valuable set of minimum standards. Faced with demands for larger buildings and wider bays, they increased the dimensions of their structural members until the posts were often 15″ in cross section and beam depths were in proportion.

In the midwestern adaptation the columns were not round, as suggested by Kidder, but square with the exposed edges chamfered. All sorts of details were worked out to reinforce the joints where the load was greatest. Sometimes an extra piece of wood was used as a kind of impost block. Sometimes a cast iron plate was added; these details were usually bolted rather than screwed. In some buildings one floor might be in mill construction, while the next would be done in cast iron. The choice appears to have depended on cost considerations, the nature of the problem, and the preference of the owner. Very often the purest mill construction is found in structures devoted to wholesale hardware and farm machinery, but this generalization is by no means invariable.

Aside from its fire-resistant nature and flexibility, the system had other advantages; ceiling heights could be varied by the simple expedient of specifying appropriate dimensions and inexpensive timber from the forests of Minnesota and Wisconsin, moved easily over the newly established railway lines. Most of the warehouses and factories in Gateway City were, therefore, of mill construction up to World War I. The structural system itself was thus not new but the lengths to which it was pushed certainly were.

The structural development of the American warehouse is, therefore, a beautiful corroboration of the theoretical insight of James Fitch, offered three decades ago. In 1958 Fitch noted that Americans have always avoided the load-bearing mass masonry wall which was our dominant heritage from Europe:

> The structural form which we did adopt, and which we have cultivated ever since, is the skeleton. There were two great virtues to skeletal structures. The first was purely technical; it was more efficient than mass masonry in resisting loads and because of its specialized curtain walls, could be made much more effective in repelling climatic attack. The second virtue was economic. The skeleton was *possible* in America as nowhere else in the modern world, because ample supplies of the proper materials, wood

and steel were at hand. But it was *desirable* because the skeleton frame and its curtain walling are subject to a high degree of rationalization. The economics in labor were so pronounced that it has remained for three centuries our most popular structural form.[18]

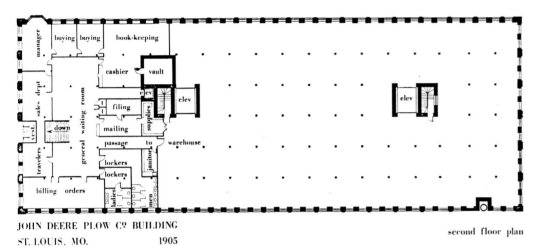

JOHN DEERE PLOW C⁰ BUILDING
ST. LOUIS. MO.   1905
                                    second floor plan

Fig. 1.4. St. Louis warehouse, plan. Redrawn from original blueprint by Robert Daverman.

Fig. 1.5. St. Louis warehouse, longitudinal section. Redrawn from original blueprint by Robert Daverman.

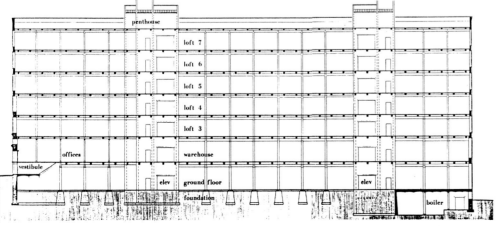

longitudinal section

The system of mill framing may be seen well in a pair of warehouses that Oscar Eckerman did for the John Deere Plow Company in St. Louis in 1902–1903 (see Figs. 1.6–1.9). In effect they are gigantic brick and timber cages. The extremely heavy sill beams are bolted together and the upright members are chamfered to diminish combustible surface in the event of fire. The exterior walls are simply screens. The massive timbers necessary for the construction were moved easily by rail, and building with them was easy, rapid, and economical—important considerations for a company whose chief executive was deathly afraid of deficits. "What worried Mr. Deere," wrote an associate, "was that a spending spree would run away with itself. He always wanted to be on the safe side financially."[19] So much for problems of construction—until the advent of the reinforced concrete slab.

Fig. 1.6. Oscar Eckerman. Warehouses for Deere & Co., St. Louis, Mo. Construction photograph, Oct. 16, 1905. Photo: Deere & Co.

Fig. 1.7. *Construction photograph of St. Louis warehouses, Oct. 21, 1903. Photo: Deere & Co.*

Fig. 1.8. *Construction photograph of St. Louis warehouses, Oct. 21, 1903. Photo: Deere & Co.*

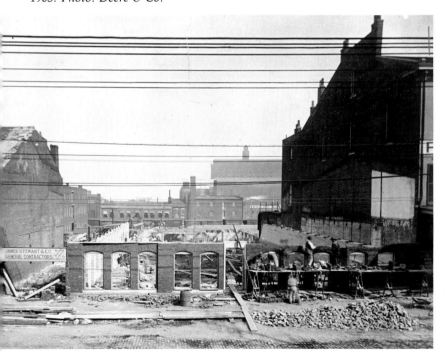

The Warehouse: Problems of Design

To a considerable extent the architects of Gateway City were admirers of the commercial style in Chicago, but ironically the single most influential building in that city was unquestionably the Marshall Field Wholesale Store of 1885–1886 by the Bostonian H. H. Richardson (Figure 1.10). This building, now destroyed, was a favorite of Louis Sullivan, the leading theoretician of the Chicago School, and it served as a model for Sullivan's own Walker Warehouse of 1888. John Root, Sullivan's talented contemporary, also thought highly of Richardson. There is a strong Richardsonian element in many of his best buildings, especially the offices and warehouse for McCormick-Harvester of 1884–1886. These structures would have been known to the Gateway designers through publication or through personal acquaintance. They offered the appeal of disciplined massing and the opportunity to organize an elevation through tiers of rhythmically related arches. This, of course, was the Richardsonian Romanesque, which, as many critics have remarked, was more Richardsonian than Romanesque.[20]

Fig. 1.9. *Unfinished interior of St. Louis warehouse. Undated. Photo: Deere & Co.*

Fig. 1.10. H. H. Richardson. Marshall Field Wholesale Store, Chicago, 1885. Photo: Chicago Historical Society.

It should be noted that the architects of Gateway City were fortunate in their proximity to Chicago. Nowhere else in the western world was there such a concentration of first-class commercial and industrial architecture. Sullivan and Root were simply the leaders of a group of men whose work was as notable for its quality as its quantity. Standards in design were exceptionally high. Because of the great fire of 1871 and the poor soil conditions of the city, there was a lively interest in building technology, and the architects and engineers coop-

erated closely on all major projects. It is not surprising, then, that the warehouse district of Gateway City contains a large number of buildings which are outstanding in design and structure. Some of its architects emerge as worthy personalities in their own right. They accomplished a number of significant variations on the themes stated by the Chicago masters and produced many highly original buildings of their own as well.

Several important facts may be noted concerning the architects of Gateway City in these post–Civil War years. Very few of them had a professional education. The first American school of architecture at MIT did not open its doors until 1865, and not many of its graduates found their way as far west as Gateway City. Hence immigrant architects, trained at European schools, formed a small but important minority. Later, around the turn of the century, when architecture had become a more recognized profession, a few of the sons of Gateway's aristocracy would go abroad, study at the École des Beaux Arts in Paris, and return, bringing with them an entirely different point of view, but that day was at least three decades away.

Nonetheless, to say that these early architects were not graduates of conventional schools is not to say that they were incapable of good building. Most of them had come up through the construction trades, and some, like Dankmar Adler and William LeBaron Jenney, had Civil War experience which gave them a maturity far beyond their years. Without having read Viollet-Le-Duc or Gottfried Semper, they had a deep respect for the facts of construction and for the brick, wood, cast iron, cut stone, and terra-cotta which were their materials. They *did* read, so far as one can judge, the major American architectural periodicals: *The American Architect and Building News* (Boston), *The Inland Architect* (Chicago), and *The Northwestern Architect and Building Budget* (Minneapolis, 1882–1894). *The Inland Architect*, which first appeared in Chicago in February 1883 under the gifted leadership of Robert Craik McLean, was particularly important since it stressed the latest work of Root, Jenney, Sullivan, and the other leaders of the Chicago School. McLean played an important role in the formation of the Western Association of Architects in 1884. When the organization merged with the older American Institute of Architects in 1889, it contributed the greater share of vitality and ideas to the merger.

The architects of Gateway City, then, may have been located in the provinces, but their outlook was in no sense provincial. Their relationship to the architects of Chicago was, in fact, rather like the relationship of the architects of Bath, Bristol, and Edinburgh to the great designers of eighteenth-century London. The magazines kept the Gateway designers in close touch with what was going on in the great world of architecture. H. H. Richardson's Cheney Block of 1875–1877 in Hartford would, for example, have been well known to them; it may have been the most important commercial work of the period because it was the first indication of the possibility of adapting the round-arched forms of the Romanesque to contemporary commercial problems.

Furthermore, the men of Chicago actually gave demonstrations of their skill in cities like Gateway. John Root built one of his finest structures, the Board of Trade, in Kansas City, and S. S. Beman did important buildings in St. Paul and Grand Rapids, Michigan. Their organizations were small versions of Burnham and Root or Adler and Sullivan in Chicago. In times of pressure the office forces might be augmented from a travelling group of draughtsmen-designers who floated through the Midwest working at various places in the region. Of these, by far the most gifted was the talented but alcoholic Harvey Ellis, a specialist in ornament. (Ellis may or may not have worked in Gateway; his trail is almost impossible to follow.) At the turn of the century, in any event, the senior partners of the city's leading firms were men of standing in the community, their biographies duly featured in the compendiums of Prominent Citizens which began to appear at about this time.

Practice in these early Gateway City offices presents an interesting combination of the sophisticated and the casual. After the initial design had been set by the partner in charge, it was often further refined by the draughtsman in charge of preparing the working drawings, who might make a considerable contribution; here it is well to note that the period did not make the sharp contemporary distinction between draughtsman and designer. The working drawing itself was frequently rather sketchy, and one has the impression that the architects tended to rely heavily on the traditional skills of the carpenters, brickmasons, and stonecutters in the vicinity. This would have been a necessity in a period which was just seeing the introduction of the general contractor system; O. W. Norcross, Richardson's chief builder, was a pioneer in this regard. On the other hand, the client could expect a finished pen and ink or wash drawing of his building, and from the hands of someone like Ellis this might be a work of art in itself. In office buildings a great deal of attention would be paid to detailing such objects as elevator grills, stair rails, and hardware of all kinds. These objects were individually designed and locally fabricated. There was no *Sweets Catalogue*.

In structure the architects of Gateway City were neither particularly daring nor particularly conservative. While they admired the bold experimentation with the steel frame of their brethren in Chicago, they viewed it as a special solution brought about by soaring real estate values and uncertain soil conditions. They were generally wary of concrete because its essential properties and behavior were unknown. When these properties did become established, after 1900, they were quick to adapt it. Minneapolis, in fact, was a center of development for this material.

The Future of the Warehouse District: Adaptive Use and Continuing Function

The years 1880-1910 left Gateway City with a remarkable stock of architecturally significant buildings in the warehouse district. Today the use of those structures is a matter of prime concern to all those who are interested in the city as a humane environment. Gateway itself has grown into a metropolis of 250,000–500,000 people, and while its problems are by no means so overwhelming as those of New York, Philadelphia, and Detroit, they are serious. The warehouse district can be a real asset to their solution.

It is, of course, a very different place from what it was in the great days of the jobbing trade. The reason is that wholesaling itself has changed in character. Technological and social factors have played major roles in this change. Perhaps most significant is the development of alternative means of transport. A large percentage of the goods which formerly moved by railroad now go over the highways in trucks. It is convenient for these monsters to pick up freight at terminals on one of the superhighways encircling the city. The chain groceries cannot do without the warehousing function, but they have changed its location. Interestingly, no critics have claimed any architectural distinction for these buildings, which are usually a single story in height and spread over several acres.

Wholesaling has changed in other ways. The advent of the sewing machine in millions of American homes and the use of sophisticated patterns have made dry goods jobbing a thing of the past. The emergence of New York as the preeminent fashion center and apparel mart of the United States has been almost as important. Farm machinery distribution has also changed significantly. Plows and hayrakes have become complicated machines which no longer come in bundles. The farmer is no longer expected to assemble this equipment by himself, and the industry has become computerized and decentralized. The customer does not travel to a branch house to make his selection from the machines on display. Instead, he goes to a local dealership for initial purchase and for continuing service.[21]

All these developments and others too numerous to list have worked great changes in the wholesale district of Gateway City. Notwithstanding the disappearance of jobbing in groceries, it is by no means an inactive area. Its buildings are excellent architecture, and they are not empty shells. As farm machinery, groceries, and dry goods have moved out, other businesses have moved in. Typically these have been light manufacturing enterprises which do not require buildings that can sustain heavy floor loads. In this connection it should be noted that the load-bearing capacity of buildings in mill construction is substantially less than that for structures done in flat slab concrete. In 1945 the 18'6" square bays of the George D. Wood Warehouse in Winnipeg were certified for a uniformly distributed live load of 82 lbs per square foot on the first floor and 55 lbs per square foot on the fourth level. In contrast, Deere & Company currently calculates the permissible live load on all eight floors of its Omaha warehouse at 275 lbs per square foot.[22]

The discrepancy between these figures suggests a considerable range of possible uses for the buildings of the wholesale district. Small manufacturing operations, such as those of the apparel industry, can be easily fitted into the heavy timber frame of such buildings as the Woods warehouse. This has happened to a considerable extent in Winnipeg. In 1974 the fashion industry in that city absorbed about one thousand new people a year, and the figure has evidently risen since

that date. Typically the upper floors of these loft buildings now contain long rows of light wooden tables on which fabrics are spread out for the workers to cut and stitch. A sewing machine is probably the heaviest piece of equipment the visitor sees. With re-enforcing, however, the buildings can be made usable for heavier types of machinery, such as those employed in printing shops. This kind of recycling for industrial purposes has been going on quietly for a long time, and no one has made much fuss over it. It should certainly be encouraged since it provides workplaces for all kinds of people, some of them otherwise difficult to employ. In addition to sewing machine operators, there are freight handlers, shipping clerks, and various others in the wholesale hardware and plumbing fixture warehouses who still find the area attractive. Experience has repeatedly shown that it is sensible not to disrupt an area of this kind, particularly when it contains buildings of architectural merit, of which Gateway City has too few. This is traditional wisdom and it is entirely sound. Happily there appears to be a revulsion against redevelopment by demolition, but the cost has been horrendous.[23]

When I first sat down to write about warehouses in 1977–1978, I included a section in one essay which was an appeal, perhaps too strident, for the preservation and adaptive reuse of these fine old structures. I may have been influenced by my feelings about the loss of H. H. Richardson's Marshall Field Wholesale Store. It would be near the top of my list of vanished American buildings, which, given the opportunity, I would like to reerect. In any event, it was clear to me that, at least since the Second World War, the centers of our midwestern cities have looked less and less like humane environments. I wanted to point out that the warehouse districts of these places should be considered as huge reservoirs of usable space located close to the financial and shopping areas. I urged architects and developers to look long and hard at old industrial buildings, especially warehouses. I pointed out that the cost of new construction was soaring and that many studies showed the dollars and cents advantages of recycling. I had no idea that federal legislation, especially the tax credits which began in 1978, would produce the results I saw as desirable. Having revisited Gateway City in 1987, I have been impelled to rewrite my essays. They are now partly architectural history and partly reportage on current developments.

The case of the M. E. Smith warehouses in Omaha may serve as an illustration. When I visited the city in 1975 and 1976, this pair of buildings were owned and used by McKesson Robbins and Pendleton Woolen Mills. Unknown to me (I only looked at the buildings), the city's leaders had already recognized that the new satellite office complexes in the western suburbs were causing the downtown to lose its dominance as a shopping and financial center. They commissioned a study from Lawrence Halprin Associates of San Francisco, who recommended a linear park connecting the downtown and the river, about nine blocks east, through a deteriorating area of old commercial structures. Many of these I had admired. The study recommended, however, that "Omaha's stock of late nineteenth and early twentieth-century buildings might provide good housing opportunities."[24] Taking advantage of federal grants under the Open Space and Community Development Programs, the city purchased and cleared a stretch of land a block wide and four blocks long. The *New York Times* reports that:

> On this was created an urban retreat excavated below ground level, 20 feet in places to mask street noise, and filled with trees, grass, waterfalls and a lagoon. Part of the rationale for creating such a park was that its presence would encourage revival of the area, many of whose buildings were vacant. In the years since its completion, the neighborhood has in fact improved, and property values have increased.[25]

In the process one of the Smith buildings was lost, but the other was retained because of its National Register status.

Initially the city intended to use the warehouse for a civic recreation center or housing, but could not raise enough money for the project so in 1983 it invited bids from developers. The Schneider group in Ann Arbor was selected and bought the structure for $545,000. The firm proposes to convert it to some 135 apartments, some of them two stories high, ranging in size from 900 to 1300 square feet. Rents will run from $600 for a one bedroom to near $1000 for two bedrooms. This is substantially above the level in Omaha, but Mrs. Estelle Schneider expects to appeal to a group of people who work downtown and are looking for a premium location and a great view of the Missouri River. Schneider is a developer with a proven track record in Baltimore and elsewhere. I believe that success is likely. If such projects do nothing else, they will allow the residents to avoid the incredible nuisance of commuting on the superhighways. This is one of the least attractive features of living in many places in the United States today.[26] It remains to be noted that "Green House," as the Smith Building has been renamed, would be impossible without tax increment financing by the city of Omaha, a $700,000 gift by the local Peter Kiewit Foundation, and, very importantly, the federal tax credit for the adaptive reuse of buildings on the National Register.

So several of the buildings discussed in these chapters are much better known, at least locally, than they were when I "discovered" them in the mid-1970s. I should add, of course, that my recipe for the revitalization of downtown in Gateway City does not stop with adaptive reuse in the warehouse district. It includes new urban parks and the overhaul of places like Loring Park in Minneapolis, which I knew as a boy. And it includes the building of a certain number of absolutely first-class new commercial buildings. The businessmen of Gateway City need to become tougher and more knowledgeable patrons of architecture, less willing to accept what the prima donnas of the architectural profession offer them. Limited competitions are valuable. Here the example of the Humana Corporation in Louisville is very much to the point. The owners of the company held their own competition, awarded the prize to Michael Graves, and obtained a building which is a civic monument of the first order. I should add that I did not expect to like the Humana Building. Over a period of five months I studied it carefully and came to like it enormously. I wish I could say the same thing about the new office buildings in the cities mentioned in these essays.

Obviously my heart is very much with the Gateway Cities of middle North America. I hope that they will continue with judicious recycling, leave going enterprises alone, secure more urban parks, and obtain really excellent new buildings. Then they will become better places to live.

2

St. Joseph and the Western Trails

I shall always remember the city of St. Joseph, Missouri, with a certain degree of affection. I recall very well my excitement at discovering the architectural riches of the town and the warm reception of a few dedicated preservationists, especially Mrs. Bartlett Boder. Much of the extant work of Eckel and Mann, I thought, was very fine, and Eckel himself was such an interesting personality that I decided to include a section on his firm in my essay on warehouses. As I was well aware, studies of building types are notorious for the pitfalls they offer the architectural historian. My object was to examine the development of the warehouse in a restricted geographical area and during a relatively brief period when it became a type of exceptional architectural interest. In seeking the causes of this situation I was led to concentrate on problems of structure, of function, and of patronage. Structure and function are important and a major part of the story but are easier to deal with than patronage. The historian who goes after the *reasons* that cause a man, a woman, a partnership, or a corporation to put up an exceptional bit of architecture has set upon a difficult job. The task almost inevitably leads to a discursive treatment in the search for that elusive and indefinable essence called "character." I know very well that there are a lot of details in my accounts of James McCord, Rufus Lee MacDonald, John D. Richardson, and the Krug brothers. Some of these details may seem to the reader irrelevant

to the buildings those men erected. In the aggregate they seem to me to add up to a representation of a typical member of the mercantile elite.

At the same time that I enjoyed the hospitality of Mrs. Boder, I was conscious that there were many problems with the preservation of St. Joseph's architectural heritage. The business community did not seem to be at all enthusiastic about the idea. On my first visit I took a picture of Eckel and Mann's fine building for the Turnverein. On my second, it was gone, destroyed to make way for a parking lot. For reasons of convenience and price I stayed in a fine old hotel, the Robidoux, not far from the warehouse district. People asked me why I had not chosen one of the newer motels on the outskirts of town. I noticed that the occupancy rate of the Robidoux was low and wondered if it would survive. (It has gone too.) Nearby warehouse row, the best surviving block of Italianate structures from the 1870s and 1880s, was obviously in some danger. Recently I secured the National Register nomination of these buildings as a historic district (1976) and was not surprised to read, "The weakening affect of slow deterioration is augmented by a general lack of interest in preservation of the area by a majority of the business community." In the 1970s, at any rate, St. Joseph was a city which wanted "progress," without any reference to its historic past. I was fortunate to find a few warehouses well preserved and still functioning effectively as business buildings and to be able to spend some time working in the archives of Brunner and Brunner.

The warehouses of St. Joseph are particularly interesting because they show the building type in a richly decorated late nineteenth-century form. Among architectural historians it is an accepted generalization that the nineteenth century loved decoration. Sometimes the sources of this decoration were in the historic styles, chiefly Gothic and Renaissance. Sometimes, in a much more sophisticated way, as with Sullivan and Wright, the sources were found in nature and especially in plant forms. In any event, ornament was something the St. Joseph wholesalers evidently wanted in the buildings which housed their enterprises and which Eckel and Mann were happy to provide. Certainly it made the buildings somewhat more expensive than unadorned brick boxes, but the merchants and their architects evidently thought it a worthwhile investment. Why? With some diffidence I suggest that the reason is to be found in the attention the contemporary press paid to these buildings and in the characters of the jobbers themselves. The wholesale trade was seen as a highly respectable calling. The buildings which contained it were therefore serious architectural endeavors and emblematic of business soundness and solid worth. In this essay, and those which follow, the reader will therefore find an abundance of contemporary descriptions of warehouses and character sketches of their builders. In each case my method has been to supply a succinct urban history of the place and then to proceed to those factors in that history which made it an important wholesaling center. An analysis of the warehouses, their builders, and their architects forms the main body of each essay.

At the beginning of the nineteenth century French fur traders were already active close to the site of the present city of St. Joseph. Among the most energetic and successful of these was a certain Joseph Robidoux, an agent of the powerful Chouteau family of St. Louis, which, as the Missouri Fur Company, had almost a monopoly of trade with the Osage Indians south of the Missouri River. By 1804 he had built a stockade and some cabins, which were pointed out to Lewis and Clark by one of their boatmen, as they worked their way up the river. When they returned down the river in 1806, they met Robidoux himself, who was trading with the Indians at the mouth of the Wolf

River in Doniphan County, Kansas; they asked to see his credentials, which were perfectly in order. For some years thereafter Robidoux, who was born in 1784, divided his time between his trading post and the old family home in St. Louis, where the first Missouri legislature met in 1812 and where his second wife, Angelique, lived for many years caring for his numerous children. Robidoux must, in fact, have been one of the most successful fur traders of his time. In 1809, after his father's death in St. Louis, he went up the river with a new stock of goods to Council Bluffs, where John Jacob Astor's American Fur Company was firmly entrenched. He was so respected by the Indians that within a few years he controlled a large part of the trade from the Blacksnake Hills, near the site of St. Joseph, to the Bluffs, and in 1822 Astor offered him $1000 a year for three years to stay away.

As the years wore on, however, the gentlemen of London and Paris ceased to wear beaver hats, the fur trade declined, and by the early 1840s Robidoux was thinking of laying out a town which could be essentially a supply point for the farmers who were filling up the territory. The Platte Country had passed to the United States by a purchase treaty signed at Fort Leavenworth on September 17, 1836. (The United States government was represented by Joseph E. Robidoux, his father's namesake and associate in the fur trade.) The agricultural possibilities of the area and the potentialities of the townsite were noted by John James Audubon, the great naturalist and artist, when he traveled up the Missouri to the Yellowstone in the spring of 1843 in a boat lent to him by Pierre Chouteau, Jr. In his journal of May 5, 1843, Audubon wrote:

> At half-past twelve we reached the Blacksnake Hills settlement, and I was delighted to see this truly beautiful site for a town or city, as will be no doubt some fifty years hence. The hills themselves are about 200 feet above the river, and slope down quietly into the beautiful prairie that extends over some thousands of acres, of the richest land imaginable.[1]

Audubon's prophecy was fulfilled sooner than he expected. Later in the summer of 1843 Chouteau helped Joseph Robidoux to lay out his new town of St. Joseph with a loan of $6,372.57. Two surveyors solicited the founder's favor by submitting competing plats. They were Simeon Kemper and Frederick W. Smith, and the Smith plat won out. According to some local historians the Kemper plat was rejected because he had made the proposed streets too wide and Robidoux had the traditional French preference for narrow streets. Majority opinion seems to hold that the Smith plat was accepted because he had proposed the name of St. Joseph, the old man's patron saint.

On January 24, 1848, fifteen hundred miles to the west, an event took place which was to have a profound impact on the fortunes of the little settlement. James W. Marshall discovered gold at the site of Sutter's Mill on the clear, swift south fork of the American River in Placer County, California. A year later, in the spring of 1849, twenty thousand emigrants were camped around St. Joseph awaiting green grass for their horses and oxen. Fortunes were to be made from provisioning these people, and St. Joseph's merchants, craftsmen, saddle and harness makers, hemp growers, gunsmiths, and pork packers supplied the forty-niners at handsome profits.

It was at this time that the foundations of many large fortunes of St. Joseph were laid, notably that of the Tootle family. Because of an outbreak of cholera at Independence and Westport, which were the rival points of departure for the Santa Fe trail, the greater number of emigrants took the northern route. St. Joseph thus emerged as the major wagon train and supply depot. Between April and June 1849, approximately fifteen hundred prairie schooners crossed the Missouri at St. Joseph and thousands more crossed on the ferries above and below the town. Rudolph Kurz, a Swiss artist, who happened to be on hand, wrote in his journal that so many tents were pitched on the riverbank and around the city that it seemed they were besieged by an army.

While the forty-niners sang around their fires, boom times came to St. Joseph. Despite the increasingly tense political atmosphere of the period, building went on apace. This outfitting of wagon trains was short-lived but it established the basis of many enterprises which were to be of major significance. It meant that the merchants of the city very early saw the possibilities of the wholesale trade. They were strategically placed for this business not only in relation to the western trails but also to the river. The 1850s were, as Mark Twain so beautifully depicted them on the Mississippi, the great decade of the steamboat. For most of those years more than twenty steamers a day paid the $5 wharfage fee at St. Joseph, and most of them were laden with goods which had to be stored awaiting further shipment overland. To add to the prosperity, in 1858, just when the California excitement was dying down, gold was discovered in Colorado, and a new horde of emigrants poured through the city. Truly, the future must have seemed golden.

It is not surprising that all this activity stimulated the construction of a railroad. Aided by the usual federal and state land grants, the Hannibal and St. Joseph Railroad reached the thriving town in 1859, and the customary golden spike was driven by first citizen Joseph Robidoux. Thus, St. Joseph had the tremendous advantage of being the last western railroad terminal, and moreover, the connecting point for John M. Hockaday's famous stage line to Salt Lake City, one thousand miles away. Since this venture had been initiated to strengthen the connection between the War Department and the small body of troops in Utah, it sought dependability rather than rapid service. Speed, on the other hand, was a necessity if California was to be saved for the Union. Out of this situation emerged the Pony Express, whose history was one of the most colorful, if brief, episodes in the history of the city. Service was begun April 3, 1860, with St. Joseph as the eastern terminus and Sacramento as the western. Riders left both places the same day, and on April 14 the eastbound rider reached St. Joseph with the western mail. While the Pony Express was displaced within two years by the overland telegraph, the railroad mail car was a direct outgrowth of the need to sort mail quickly for the outgoing riders. The first such car was built for the Hannibal and St. Joseph.

Among all the young cities of the Midwest St. Joseph was most brutally affected by the Civil War. Buchanan County was largely southern in its sympathies. More than two thousand slaves were owned here, and when crusading abolitionists encouraged some and aided others to escape into "Free Kansas," feelings ran high. In 1859 a certain Dr. John Doy was intercepted in an attempt to spirit a group of slaves out of Missouri, and the case was brought to St. Joseph for trial. "Shortly before the trial, however," says an unknown chronicler, "a party of Kansans, 'secured' the jailer and escaped with Doy into Kansas."[2]

In the tense spring of 1861 a proslavery mob headed by M. Jeff Thompson, a local real estate dealer, tore down the United States flag at the post office. This incident suggests the intensity of southern sentiment in the town; it was so strong that a local newspaper actually published the names of the four hundred individuals who had the temerity to vote for Lincoln in 1860! Thompson became a general in the Confederate forces, was widely known for his skillful guerrilla tactics, and at the conclusion of hostilities, in an unknowingly symbolic gesture, surrendered his sword to Gen. Grenville M. Dodge, the famous railroad builder. Until 1864, when troops were quartered in the town, schools were closed and business almost disappeared. Nonetheless, when Joseph Robidoux, the patriarch of St. Joseph, died in 1868, prosperity had returned. Texas cattlemen began to move eastward to market, and they brought with them not only meat animals but also new breeding stock. A St. Joseph company built a toll and railroad bridge across the river. Finished in 1873, it served until 1929. In the quarter century after the war five more railroads entered the city, and by 1889 their tracks totaled more than thirty-five thousand miles. Almost unnoticed, however, Kansas City had bridged the Missouri in 1869, and within a few decades the bustling city a few hours to the south of St. Joseph had overtaken its northern neighbor.

In the 1880s St. Joseph was at the peak of its postwar prosperity. It was a regional center for the cattle business, and its flour mills, packinghouses, and horse and mule markets were of interstate importance. *The Daily News History of Buchanan County* (1899) considered that the years from 1885 to 1893 were the most momentous period in the city's history. During this period the Rock Island, the Chicago Great Western, and the Atchison, Topeka, and Santa Fe reached the city, and there had been an immense amount of construction. In addition to several office blocks, a YMCA, a theater, a police station, and a building for the local Turnverein (German gymnastic society), there also went up those massive piles of brick, stone, and terra-cotta occupied by Tootle, Hosea & Company, the C. D. Smith Drug Co., and many others.

These last were the great wholesale firms which were the real key to the city's prosperity. Most of them were designed by the firm of Eckel and Mann, which also did splendid romantic mansions for their owners on the bluffs overlooking the Missouri River. In these houses Eckel may very well have given Harvey Ellis, who arrived in St. Joseph in 1888, a freer hand than in the commercial work, where structural problems and strict adherence to a restrictive program were ne-

cessities. The importance of St. Joseph as a jobbing center is suggested by the fact that in 1897 more than one thousand travelling salesmen lived there. A brochure issued by the United Commercial Travelers in that year illustrated the great building of the Tootle firm and remarked that it was the oldest wholesale house in the West.

In St. Joseph, then, we have a city whose economic life depended primarily upon the success of a handful of great wholesale firms which were primarily family enterprises. The careers of the men who managed them have so much in common that it is possible to draw a kind of composite portrait. The typical St. Joseph merchant came originally from the Upper South: Virginia, Kentucky, or Tennessee. He was born in the 1820s or 1830s, went west with his family, and while still a boy, began to help out in a Missouri country store. Savannah, River Forest, and Oregon, Missouri, were common places in which to get started. He had little formal education but in the 1850s often saw a good deal of the world.

Because he was a young man of promise, his employers often trusted him with substantial responsibilities. Sometimes he took a shipment of goods to California, sold them there, and returned to Missouri via the Isthmus of Panama and steamer from New Orleans. He rose rapidly in the business world and usually married into the family of his employers or one of his future partners. Just before the Civil War or shortly after its conclusion, he moved to St. Joseph, as he was impressed with its commercial advantages.

His business was at a standstill during the war, but after peace was signed he again plunged into the jobbing trade and was shortly doing very well indeed. In fact, his greatest failing as a business leader was undoubtedly his inability to see the profound significance of the transcontinental railway. True, he was excited by the arrival of the Hannibal and St. Joseph in 1859, but he was already doing so well fitting out wagon trains and selling to country storekeepers that he did not throw himself into a campaign for the city to become the eastern terminus.

His prosperity, in fact, caused him to think of his business headquarters as a family emblem. The building was likely to be displayed on the firm's circulars, so great care had to be taken with the design. This attitude, and the fortuitous presence of Ellis, who was a genius in the design of ornament, led to a version of the warehouse remarkable for its architectural richness. By comparison the warehouses of our other Gateway Cities seem extremely severe.

In the long run, then, this dependence on the jobbing trade worked to the detriment of St. Joseph. It meant that the city did not have a strong industrial base, and so it could only look on enviously as Kansas City forged ahead. A significant note in *The Daily News History of Buchanan Country* remarked that certain manufacturing ventures had been launched but did not survive. These included a steel car works, a stove company, and nail mills. St. Joseph did not become an industrial center, but it was the first, and for a long time the greatest, jobbing center for the trans-Missouri West.

Edmond J. Eckel and His Office

For a surprisingly long period Edmond Jacques Eckel and his partners were the dominating firm in St. Joseph, and their influence was felt throughout the entire Missouri Valley. Eckel himself was born in 1845 in Strasbourg, France, where his father, formerly a professor at a local military institute, ran a successful toy manufacturing establishment. His early schooling was at the city's Protestant lycée, and at the age of fourteen he went to work for a relative who had a substantial contracting business. This early experience with the practical side of building was to serve him well; in later years he was famous for the integrity of his structures. In 1863 he entered the Atelier Paccard in Paris, and on the death of M. Paccard, joined the Atelier Vaudoyer, taking his diploma at the École des Beaux Arts in 1868, in which year he came to the United States. After landing in New York, Eckel went directly to Cleveland to meet a brother, and together they went west, arriving in Omaha just at the time the Union Pacific Railroad had made its connection with that city. They had intended to go to Kansas City but were detained in the woods just north of St. Joseph by a bridge washout. They arrived in St. Joseph on a Saturday afternoon, only to discover that the trains did not run on Sunday. Eckel, however, liked the town and decided to settle there. Thus St. Joseph gained a highly trained architect at just the point in its history when it could use one.

Exactly why Eckel emigrated remains a mystery. Not many architects left France for the United States in the 1860s; the invasion was to come several decades later. A possible explanation is that Eckel was a Protestant and that he may have anticipated some difficulty in securing the official commissions which are such an important part of architectural practice in France. The presence of the older brother in the United States may also have been an attraction. In any event, we have the somewhat curious case of a highly trained Beaux Arts man going into architecture in a town of about ten thousand population only two decades or so removed from the frontier stage. One other aspect of his European background should be noted here. In the bilingual city of Strasbourg Eckel grew up speaking German as easily as French, and this ability may well have helped him in his dealings with St. Joseph's German community.

One of his first jobs was with the local firm of Stigers and Boettner, where much German must have been spoken. In a few years Stigers retired, and the firm became Boettner and Eckel. In 1880 Eckel associated himself with George R. Mann, a native of Indiana and a graduate of the recently founded school at MIT. For the next twelve years the firm was exceedingly active, and it was in this boom period that the great warehouses of Wyeth Hardware, the Nave-McCord Mercantile Company, and Tootle, Hosea and Co. were built. From 1888 to 1892 they employed the gifted but alcoholic Harvey Ellis, who was probably responsible for the decorative detail on the last named building. Ellis was also undoubtedly in large measure responsible for many of the imposing mansions which the firm built. His role in the production of the firm can, however, be overstated. Eckel and Mann employed other designers, and at least one important house, customarily assigned to Ellis, should certainly be credited to young John Richmond on the basis of a signed drawing in the archives of the firm. Furthermore, Eckel himself was not only a domineering personality but also an expert on structure. It is extremely unlikely that he would have trusted Ellis with a foundation or the handling of the mill framing system in one of these great buildings. On the other hand, he was undoubtedly happy to use him on decorative detail, where Ellis was an acknowledged master.[3]

The problem of style in Eckel's office is, in fact, extremely complicated, and has several ironic twists. On the basis of the extant work with which Eckel himself can be credited, his early preference was certainly for the academic manner of the École des Beaux Arts in the

1860s and 1870s. The Cedar Rapids, Iowa, Court House of 1885 is a good example; with its mansard roofs and imposing entrances it is very much Parisian Second Empire. In this same decade, however, he was confronted with the fantastic American enthusiasm for Richardson, which endured into the 1890s. Eckel was quick to understand its significance; his own drawing for the St. Joseph Railroad Station of 1895–1896 (now destroyed) is extremely Richardsonian. Nonetheless the building of which he was most proud was his winning design in the competition for the St. Louis City Hall in 1891. His granddaughter recalls that he frequently said that he had let no one else touch those drawings. The building itself is a French Renaissance concoction with an imposing and exceedingly picturesque collection of gables, towers, and spirelets.

After 1900, of course, he was confronted by a resurgent American neoclassicism, and this development he must have found thoroughly congenial. His second important partner was Will Aldrich, a New Yorker, graduate of MIT and thoroughly schooled in the academic manner. Eckel thus lived to see the triumph of those ideals which he had brought to the West as a young man, but he will probably be best remembered for the great warehouses of the 1880s and for the handful of buildings on which he gave Harvey Ellis free rein.

Part of the significance of Edmond Eckel lies in the sheer volume and range of his work. A newspaper article of 1931 remarked that if it were possible to remove all the buildings designed either by Eckel himself or his firm, the city would resemble to a great extent the small town of ten thousand people in which he had arrived sixty-two years previously. The work of the firm extended through fifteen states and in addition to the St. Louis City Hall and the Cedar Rapids Court House, included the Paxton Hotel in Omaha, the City Hall at Columbia, Missouri, and very late in Eckel's life, a factory for the National Biscuit Company in Los Angeles, with which that concern was especially well pleased. Though small in stature, Eckel was a man of great energy and endurance and continued in practice almost to the very day of his death in 1934. Pictures taken in his maturity show him to have been immaculately groomed and neatly bearded—the very model of a French chef d'atelier—and there is no doubt that he insisted on the highest professional standards in all his work. He was an active member of the Western Association of Architects, later a Fellow of the

A.I.A., and an entire issue of the *Western Architect* was devoted to his buildings. Quite possibly his achievement deserves greater notice in histories of American architecture than it has hitherto received.[4]

NAVE-McCORD MERCANTILE COMPANY
(Eckel and Mann, 1882–1883)

Among all the great wholesale houses of St. Joseph, the firm of Nave-McCord was probably most important in groceries. While it is difficult to assign responsibility, it is probable that the junior partner, James McCord, was the more active in the business. A Virginian by birth, he was born in 1826 in Albemarle County, where his father practiced law. In 1836 the family decided to go west, travelling by steamboat down the Ohio and up the Mississippi to Cape Girardeau, Missouri, and thence to Versailles, where William McCord resumed the practice of law in 1838. He died, however, in the following year, and it was necessary for his son to leave school and get a job. Hearing that he could obtain a position in a country store in Calhoun, sixty miles away, he walked the distance and for the first year worked for his board alone. For the next few years he learned the storekeeper's trade and gradually acquired his employer's confidence with the result that he was sent as an agent on buying trips to St. Louis and New Orleans. During this period he visited the newly opened Platte Purchase and evidently made a careful study of business conditions there, particularly in Savannah and St. Joseph.

In 1841 his sister, Lucy, had married Abram Nave, a merchant of Savannah, and by 1846 McCord felt himself sufficiently experienced (he was twenty years old) so that he entered a partnership with his brother-in-law in that town. This business association and personal friendship was to continue unbroken for fifty-two years. The firm opened a branch in the town of Oregon in Holt County, which McCord managed, while Nave was in charge in Savannah.

Like most of his contemporaries, McCord had interests not immediately related to his country stores. He made several trips across the plains driving cattle, returning to Missouri by the Isthmus of Panama. In later years he was interested in the Henry Krug Packing Company of St. Joseph and participated in the organization of the C. D. Smith Drug Company and in the ownership of a one-hundred-thousand-acre cattle ranch in Texas. The center of his business activity, however, was always in the wholesale grocery firm of Nave-McCord, which the partners moved to St. Joseph in 1857. Despite the upheavals of the next decade, it prospered enormously because of its aggressive, honest, thorough, and conservative methods. Branches were established in St. Louis, Kansas City, Omaha, Pueblo, Fort Worth, Oklahoma City, Topeka, and Hutchinson, Kansas, and these afforded ample opportunity for the business education of McCords' six sons, all of whom went into the firm. McCord died at his home in St. Joseph on September 24, 1903, and the newspaper obituary was, in the manner of the time, somewhat fulsome:

> Modest almost to a fault, moving on day after day, attending to his own business and medling [sic] with no other man's, giving counsel to the younger men who sought his advice, temperate and industrious, kind and gentle, yet dignified and firm, Mr. McCord had been for over half a century, the one distinct, leading figure in the world of merchants in the great West, and the pride and admiration of his many friends.[5]

More to the point is the fact that, as a token of appreciation, his employees gave him a gold-headed cane on January 1, 1880, to celebrate the New Year.

McCord's partner, Abram Nave, was, like himself, a southerner, born in Cooke County, East Tennessee, in 1815. His parents brought him to the newly organized territory of Missouri when he was a boy, and at age twenty-six he went to Savannah, where he subsequently met his future brother-in-law. In 1872 he went to St. Louis to superintend the partnership's business there and did not return to St. Joseph until 1882. While his son, Samuel M. Nave (1849–1901), was one of the most important businessmen in St. Joseph, Abram Nave does not seem to have been as important in the development of the wholesale business as James McCord. The simple difference in ages may partly account for this variation in achievement. He was more than a decade older than his partners, and it was the younger, more energetic men who presided over the expansion of the house.

The superb building which Nave-McCord commissioned in 1882 (Fig. 2.1) was at least the fourth in the history of the firm.[6] After their first small beginning in 1857, they moved to a structure from which they were burned out in 1860, probably in the commotions attendant on the outbreak of the Civil War. About 1880 they secured property on South Third Street close to the railway lines of the Missouri Pacific and the Burlington and began building there. The partially finished edifice was destroyed in a curious accident. A handcart loaded with nails crashed through the supporting timbers and set fire to the building by crashing into a section in which matches were stored. This episode evidently impressed the partners, particularly McCord, with the need for an exceptionally strong building, and the edifice designed by Eckel and Mann is a classic instance of fire-resistant mill construction (Fig. 2.3). The heavy beams are framed directly into the brick piers of the facade; most joints are bolted, and there is very little nailing.

Fig. 2.1. Eckel and Mann. Nave-McCord Mercantile Co., 1882–1883. From George R. Mann, Selections from an Architect's Portfolio *(1893).*

Fig. 2.2. Nave-McCord Building, facade detail. Photo: Steve Slater.

Fig. 2.3. Nave-McCord Building, structural system. Photo: Steve Slater.

The facade itself is a powerful expression of the heavy construction within. The brick detailing is magnificent, and it is set off by delicate bands of terra-cotta and stonework (Fig. 2.2). On the facade the designer attempted a very interesting articulation of the wall. The windows are simply nicely proportioned openings in the brick surface, but the elevations are enlivened by the delicate brick corbelling which was necessitated when the heavy 4″ x 10″ floor joists were slotted into the bearing wall. Here is a fine example of a designer accepting a necessary structural feature and making it into something beautiful. At the rear are the large doors necessary for easy movement of goods to

and from the adjacent railway line. The entire structure brings to mind the perceptive comment of a writer in the *Western Architect* who reviewed Edmond Eckel's work in 1911:

> The early clients of Mr. Eckel were those sturdy pioneer merchants who were laying the foundations for immense wholesale businesses in the west, while at the same time they were laying the foundations for the magnificent buildings that now house their stock. Conservatism was the rule in their business transaction and the same rule was applied to other phases of life.[7]

One is, however, tempted to assign at least some credit for the design of this fine building to George R. Mann, who published it in his *Selections from an Architect's Portfolio* (1893). Mann was a graduate of MIT and would presumably have been familiar with the system of mill construction as it had been developed in the East. On the other hand it is only fair to add that Eckel himself had the traditional Beaux Arts respect for structure and that he undoubtedly knew a good thing when he saw it.

TURNER-FRAZER MERCANTILE COMPANY
(Eckel and Mann, 1882–1883)

A close neighbor to the Nave-McCord Building is this handsome structure of approximately the same dimensions (five stories and 80′ × 130′). The business was founded in 1854 in Oregon, Missouri, by Richard E. Turner, who was born in Culpepper County, Virginia, in 1830. His family moved west and he attended schools in Ohio and Missouri until age fourteen. "Such education as he has since received," said a biographer, "has been through contact with the world,"[8] and indeed this was the normal situation for most of his contemporaries. At age fourteen he was clerk in a country store at Millersburg, Missouri, and in 1848 he took charge of the mercantile house of T. P. Bell in Cooper County, which he managed successfully for some time. In the spring of 1850 he accepted a position with Abram Nave, and the following year went to Salt Lake City with a stock of goods owned by Nave, spending the winter in the Morman capital. In the spring he exchanged the merchandise for horses, cattle, and mules, which he took to California and disposed of profitably, returning to Savannah in November 1852 by way of the Isthmus of Panama and New Orleans. In 1854 Nave and his partners sent Turner to California in charge of a second expedition consisting of thirty men, sixteen wagons, fifty horses and mules, and seven hundred steers. Today this would be considered a substantial responsibility for a man of twenty-four, but Turner safely conducted the wagon train to a ranch on the Sacramento River. He returned to Savannah by way of Nicaragua and New York.

From 1855 to 1860 Turner was a partner of Nave and James McCord, and in the latter year purchased their interests in the firm, which was at that time located in Forest City, Missouri. In 1860 he formed a new partnership with H. L. Williams and John M. Frazer under the name of Turner, Frazer, and Company. The new firm was in business at Forest City until 1864 when they moved to St. Joseph, just in time to escape the shift in the channel of the Missouri River which so damaged the prospects of the little town.

After doing business in three other locations, the partners built, in 1882–1883, the handsome structure which is shown here (Figs. 2.4–2.6). A contemporary writer caught the spirit of the building when he remarked that its solidity showed the solid worth and extensive ramifications of the company's operations. It was steam-heated, had elevators for conveying freight from one floor to another, and every convenience for handling heavy goods. It had platform space where several freight cars could be loaded and unloaded at once; on its side tracks twenty cars could stand easily. The offices were spacious and well appointed, and the staff was noted for its politeness. There were about forty inside employees—porters, clerks, and salesmen—and a large and experienced corps of travelling representatives, each of whom carried a full line of samples. The somewhat exotic character of the business is suggested in the following language:

> On the numerous floors and in the rooms of their spacious establishment will be found the edible products and preparations of every zone and country, necessities and luxuries used by civilized men, from the teas of Asia, the coffee of South America, through Havana and domestic cigars, European fruits and jellies, to the canned goods of our home factories, the butter and cheese of our Missouri farms, all we remark of best quality, at prices seldom duplicated elsewhere.[9]

The firm seems to have had a notable reputation for meeting its financial obligations on time and for fair dealing with its customers.

In the classic pattern of the American businessman, Turner's avocation was business. In addition to his interest in the wholesale house which bore his name, he was president of the Merchant's Bank of St. Joseph for three years, was instrumental in building the first street railway line and the first electric plant in St. Joseph, and was president of both utilities for considerable periods. He was also a promoter of the St. Joseph and St. Louis Railway and served as vice-president when the road was built, was connected with the company that built the St. Joseph and Grand Island, was president of the first Board of Trade in St. Joseph, and was a large stockholder in the Jones Payne Hat Company. Despite all these activities he does not seem to have ranked as one of the town's wealthiest men. His biographer remarked that he was satisfied with moderate gain annually.

He may well not have been St. Joseph's most successful merchant but his building is a remarkable memorial. It is of interest that in July 1974 Mr. John Clayton, president of the Sheridan-Clayton Paper Company, which has occupied the building since 1903, told the writer that he had once remarked to his insurance agent that he was worried about the possibility of fire in his old wooden building. The reply was that, equipped with an automatic sprinkler system as it is today, the building was much safer than the majority of comparable industrial structures. His rates were lower, too.

Fig. 2.5. Turner-Frazer Mercantile Co., facade detail. Photo: Steve Slater.

Fig. 2.6. Turner-Frazer Mercantile Co., structural systems. Photo: Steve Slater.

Fig. 2.4. Eckel and Mann. Turner-Frazer Mercantile Co. From Selec-tions from an Architect's Portfolio (1893).

BLOCK OF WAREHOUSES ON NORTH FOURTH STREET
(Eckel and Mann, 1880–1898)

This series of warehouses on North Fourth Street at one time housed three of the major dry goods firms in St. Joseph. The earliest was built in 1880 for Rufus Lee MacDonald, who, like most of the leading merchants of the city, was a southerner by birth. He was born in Harrodsburg, Kentucky, in 1832, was educated in the local schools, and came to St. Joseph in 1851 to visit an uncle, who was a doctor in the city. MacDonald wanted to get a job with the merchandising firm of Donnell and Saxton, then the leaders in the city, but was told that they had no place for him. Fortunately, his uncle's wife, who was the sister of one of the partners, interceded for him, and he was taken on at no pay in order to learn the business. By all accounts the young man was a hard worker. He slept over the store, and when one of the partners worked late, MacDonald asked to sit at his side to see what he was doing. In this way he learned bookkeeping. As a result of his industry, the partners decided to pay him $12 a month and board. Three years later he was taken into the firm. In 1857 Donnell and Saxton decided to open a bank, and they offered to sell the store to MacDonald. Although he said he had no capital, they replied that they trusted him and that he could pay them off as he was able. So he bought the store, enlarged it, and it grew and prospered.

One of the characteristics of the pioneer merchant was ingenuity, and this was never better demonstrated than by MacDonald during the Civil War. At that time the city was filled with "Bushwackers," who would come into the stores, take the merchandise off the shelves, and walk away, paying nothing. It was almost impossible to continue in business this way. The MacDonald family situation was particularly strained by the presence of numerous relatives. Many of these were women and children, sent out from Kentucky and Virginia to escape the active seat of war. Mrs. MacDonald was in effect feeding a refugee camp. Pondering his problem, MacDonald went out into the countryside to buy as many young Missouri mules as he could find. These animals were not yet ready to work and had to be fed. They were not worth stealing. People thought MacDonald was crazy to put his money into them, but he arranged for his son and employees to take the mules and a wagon train across the plains to California. The mules fed on the fresh grass, and by the time they reached the coast

were large enough to break and sell. MacDonald went by stagecoach to Salt Lake City, met the train there, took them through the mountains, sold the mules at a handsome profit, and returned to New York by way of Panama.

With his new capital he purchased a fresh stock of goods, and in 1865 opened up the wholesale business of R. L. MacDonald and Company. His enterprise flourished, and in 1880 he moved into the building shown here (Figs. 2.7 and 2.8), at that time the largest mercantile house in the city with 70,000 square feet of floor space. In 1886 he bought the old Patee House, St. Joseph's first large hotel, converted it into a factory, and began manufacturing shirts and work clothes; the "Red Seal" overalls were a particular success. He also operated a large farm in Andrew County, in the present Country Club district outside St. Joseph, and owned substantial wheat acreage in Western Kansas. Finally, he was a director and vice president of the First National Bank.

Fig. 2.7. Eckel and Mann. Block of warehouses on North Fourth Street, 1880–1898. Photo: Steve Slater.

Fig. 2.8. R. L. MacDonald Co. and first unit of Englehart, Winning, and Co. Photo: Brunner and Brunner.

The next pair of buildings were the headquarters of Englehart, Winning, and Company, the leaders of the wholesale millinery trade. The firm's leading figure was George J. Englehart, who surely had as colorful an early career as any of the city's merchants.

Born in the small town of Hohensultzen near Worms, he came to the United States as a child with his parents, who settled on a farm near Mansfield, Ohio. At age sixteen he got a job in a dry goods store in nearby Mt. Vernon, worked there and in Cincinnati for a few years, and in 1855 went to California to pan for gold. Three years later he returned to New York on the steamer *Golden Gate*, subsequently deciding to locate in Kansas. He came up the Missouri River as far as Iowa Point and walked to Hiawatha, where a brother was

farming. Hiawatha was only a small place, but Englehart saw an opening for a general store. He went to St. Louis and purchased stock with gold that he himself had dug. After six years he sold his interest and came to St. Joseph in 1865, buying a partnership in the house of Tootles and Fairleigh. The following year he entered the hat and cap business, which had been established in the city in 1850 by Samuel Lockwood, a journeyman hatter.

Englehart is a good example of a man who saw the advantages of specialization. He went into partnership with Lockwood, and, says a contemporary account, "brought the millinery and notions part into the business, from which time on they led an exclusively jobbing trade."[10] In 1878 Robert Winning, a Scotsman, joined them, and two years later John A. Johnston came in. In 1885 the senior partner retired, and for the next two decades the firm was known as Englehart, Winning, and Company.

There is no doubt that Englehart was the driving force in the expansions of the business. They moved several times and in 1880 Englehart finished the building next to MacDonald; five years later he leased the adjoining structure, and in 1898 added an additional story to his original premises (see Fig. 2.8). He thus obtained a frontage of 80' and a depth of 140' feet, ample for his purposes. Both buildings were five stories with basement. The same contemporary account gives an excellent description of the interior layout.

These premises are spacious and lofty in their aspect, everything is kept as neat as a pin, and they are quite a pleasure to visit. The basements are used for billing, packing, and shipping. On the first floor of the millinery and notion house we find an array of notions in which the inventive genius of the milliners and artisans of all nations is displayed; on the second floor from the varied colors of the numberless flowers, it is but a short step to the beauties of a tropical forest; the third floor is devoted to ladies hats, trimmings and patterns, and the fourth and fifth to duplicate stock. On the hat and glove side of the house on the first floor, we find fur goods of every description, the corner being laid off in well appointed offices; above we find silk, felt, and wool hats in the latest fashions; on the third floor are caps, straw goods and gloves; the fourth being set aside for duplicate stock in unbroken boxes.[11]

The house's trade extended west to Utah and Idaho and south through the Indian Territory to the Rio Grande. It kept fourteen men on the road selling millinery and notions, and twelve others marketed hats, caps, and gloves. Sixty-five clerks and sales personnel worked inside the building. An interesting innovation was the development of a corps of female stylistic representatives. These ladies did not sell, but kept the country storekeepers informed on the latest trends in fashion.

Englehart himself found time for politics, and he was unusual among his fellow merchants in that he was a Republican. In 1886 he was nominated for state senator but declined to run for business reasons. He was also president of the first Federal Grand Jury in Buchanan County.

As of the summer of 1987 this block of buildings still exists, preserved as a National Register district. The Englehart buildings have been gutted in preparation for reuse, but have not been finished, leaving the structure open to the elements.

RICHARDSON, ROBERTS, AND BYRNE WAREHOUSE
(Eckel and Van Brunt, 1891)

Born in 1847 in Dorchester County, Maryland, John D. Richardson came to St. Joseph in 1870 and secured a post as accountant for Donnell and Saxton, who were then active in railroad contracting for the line which later became the St. Joseph and Grand Island Railway. Attracted by the possibilities of the jobbing trade, he joined John S. Brittain in a wholesale dry goods firm, whose building we have mentioned earlier. In 1890 Richardson withdrew from the business and organized Richardson, Roberts, and Byrne Wholesale Drygoods, which in time became one of the largest jobbing houses in the Missouri Valley.

The headquarters of this new firm was the large building shown here in the original illustration from *The American Architect and Building News* of 1892, and in a recent photograph (Figs. 2.9 and 2.10). On this occasion Richardson went not only to Eckel but also to Henry Van Brunt of Kansas City, who was also a specialist in commercial building. Together they produced a structure whose elevations have a pronounced resemblance to those of Adler and Sullivan's Auditorium Hotel in Chicago of 1886–1888, which both firms must have

known well. Particularly close in design are the rising arches at the corners and the groups of arches which fill the center sections of the building. The rustication at ground level is also very similar to the Sullivan treatment.

Fig. 2.9. Eckel and Van Brunt. Warehouse for Richardson, Roberts, and Byrne, 1892. From American Architect and Building News *(May 1892).*

30

Fig. 2.10. Richardson, Roberts, and Byrne Warehouse. Photo: Steve Slater.

Fig. 2.11. Eckel and Mann. C. D. Smith Wholesale Drug Co., 1888. Photo: Steve Slater.

In structure the building is a combination of the older mill construction and the newer forms of metal framing. The entrance on the corner, marked out by its single column of polished granite, is somewhat peculiar, but we must remember that wholesale firms usually wanted imposing entryways and that there was a sharp distinction between office space and loft space. In its elevations the building is extremely close to another structure of approximately the same size, the Melvin J. Clark Building of Grand Rapids built in 1896. The Auditorium image was evidently extremely persuasive.

Richardson himself was evidently a rather quiet personality, active in the affairs of his church and for many years a trustee of Noyes Hospital. He had no children and was known for his charities. He died in 1924.

C. D. SMITH WHOLESALE DRUG COMPANY
(Eckel and Mann, 1888)

The C. D. Smith Drug Company of St. Joseph is probably the only wholesale house in the United States which still operates from its original premises. The founder, Charles Daniel Smith, was born at Waynesboro, Pennsylvania, in 1835, but his parents moved to Emmetsburg, Maryland, when he was a boy so that his early schooling was in that locality. In 1857 he went west to Iowa and thence to St. Joseph. Attracted by the possibilities of the wholesale grocery business, he was for several years associated with James McCord, while his brother, Samuel Smith, who had come to the city with him, was in the dry goods trade. In 1887 they combined forces to start a wholesale drug business and in 1888 built the excellent structure shown here

(Figs. 2.11, 2.12). Within a few years Charles bought out the interests of his brother, and since the purchase his branch of the family has carried on the business. In 1923 they bought out the Van Natta Drug Company, thus consolidating the two largest drug houses on the Missouri River. Although the same number of salesmen are no longer on the road, the firm is still highly successful. The old building has been modernized with conveyor belts, and it is to be hoped that the C. D. Smith Company will occupy it for many years to come.

This edifice is, in fact, one of the masterpieces of Eckel and Mann. The role of Harvey Ellis in the design is problematical. He was in St. Joseph working for the firm in 1888 and from all accounts extremely influential when sober. He may well have suggested the noble series of arches across the facade, now unhappily blocked in for business reasons. Probably he was responsible for the delightful moulded brick at the corners, and the glowing red terra-cotta is certainly his (Fig. 2.13). On the other hand, it is unlikely that Eckel, who was an extremely careful person, strongly imbued with the classic French respect for construction, would have let Ellis have anything to do with the structural design. George Eckel said as much to a correspondent in 1951.

Fig. 2.12. C. D. Smith Wholesale Drug Co., side elevation. Photo: Wayne Andrews.

Fig. 2.13. C. D. Smith Wholesale Drug Co., decorative detail. Photo: Steve Slater.

Fig. 2.14. Eckel and Mann. Tootle, Hosea & Co., 1888–1889. Original rendering courtesy of Brunner and Brunner.

For this building the firm returned to a pure version of mill construction, which had been used so successfully in the Nave-McCord and Turner-Frazer warehouses across the street. Like the earlier buildings, the C. D. Smith is essentially a magnificent essay in the use of brick and wood. It is a true monument to the solidity of the family enterprise.[12]

TOOTLE, HOSEA, AND COMPANY
(Eckel and Mann, 1888–1889)

Among all the merchant princes of St. Joseph, Milton Tootle was the most important. His success can be gauged by the fact that in the early days of his great enterprise in Chicago, Marshall Field paid a visit to St. Joseph and reportedly said that he hoped he would someday have as fine a business as Mr. Tootle. Born in Ross County, Ohio, in 1823, Tootle apparently never received more than an elementary education. Like Abraham Lincoln, he supplemented this with a great

deal of well-directed reading; his business education began early and was exceptionally thorough. In 1836 his father moved to Jersey County, Illinois, where Milton, only thirteen years of age and hardly able to see over the countertop, embarked upon his early training. He soon entered the employ of an uncle, George Smith, who took him to Savannah in Andrew County, Missouri, and he won the confidence of Smith to such an extent that he was indispensable to him. In Atchinson County, Missouri, he was given complete charge of another business, and after various experiences with other country stores, came to St. Joseph in 1849 at the request of Smith, who gave him an interest in the business of Smith, Bedford and Tootle.

Shortly after Tootle's arrival Smith died, and with his brothers, Joseph and Thomas, and William G. Fairleigh, Milton purchased his stock and began business as Tootles and Fairleigh. They established branches in Omaha and Sioux City, and while these were successful, Milton Tootle always regarded St. Joseph as the most stable and promising of his business ventures. Gradually the other brothers and Fairleigh withdrew, having amassed substantial fortunes, and able young men like Joshua Motter, an aggressive native of Pennsylvania, took their places and made fortunes in their turn.

Tootle, who left an estate of $5 million, was an interesting personality. A newspaper account noted that even in the early, rough days of the city he was immaculately dressed, wore a top hat, a frock coat, pressed trousers, and kid gloves every day to business. The writer added that Milton Tootle was not a society dandy; his dress was simply the reflection of an orderly mind. A fondness for the arts ran through the family. In 1872 Tootle gave to the city an opera house which contributed much to the reputation of St. Joseph as a cosmopolitan place, and his oldest son, also named Milton, had an almost professional knowledge of architecture; in later years he was largely responsible for the city's excellent system of boulevards and parks. It may be noted that the Tootles were prolific, almost in the manner of the great Dutch merchant families of the seventeenth century, so that until the wholesaling trade began to fade away, there was always a young man ready to look after its interests in Helena, Montana, or wherever the need might be. They also naturally branched out into peripheral fields such as banking and real estate. These became more important as the jobbing business diminished.

Since Milton Tootle died in 1887, it was not he who commissioned the superb building shown in the fine rendering from the office of Eckel and Mann (Fig. 2.14). Credit must rather be assigned to his wife, Kate M. Tootle, who for some years remained active in the affairs of the firm, and to his partner, William E. Hosea. It was he who took out the building permit for the new structure at the corner of Fourth and Jule Street on August 8, 1888, for $54,000. The building is therefore properly known as Tootle, Hosea, and Company.

Fig. 2.15. Tootle, Hosea and Company. From George R. Mann, Selections from an Architect's Portfolio *(1893).*

For the design of this structure, the most ambitious and finest of the St. Joseph warehouses, Eckel and Mann followed closely the elevation of Burnham and Root's Rookery (1885–1886) in Chicago (Fig. 2.16). The Rookery, of course, was one of the most widely admired office buildings of the decade. Its facade was also emulated in the Cleveland Arcade of 1890 (George H. Smith, architect, and John M. Eisenman, engineer) and in the St. Paul Pioneer Press Building (Solon S. Beman, 1888–1989).

Fig. 2.16. Burnham and Root. The Rookery, Chicago, 1885–1886. Photo courtesy Donald Hoffmann.

The Eckel and Mann version varies from the original in several respects, but its debt to the Chicago building is clear. The organization of the interior space is, however, very different. The Rookery is an open core building with offices arranged around the periphery. The headquarters for Tootle, Hosea, and Company was mostly loft space. The permit shows a structure of iron columns at the first, second, and third levels and wooden framing above. As we have noted elsewhere this combination of wood and iron was by no means unusual in warehouses of the time. Since the building was subjected to numerous alterations, we show it in an illustration from the 1893 publication of George Mann, from which some idea of its somber magnificence can be gained (see Fig. 2.15). Although the building has been demolished, it survived until 1975. A photograph taken the preceding year shows a portion of the decorative extravaganza with which Harvey Ellis adorned the Fourth Street elevation (Fig. 2.17). A picture taken during demolition reveals the framing system (Fig. 2.18).

Fig. 2.18. Tootle, Hosea & Co., demolition. Photo: Steve Slater.

Fig. 2.17. Tootle, Hosea & Co., decorative detail. Photo: Steve Slater.

GERMAN-AMERICAN BANK
(Eckel and Mann, 1889)

As every student of American history knows, one of the primary needs of the West was a reliable system of banking. The early history of St. Joseph has its share of "wildcat" episodes, but by the 1880s conditions had settled down. Because of the prosperity of the city there was a growing need for banking services. It remained for two immigrant brothers, Henry and William Krug, to put up the only bank which can compete in architectural distinction with the warehouses.

Born at Spielmass, Germany, in 1822, Henry Krug was the elder by two years. Both boys attended local schools and about 1841 were sent by the family to Vienna to serve apprenticeships. Henry worked in a large hotel and evidently ended up in charge of meats and wines. He stayed in Vienna for seven years, until the revolutionary outbreak of 1848, and then returned home, resolved to try his fortunes in America. Reaching New York in the spring of 1849, he went up the Hudson to Albany and thence westward through Buffalo and Cincinnati to St. Louis. There he learned that the community of Glasgow, Missouri, was looking for a butcher. Feeling himself well qualified despite his limited knowledge of the language, he bought two animals and found the area in such need of fresh meat that he was able to do an excellent business.

The further adventures of Henry Krug resemble those of his contemporaries in the jobbing trade. He went to California in 1851, panned for gold unsuccessfully, lived in poverty for awhile, and finally found a job in a boardinghouse where he replaced two Chinese cooks. He was paid $100 a month and board and was soon able to purchase an interest in a bakery supplying bread and pies to the mining camps. This was a successful business; he added groceries, purchased a team of horses for deliveries, and cleared $5,000 in his first year. In April 1856 he returned to Germany to see his family and learned that his brother William had left to join him in the United States. The two finally made contact in Cincinnati in the fall of that year.

The real success story of the Krug brothers started when they arrived in St. Joseph in April 1859. After farming for about two years in Chilicothe, Missouri, they decided to start a grocery business there with a branch in Denver. At that time merchandise was brought to St. Joseph by steamboat and transported west by wagon train. Henry carried on operations in St. Joseph, while William carried goods west, several times escaping from hostile Indians. In 1868 the two brothers started a meat packing business in St. Joseph, and by 1877 it had grown large enough to be incorporated as the Henry Krug Packing Company. Their substantial plant continued in operation until 1904 when it was purchased by Swift and Company. The Krugs were also original backers of the Union Street Railway Company and in June 1887 were joined by J. G. Schneider and John Donovan, Jr., in or-

ganizing the German-American Bank with a paid-up capital of over 100,000 dollars. In temporary quarters for its first three years, it moved to its fine new building in September 1890 and less than a decade later had deposits of almost a million dollars.

Fig. 2.19. Eckel and Mann. German-American Bank, 1889. Photo: Steve Slater.

The original program for the bank included both the customary banking facilities of the day and three floors of office space. It was thus analogous to Sullivan's Prudential Guaranty Building of 1895 in Buffalo, New York, rather than to his Wainwright in St. Louis, which was office space alone. The site was an important corner in the commercial center of St. Joseph, and the structure naturally took on the shape of a rather wide slab (Fig 2.19).

Fig. 2.20. German-American Bank, cross section. Courtesy of Brunner and Brunner.

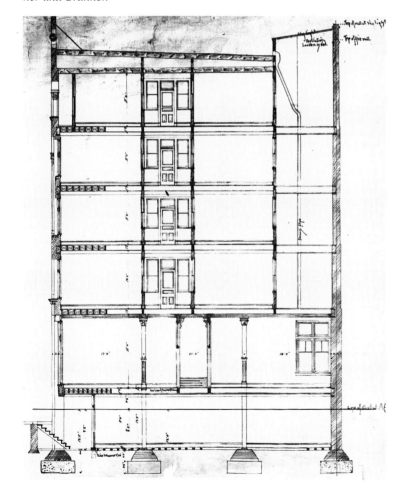

The structure which was devised to accommodate this program was, however, most peculiar. In a certain sense it was an equivalent in metal of the mill constructions with which Eckel and Mann were so familiar. Their drawings show steel I beams running at right angles to the main axis of the building as the major bearing members. These lateral elements are slotted into a heavy brick bearing wall, exactly like the 4″ × 10″ joists in the firm's warehouses. The vertical supports are cast-iron columns, running down to stone piers (Fig. 2.20).

As we have previously noted, many fine business buildings featured an interior court. Such a court could provide light and air, and it offered all sorts of possibilities for architectural dramatization. In the German-American Bank, however, the plan forces this court to the western side of the building; the offices on this elevation do have an exterior exposure. They look out on nothing more than a series of I beams butting into a blank wall. There is, in the surviving record, no explanation for this curious treatment. One wonders if the Krugs had wanted to do something with the light court and then found that money was running out.[13]

The true glory of the building lies in the magnificent treatment of the exterior. It is clad in the wonderful tawny red brick of St. Joseph with imposing entrances in carved red granite. Above the Felix Street entrance were originally the arms of Imperial Germany and the United States; the German emblem was obliterated during the First World War at which time the bank's name was changed to the American National (Fig. 2.21).

At the upper levels of the elevations there is an abundance of carving, almost Moorish in its fantasy, which again suggests the hand of Harvey Ellis. Although his name nowhere appears on the drawings for the bank, I am inclined to think Eckel turned him loose on the decorative aspects of the building, as he undoubtedly did on the warehouse of Tootle, Hosea, and Company. In the handling of the arcade and frieze there is a fine balance between plain wall surface and decorative enrichment. In this respect it would, in fact, be difficult to find a better building in the entire region.

Henry Krug himself succeeded John G. Donovan as president of the bank in 1893 and continued in that post until his death in 1904, when he in turn was succeeded by his brother William, who ran the bank until his death in 1913. Not without reason was the institution known as "the Krug Bank," and certainly the wise policies of the family had much to do with the way in which it weathered the financial storms of the day.

Aside from the bank, the Krugs left another fine legacy to St. Joseph. Henry Krug gave twenty acres adjoining his home to St. Joseph for a park, and after his death Mrs. Krug asked her son to add to the park acreage, which he did in three gifts until the park totalled 158 acres. A generation later a second major gift to the citizens of St. Joseph by George Bode was admittedly greatly influenced by the philanthropy of the Krugs. In their combinations of business activity, artistic interest, and civic responsibility, the Krug family beautifully exemplifies the best traditions of the merchant aristocracy of St. Joseph.

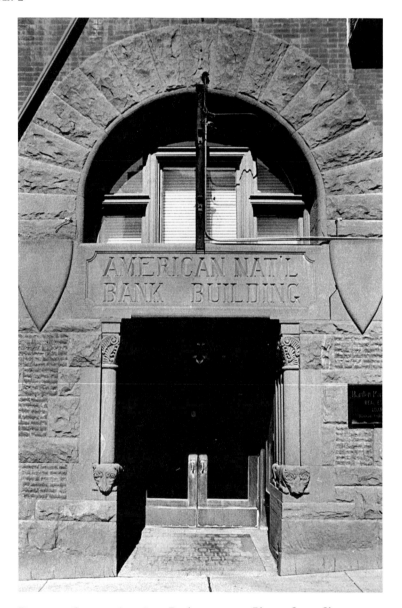

Fig. 2.21. German-American Bank, entrance. Photo: Steve Slater.

3

St. Paul and the Vision of James J. Hill

The beginnings of the city of St. Paul are associated with a group of squatters who were ejected from the military post at Fort Snelling in 1840. One of these squatters was Pierre Parrant, a French Canadian of sinister appearance, nicknamed "Pig's-Eye." (Tradition has it that he had lost an eye in a fight at Sault Ste. Marie.) He seems to have been engaged in various illegal activities, of which the most important was the selling of rotgut whiskey. When a certain officer on the post thought Parrant's presence was no longer desirable, Parrant simply moved his operations a few miles away to a spot named Fountain's Cave. A survey, however, showed that this, too, was within the limits of the military reservation, and so Pig's-Eye moved to a location near a prospective steamboat landing in the heart of what is now downtown St. Paul. He thereby became the first settler in Minnesota's capital city and may in a sense be considered the founder of the town.

His story gave rise to a popular quip in the writer's youth that, "Minneapolis was born in water power and St. Paul in whiskey." Today this remark is rarely heard, but the marvelous words of Mark Twain, who visited the city in 1882, should not be forgotten:

How solemn and beautiful is the thought that the earliest pioneer of civilization, the van-leader of civilization, is never the steamboat, never the railroad, never the newspaper, never the Sabbath-school, never the missionary—but always whiskey! Such is the case. Look history over; you will see. The missionary comes after the whiskey—I mean he arrives after the whiskey has arrived; next comes the poor immigrant, with ax and hoe and rifle; next, the trader; next, the miscellaneous rush; next, the gambler, the desperado, the highwayman, and all their kindred of sin of both sexes; and next, the smart chap who has bought up an old grant that covers all the land; this brings the lawyer tribe; the vigilance committee brings the undertaker. All these interests bring the newspaper; the newspaper starts up politics and a railroad; all hands turn to and build a church and jail—and behold! civilization is established forever in the land.

In the case of this city, Twain's eloquent passage is accurate. The place got its name from a French missionary priest, Father Lucien Galtier, who built a church near the landing and dedicated it to "St. Paul, the Apostle of Nations." Soon the village which grew up on the site was known as St. Paul's and then simply as St. Paul.[1]

The crucial fact about the location, which Pig's-Eye probably did not grasp, was that it was the head of navigation on the Mississippi. Above the St. Paul landing the falls, which Father Hennepin had discovered in 1682, made steamboat traffic impossible, and in an age which depended heavily on the waterways for transportation, this was a matter of immense importance. Henry H. Sibley, the Minnesota territorial delegate to Congress, successfully urged its designation as the capital. In the spring of 1849 when the first governor, Alexander Ramsey, arrived, boom was in the air. Although the place had at that time by generous estimate a population of about 910 souls, Ramsey, a Whig politician from Pennsylvania, foresaw a great future for the city and the state. A regular steamboat line was already in operation, and within a few years there was even a fashionable tour upriver from St. Louis and New Orleans. (Among those who took it was Henry David Thoreau, who came to Minnesota in search of health.) In 1855 there were more than one hundred steamboat arrivals, and despite the nationwide depression, there were more than a thousand only three years later when Minnesota became a state. The rich farm lands were filling up with easterners and immigrants from northern Europe, and it was obvious to any observer that St. Paul had a great future. In an age when transportation was a key to economic development, it was strategically situated.

This fortunate location had many important consequences. In 1849, the year of Ramsey's arrival, St. Paul became the regional headquarters of the American Fur Company, which transported its valuable products from Pembina on the Red River in convoys of great, creaking carts which could be heard for miles as they rumbled over the trails. By 1861 the Hudson's Bay Company was shipping furs to London by way of St. Paul, and as early as 1853 a newspaper noted that a large part of the city's trade was already a wholesale business and that its merchants were displacing those of Galena as suppliers to the region's retailers. In the next decade the wholesale houses began to specialize; some concentrated on drygoods and clothing, others on groceries, and still others on hardware and farm machinery. This development of the jobbing trade created a demand for credit and banking facilities. The early years of the state were characterized by the usual proliferation of wildcat banks, but in 1863 the fledgling Bank of Minnesota was reorganized as the First National Bank of St. Paul. For the next two decades most of the area's leading banks were headquartered in the city, and the insurance companies were there as well. In the early days capital came largely from Galena and St. Louis, but as time wore on, St. Paul's bankers turned eastward, and soon developed connections with the great banking houses of New York—another

feature in the city's eastern orientation. It is a tribute to the soundness of their business instincts that none was seriously affected by the panics of the late nineteenth century. In fact, these panics essentially strengthened the area's provincial institutions. In 1884 none was affected by the failures in New York City, and the newspapers commented on their stability. The major depression of 1893 enabled the St. Paul bankers to entrench themselves even more solidly.[2]

While the Civil War and the Indian uprising of 1862 slowed the growth of Minnesota and of St. Paul, the economic vitality of the region was such that the census of 1870 actually showed a considerable increase in population and wealth. For St. Paul the great event of the decade was its connection with the outside world by railroad. This was achieved in 1867 when the Milwaukee and St. Paul interest, which for ten years had wanted to extend its lines into Minnesota, bought the railroad property—not the land grant—of the Minnesota Central, and built northward from McGregor, Iowa, opposite Prairie du Chien, Wisconsin, to connect with track already laid. A pontoon bridge across the Mississippi connected those towns, and St. Paul thus became only thirty hours from Chicago.

The next great connection took place in 1871 when the Lake Superior and Mississippi Railroad opened for business. So enthusiastic was St. Paul about this line that it granted a quarter of a million dollars to it through a municipal bond issue. Minneapolis businessmen did not share the feelings of their St. Paul counterparts, since the terminus would not be in their city. Already the rivalry between the two places was intense. The railroad also received a land grant from the state legislature, and an important decision was made to give the road a terminus on the Minnesota side of Lake Superior Bay. This ensured that the major city of the lake would be Duluth. Some idea of the importance of the route can be gained from the report of the state railroad commissioner that two million bushels of wheat were shipped over the Lake Superior and Mississippi during its first year. Shippers using the line saved five cents a bushel in freight charges. It was leased to the Northern Pacific a year after it was opened. In short, St. Paul and its neighbor, Minneapolis, became the center of a web of railroads flung south, southwest, west, northwest, and northeastward to the shores of Lake Superior.

All this, however, was but a prelude to the era of expansion which began in 1878 when James J. Hill, together with his fellow Canadians Norman W. Kittson, Donald Smith, and George Stephen, purchased the bonds of the old St. Paul and Pacific and thus laid the foundations of the Great Northern Railway. Born near Guelph, Ontario, in 1838, Hill came to the city in 1856 with the idea of joining a brigade of Red River carts to Pembina and Fort Garry. Happily for St. Paul, he missed the last group of the season and settled down to a job as a steamboat shipping clerk. Within a few years he was an independent businessman, bought a warehouse, went into the river freight business and, ultimately, into fuel supply.

After the Civil War the scope of Hill's activities widened; he served as agent for the St. Paul and Pacific, built a new warehouse, and began to sell coal instead of wood as fuel for engines and stoves. Hill can be understood as the complete transportation genius. Blegen writes:

> When Hill entered the railroad picture, his ability as an organizer and executive, his understanding of the region, his skill in meeting problems, and the sweep of his interest in agriculture, industry, and trade made him a true "giant in the earth."[3]

There is obviously no space here for a detailed chronicle of Hill's career, but it may be noted that by 1883 he himself was in control of the Great Northern, by 1887 it had been pushed across the Dakota Territory to Great Falls, Montana, and that in 1893 it was through to Seattle, 1816 miles from St. Paul. In Hill's mind the capital of Minnesota thus became the headquarters of an imperial domain stretching to the shores of the Pacific. It was wholly appropriate that the Great Northern's crack train, *The Empire Builder*, was named after him.[4]

Hill's impact on St. Paul—on its buildings, its business community, its culture, and its ethos—can scarcely be overestimated. He built the city in almost the same sense that he built the entire country through which his railroad passed. To Jim Hill it appeared that the best way to build a railroad was to settle the country as you built. He found that the Scandinavians made the best settlers, and so he imported them by the boatload. He had a furious temper and an imperious will. (The editor of the *St. Paul Pioneer Press* characterized him as

"the most even tempered man I ever saw—always bad.") His immigrants settled where he told them to, and if they practiced the crop diversification he preached, they generally prospered.

In 1912 he decided that the time had come to found a financial institution which would extend credit to the farmers and free the Northwest from the lurking menace of Wall Street. At various times a director of the First National of New York, the Chase National, the First National of Chicago, and the Illinois Trust and Savings, he had been a member of the board of the First National of St. Paul. He would have preferred simply to take it over, since it was in good condition, and the president, E. H. Bailey, was a close friend. "But its stockholders," says his official biographer, "were not inclined to make terms satisfactory to Mr. Hill."[5] He therefore simply turned to the Second National Bank and bought control of its stock for $1,240,000. In the meantime negotiations with the First National were reopened, and certain heirs of estates concluded that with Hill at the head of a rival institution, they would prefer to sell. The two banks were merged, and the First National became "Jim Hill's Bank" as the Great Northern was "Jim Hill's Main Line."

This legendary character took the same care with everything he built. The superb (and innovative) construction of the Great Northern headquarters, today the Hill Building, is symbolic. Probably Hill's finest memorial is the great stone-arched railroad bridge across the Mississippi at Minneapolis, which, he declared, was the most difficult work he ever undertook. He imported the Boston firm of Peabody and Stearns to design a huge mansion on Summit Avenue, but it is unlikely that he gave it the same intense personal supervision as the bridge, which is his real monument. Still, one senses that the rough quality of the Richardsonian masonry and the solidity of the construction were perfectly adapted to Hill's personality. The style was well suited to be his personal vehicle. And the same quest for boldness of form and stability of construction can be found in the warehouses of the leading St. Paul jobbers, several of whom were Hill's good friends. He seems to have inspired them with his ideals.

It may be noted that in the eyes of St. Paul's upper classes wholesaling was a prestigious occupation. Concerning the tight little world of one of her heroines, Louisa Denby, the St. Paul novelist Grace Flandrau wrote:

She knew more or less well, several hundred people. They lived, generally speaking, within a radius of half a mile or so and were connected with the prominent businesses. Especially the older businesses—banking, railroading, manufacturing, wholesale merchandising being among the perfectly respectable. Not retailing. In Louisa's mind the same difference seemed to exist between the wholesale trade and the retail trade that existed between the Episcopalian and the Methodist denominations. One was socially possible, the other was not. To be sure, such retailers as the Howard Nashes and the Wickhams—owners of large department stores—were brilliant exceptions. She had always known them and for this reason they were not as other retailers. Were not in fact, *really* retailers at all. Of new arrivals in Columbia those that came to be bank presidents and presidents of railroads were the only ones she knew.[6]

This passage certainly provides a clear idea of the approved occupations in St. Paul, and may indeed give some idea of the reasons for its ultimate decline in relation to its neighbor.

William Watts Folwell, who was both an excellent historian and a shrewd observer of the Twin Cities, wrote that in the beginning St. Paul had all the advantages. It had the state capitol. It had the river trade, which was of primary importance before the railroads were built. It had the fur trade until it dwindled in the middle of the 1850s. It had the Indian business until the Sioux and Winnebago were expelled from the state in 1863. It was the headquarters of a military district and for some years almost monopolized the wholesale trade of a huge area. It was the first center from which railroads penetrated the Northwest. "Its supremacy," wrote Folwell, "was long unquestioned and seemed to its citizens likely to be perpetual."[7]

The basic outlook of the city's economic decision makers was therefore extremely conservative. Louisa Denby wondered whether the prudence which had achieved St. Paul's great fortunes, fortunes built not in speculation but in trade and commerce, was not handed down from father to son. The very success of Jim Hill, who was, after all, one of the few middle western businessmen who dealt on equal terms with the magnates of the East, may possibly have affected negatively the character of the city he loved so well. St. Paul sanctified railroading, banking, wholesale merchandising, and very few other occupations. When, therefore, the citizens of St. Paul actually fell behind their bustling Minneapolis neighbors in population and wealth, they underwent a profound psychological shock. One of the results was the great scandal surrounding the questionable figures reported in the census of 1890.[8]

An observer, who was more interested in the physical structure of the city than its social aspects, was the New York architectural critic Montgomery Schuyler. He visited the Twin Cities in 1891 and commented on the cramped quality of the business quarter in St. Paul, adding that the elevator was a needed factor in the commercial architecture of the town.[9] (It is somewhat remarkable that he did not comment on a single warehouse, though some of the best had been finished by that date.) Schuyler was confronting the fact that the north bank of the Mississippi here takes the form of a series of stone terraces surrounded by hills.

The topography can be seen in an engraving done for the Winter Carnival in 1887 (Fig. 3.1). From the Wabash and Robert Street bridges (both still in place today) the terrain rises to the State Capitol, at this date already projected but not yet constructed. West Seventh Street was already an important approach to the downtown from the west, and the beginnings of the mansions on Summit Avenue, which Scott Fitzgerald was to characterize as "a museum of architectural failures," are also visible. The area known today as "Lowertown" lies directly to the west of the Robert Street Bridge close to the great bend of the river. It probably constitutes about one-third of the present downtown of the city.

The central section, roughly the portion between the two bridges is the heart of the business district. It has always had most of the city's high-rise buildings, including the fine old structure originally designed by S. S. Beman for the St. Paul Pioneer Press and discussed by Schuyler. The eastern section of the urban core, around Rice Park, is a civic center area. It contains the Ramsey County Court House, the Public Library, the old Federal Building (today the Landmark Center), the new and extremely handsome Ordway Theatre, and the Minnesota Club, the traditional gathering place of the city's power elite.

The composition of the city is thus somewhat like a gigantic sandwich, with the area between the two bridges as a filler. In the early days of the city Lowertown was a residential district, but by

Fig. 3.1. St. Paul in 1887, winter carnival view. Minnesota Historical
Society.

1887 the railroads were transforming it into a warehouse-industrial
area. It is somewhat ironic that a century later it seems to be revert-
ing, in part at least, to its original residential purpose. Among warehouse districts this one is unusual in its close juxtaposition to a business and shopping core, and in its possession of a small space, today
known as Mears Park (Fig. 3.2). On the north side of the square in
the Noyes Cutler Building (Park Square Court) are the offices of the
Lowertown Development Corporation.

No study of St. Paul warehouses would be complete without
some reference to this remarkable organization, founded in 1978 with
an initial grant of $10 million from the McKnight Foundation of Min-
neapolis. It operates in three main areas—design review, gap financing, and marketing. Its executive director is a dynamic city planner–
engineer named Weiming Lu. While Lu has been properly careful to
spread the credit around, there is no doubt that he and Mayor George
Latimer, who was first elected in 1976, have been largely responsible
for the transformation which has given Lowertown St. Paul a national
reputation.[10]

Fig. 3.2. Mears Park. Photo: Phillip James.

A personal comment is in order here. When I first studied the St. Paul warehouses in 1975-1976, one of them, the Noyes-Cutler Building, had been partially recycled, and the Merchants Bank, now the McColl Building, was also used more or less as it is today. The Hill Building contained the records of the Great Northern Railroad and a good many relics such as station masters' desks. For the most part the other structures shown in this essay were devoted to light industrial enterprises, such as the manufacture of gloves, or contained rather run-down office space. Today the entire area has enormous vitality. It has art galleries, sophisticated cafes and restaurants, and shops of all kinds. The eastern side of Mears Park is given over to Galtier Plaza, a large distinctly post-Modern, mixed-use complex, which boasts four first-run movie theatres and a YMCA. New street lighting and landscaping are everywhere. Not all of this is successful. Mears Park itself needs redesign. In 1975–1976 it was easy to see the architectural quality of the warehouses and to guess at their potential. Only a true prophet could have foreseen what actually happened, and I make no claim to prophetic insight. But as a boy I was fascinated by the stories of James J. Hill, and I think he would have been happy with what has occurred in an area he knew very well. Hence the title of this essay.

GOTZIAN SHOE COMPANY
(Cass Gilbert, 1892)

While this excellent building was erected after the death of Conrad Gotzian by his heirs, it so clearly reflects his character and the requirements of the typical St. Paul manufacturer and wholesale merchant that it should certainly be included here. Conrad Gotzian was born in 1837 in the village of Berke aus die Werra about fifty miles southwest of Leipzig in the province of Saxe Weimar. His only formal education was what he had received in the local primary school, and in 1852 he took the great step of seeking his fortune in the United States.

Arriving in Philadelphia, he apprenticed himself to a shoemaker, learned the trade thoroughly, and three years later came to St. Paul, where he was successful from the very start. At first he had a small retail shop, but by 1865 he was established in jobbing and manufacturing with 35 men in his enterprises. For the next two dec-

ades his business grew continuously; by the time of his death in 1887 there were 465 employees in the company and sales aggregated more than $1,500,000 annually. In short, Gotzian's life was the exemplary immigrant success story. He was a director of the German-American Bank, an active member of the Chamber of Commerce, the Board of Trade, of various other civic associations, and a good friend of James J. Hill. His large family continued the business for many years after his death and built the excellent structure shown here (Fig. 3.3).

Fig. 3.3. Cass Gilbert. Gotzian Block, 1892. Photo: Phillip James.

The architect for the Gotzian family was a young man named Cass Gilbert, who later went on to fame as designer of the Minnesota State Capitol and the Woolworth Building in New York. While Gilbert later worked in a neoclassic vein (his excellent Endicott Building adjoins the Pioneer Press), here he chose to emulate the commercial style of H. H. Richardson and John Wellborn Root. Although the window rhythms are slightly different within the great arches which are the organizing motif, the building is particularly close in style to Root's warehouse and office designed for McCormick Harvester in Chicago of 1884–1885 (Fig. 3.4). As Schuyler noted, Root was influential in the Twin Cities.

Fig. 3.4. Warehouse and offices for McCormick Harvester, Chicago, 1884–1885. Photo: Donald Hoffmann, Chicago Historical Society.

By opening up the side elevations so completely, Gilbert filled the building with natural light, and he put it together exceedingly well. Specifications on file with the city reveal that it has concrete foundations, cast-iron framing, and steel girders. An engraving in a 1900 publication shows that the Gotzians at one time contemplated a considerable extension. This project, however, was never carried through.[11]

After its career as a shoe factory the building functioned successfully for many years as the premises of the Milton Clothing Company. In 1985, however, it was purchased by Historic Landmarks for Living, a firm of Philadelphia developers which specializes in the conversion of warehouses and factories into apartments and condominiums. Judging by their list of successful adaptations—which includes projects in Wilmington, Baltimore, Pittsburgh, and Milwaukee—the partners, Stephen Solms and Carl Dranoff, seem to have concluded that American city dwellers will enjoy sophisticated downtown living in historic buildings. Apparently they visited St. Paul, decided that it was a city entirely ready for them, and within the space of a few months purchased the Gotzian Block and two nearby structures of perhaps less architectural quality.

Today the Gotzian Block has been transformed into "The Parkside," and it contains 53 rental apartments, most of them one-bedroom units ranging in size from 700 to 960 square feet (Fig. 3.5-3.6). The two-bedroom units are larger—up to 1,100 square feet—and offer two bathrooms, unique floor plans, and excellent views of Mears Park. This is not inexpensive housing. Rents in 1986 ranged from $465 for a studio to $900 for two-bedroom lofts. Tenants are required to pay their own heat and electricity, but parking is free in a convenient adjoining lot.

It should be noted that the neighboring building, also by Cass Gilbert, has been rehabilitated with the assistance of the Wilder Foundation, and does, in fact, provide low-cost rental units in the area. With the adjacent Powers Drygoods Company and the Hackett Block, we have a group of buildings notable for their soundness of construction, unity of scale, and sobriety of detailing. They are splendid evidence of the quality of St. Paul architecture in the late nineteenth century.

The nearby American Beauty Building, also by Gilbert and of

45

approximately the same date, has been transformed into American House apartments, a $1,880,000 project for some of the city's most difficult to house. It was designed for single, nonelderly people earning between $3,000 and $10,000 per year and has 56 furnished rooming units renting for $175 a month with shared kitchens and several shared bathrooms on each floor. The project was worked out by Asset Development Services, Inc., which contributed a $702,000 deferred loan, over 35 percent of the cost. Other loans included $680,000 from the city's Planning and Economic Development Rental Rehab Loan Program; $400,000 from the Minneapolis/St. Paul Family Housing Program, McKnight Foundation, and the St. Paul Companies; and a $97,500 grant from the project architects, Rafferty, Rafferty, Mikutowski and Associates. The Wilder Foundation manages the building and contributes any shortfalls in operating costs that are not covered by the tightly controlled rent ceilings.

This conversion is an answer to one of the unpleasant facts about downtown development: It inevitably displaces low-income workers. In St. Paul 574 rooming units were destroyed between 1976 and 1985. It is, as Mayor Latimer remarked, "the dark side of successful downtown development." St. Paul is evidently a city of good neighbors.

NOYES-CUTLER WAREHOUSE
(J. Walter Stevens, 1889 and 1909)

The moving spirit behind this fine building (Fig. 3.7) on Mears Park was Daniel R. Noyes, who was born in Lyme, Connecticut, in 1836, educated in New England, resided in New York from 1854 to 1861, served briefly in the Civil War, and came to St. Paul in 1868. Like so many other young men who arrived in the city in these days, Noyes seized upon the opportunity to expand an established business. He bought the business of S. L. Vauter with his brother Charles P. Noyes and Albert M. Pett as associates. Within a few years Pett had retired and Edward H. Cutler had joined the firm, but Daniel Noyes remained the driving force. He was its president, and by 1890 had made it into the largest and most successful drug house in the Northwest with an annual volume of over $2 million. In addition to his interest in the drug jobbing business, he was vice president of the St. Paul Trust Company, active in a local real estate title firm, and a

46

Fig. 3.5. Parkside, unfinished space. Photo: Historic Landmarks for Living.

Fig. 3.6. Parkside, typical finished interior. Photo: Historic Landmarks for Living.

director of the Equitable Life Insurance Company of New York. Among his other distinctions were the presidency of the St. Paul YMCA and great activity in behalf of that traditional St. Paul institution, the Winter Carnival. In fact, looking over his career, one feels that he was exactly the type to preside over the annual celebration as King Boreas—which he did.[12]

The main body of Steven's work shows a variety of directions, but in the Noyes-Cutler Building, as in the Germania Bank in the center of the city, he was close to Louis Sullivan. More than two decades ago Prof. H. Frederick Koeper pointed out its resemblance to Sullivan's Walker Warehouse of 1888 (Fig. 3.8).

Both buildings, in fact, derive from concepts to be found in H. H. Richardson's commercial work. Both are massive, firmly built, utilitarian structures in which large, round arches and sharply cut fenestration give rhythm and character to the facade (Fig. 3.9). In both structures decorative trim was held to a minimum, but there was a slight corbelling at the top story. In Chicago the exterior walling was smooth ashlar masonry, while in St. Paul it was red sand mould brick, which was locally abundant and considerably less expensive. (The Walker Warehouse came in at a figure between $300,000 and $400,000; the Noyes-Cutler was budgeted at $110,000 in the specifications on file with the city.) Hinkley sandstone and St. Cloud granite were the ornamental materials. Koeper noted that the building was done in two campaigns (1889 and 1909) and that the addition is well handled.

Fig. 3.7. J. Walter Stevens. Noyes-Cutler Warehouse, 1889. Photo: Wayne Andrews.

For his architect Noyes chose another transplanted New Englander, J. Walter Stevens. Though not as strong a personality as his contemporary, Cass Gilbert, Stevens was a very able architect. Along with the Astronomical Observatory at Carleton, and the first building for what is now the Moorhead branch of the University of Minnesota, he did a great many houses, business buildings, and churches. He was a close friend of Cass Gilbert, whose Hope Presbyterian Church on Summit Avenue he supervised.

Fig. 3.8. Adler and Sullivan. Walker Warehouse, Chicago, 1888. From American Architect and Building News.

47

The plan indicates that the general offices were on the first level while most of the space was given over to storage compartments carefully separated by firewalls (Fig. 3.10). It is well to remember that at this date "pharmaceuticals" included a great many highly flammable items such as horse liniment. The building had to be as fire resistant as possible; accordingly the firewalls are very substantial indeed.

Fig. 3.9. Noyes-Cutler Warehouse, exterior detail. Photo: Phillip James.

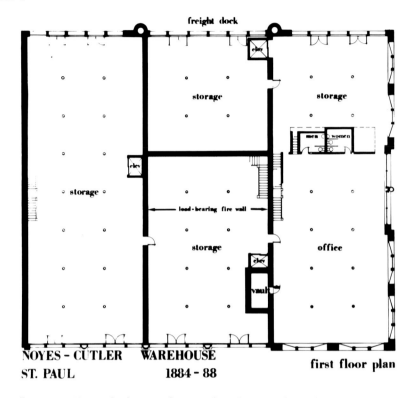

freight dock

storage

storage

men women

storage

load-bearing fire wall

storage

office

vault

NOYES - CUTLER WAREHOUSE
ST. PAUL   1884 - 88   first floor plan

Fig. 3.10. Noyes-Cutler Warehouse, plan. Drawing by Robert Daverman.

The longitudinal section shows that the building is a combination of cast iron and mill construction (Fig. 3.11). From the basement through the third floor there are cast iron columns, while the fourth and fifth stories show the customary chamfered wood posts. Although Stevens had originally intended to use steel or iron girders, all are timber, resting on cast iron plates. The beams are 3" × 14" on 12' centers. The system is clear in the accompanying photograph, which shows a portion of the building before recycling (Fig. 3.12).

48

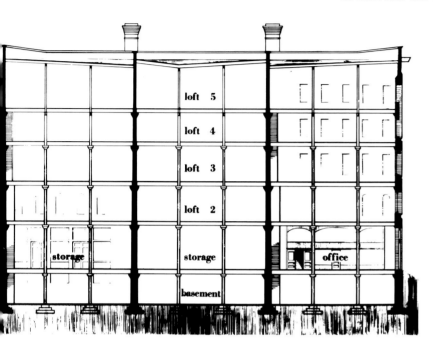

Fig. 3.11. Noyes-Cutler Warehouse, longitudinal section. Drawing: Robert Daverman.

The history of the building in the last two decades shows the need for superior architectural design in projects of this sort. An interior renovation in the early 1970s left the structure with confusing ground floor circulation, several restaurants below grade and almost invisible to pedestrians, and a two-story atrium. The Lowertown Redevelopment Corporation, which had established its offices in the building, wanted a design demonstration to persuade developers that good architecture was good business. It therefore linked a new developer with Miller, Hanson, Westerbeck, Ball Architects, the Minneapolis firm which won an A.I.A. (American Institute of Architects) honor award for Butler Square in 1976. The firm carved out a new five-level atrium in the center of the structure. This "atrium solution," by the way, is quite simple to accomplish when the architect and engineer are dealing with mill construction or the combination of timber and iron in the Noyes-Cutler. It is possible, but considerably more difficult, when the building frame is reinforced concrete. In this instance the architects regained space lost in the building's center by enclosing an alley adjoining the building on the end. And they gave the structure higher visibility and traffic by creating a new entrance facing Lowertown's main public space, Mears Park. Offices and two successful restaurants take up the available 90,000 square feet (Fig. 3.13). A popular community theatre has had to find a new location.[13]

Fig. 3.12. Noyes-Cutler Warehouse, unfinished space. Photo: Phillip James.

49

Fig. 3.13. Noyes-Cutler Warehouse, office space. Photo: Phillip James.

POWERS DRYGOODS COMPANY
(J. Walter Stevens, 1892–1893)

According to the city records, this fine old structure (Fig. 3.14) was owned by Noyes Bros., Cutler. That firm, however, never occupied the building but immediately leased it to the Powers Drygoods Company, another wholesale concern. Powers was a family business which, until fairly recent times, operated a department store in Minneapolis. In this building the company carried on a wholesale trade, dealing in drygoods, notions, and men's furnishings. It also housed two manufacturing departments which made overalls, pants, mackinaws, and ladies skirts. That the structure was feasible for this type of use is demonstrated by the fact that the next owners were Gordon

Ferguson and Robinson Strauss. Both firms were haberdashers and importers of bonnets, gloves, ribbons, etc. Mildred Hartsough noted the leadership of St. Paul in these branches of the jobbing trade in 1925. In 1976 the structure was occupied by the Globe Business College (and was generally known as the Globe Building) and also by a job printer, a stationery supply house, and a coat manufacturer.

Fig. 3.14. J. Walter Stevens. Powers Drygoods Company, 1892–1893. Photo: Phillip James.

This mixed use, so characteristic of many older warehouses, is going to change. In the spring of 1987 officials of Ameritas Inc. announced that the Powers Block would become the major part of a new project known as Park Centre. Said a reporter for the *Minnesota Real Estate Journal*:

> This will be the first Minnesota project for Ameritas, a 9-year-old firm that deals exclusively in developing office space, specializing in historic renovation. Company president John McDonald says he was attracted to the St. Paul market by healthy vacancy rates (recently estimated at about 9 per cent), a stable economy and lower property costs than many areas, particularly these in the East.[14]

The story of the entrance of Ameritas into Lowertown throws light on the mechanics of the development process in St. Paul.

McDonald was first attracted to the city by properties he did not secure: three buildings, including the Gotzian Block, which were purchased by the Philadelphia-based Historic Landmarks for Living. Not deterred, he worked with Weiming Lu to obtain the Powers Building and the structure next door, originally put up for Fairbanks-Morse and now known as the Rosenthal Building. By combining the two structures he was able to create a seven-floor, 126,650-square-foot package which, he says, made the whole project worthwhile. At about the time his company was putting the whole thing together, three metropolitan agencies were shopping for 95,000 square feet of office space on a ten-year lease. They were the Metropolitan Council, the Metropolitan Waste Control Commission, and the Regional Transit Board. Negotiations were successful, and the buildings were substantially preleased. The project could go ahead.

The next step was financing. That was provided by a $10.5 million taxable revenue bond issue approved by the St. Paul Port Authority, $2.7 million in equity capital from Park Centre Building Investors Ltd., and $527,000 in interest earnings on the construction fund and debt service reserve. This means a price tag of about $108 per renovated square foot (net). Some have criticized this figure as too costly, but others, Weiming Lu among them, point out that the approximately 350 people who will go to work in Park Centre every day will need a place to have lunch, get their cleaning done, and so forth.

Some may even live in the buildings renovated by Landmarks for Living. Thus the economy of Lowertown will be boosted further.

It should be noted that this kind of process has its critics. There are those who feel that too many St. Paul officials have become development bankers, and there are those who look askance at the bonding activity of the St. Paul Park Authority. Writing as a historian and critic, all I can say is that a large number of fine historic structures are being preserved and that their architectural integrity is being maintained. Indeed, all the buildings mentioned in this essay are on the National Register of Historic Places and the 20 percent tax credit of the Revenue Act of 1985 makes this kind of preservation attractive for the developer. I hope it continues.

Fig. 3.15. Powers Drygoods Co., exterior detail. Photo: Phillip James.

Like the Noyes-Cutler Building across Mears Park, the edifice for Powers Drygoods was designed by J. Walter Stevens, but, though continuing the Richardsonian concept, it differed in structure and detail. Somewhat less expensive ($85,000 as against $110,000) it lacked the delicate trim of Kasota sandstone and St. Cloud granite which was so effective on the older structure. It owes its effect to the excellence of its proportions and brick detailing. The window reveals are particularly fine. The most important feature, however, is unquestionably the superb relationship between the great arches and the window openings (Fig. 3.15). Altogether the building is a good example of Sturgis' "unadorned box."

On the basis of the specifications on file with the city it appears that both buildings were about equally well constructed. The frame is composed of cast-iron columns spaced 14'6" on center. Wood beams meet and rest on cast-iron cushion plates which resemble Doric capitals. The foundation is stone, and the large openings on the front and side walls are supported on 15" steel beams. The thickness of the brick walls on the long elevation ranges from 30" to 26"; on the short side it is 20" to 16". On the whole one cannot help being impressed with the sound construction of these St. Paul warehouses. In many ways they carry on the tradition of H. H. Richardson's wholesale store for Marshall Field, which was also a combination of solid masonry and metal framing. In every way such buildings are appropriate symbols for a proud and active mercantile aristocracy.

CHARLES W. HACKETT WHOLESALE HARDWARE STORE
(Clarence H. Johnston, 1891)

On February 19, 1891, a writer for the *St. Paul Pioneer Press* remarked that this building "was the most notable business improvement of the city having its inception in the year 1890," and went on to note that it was "massive in proportion and sightly in design."[15] Describing it in detail, he observed that it was 100' × 130', five stories in height (the first story is particularly tall) with a full basement, and that it rested on piles of thick concrete with massive stone piers. It was, said the architect, Clarence H. Johnston, the strongest of its kind in the city and more than capable of carrying the heavy load of goods which it would hold. The general construction was of the slow-burning mill variety.

When I inspected the building in 1975–1976 I could not avoid sharing the enthusiasm of the unknown writer in the *Pioneer Press.* The Hackett Block (Figs. 3.16 and 3.17) was a superb example of the warehouse style. Graceful round arches rose above beautifully articulated piers and were echoed in an additional series of arches at the fifth-floor level. A handsome corbel topped the whole affair.

Fig. 3.16. Clarence H. Johnston. C. W. Hackett Wholesale Hardware Store, 1891. Photo: Phillip James.

Fig. 3.17. Hackett Hardware, exterior detail. Photo: Phillip James.

WHOLESALE BUILDING FOR C. W. HACKETT, HARDWARE CO., ST. PAUL, MINN.
CLARENCE H. JOHNSTON, ARCHITECT.

Fig. 3.18. Hackett Hardware Co. Engraving from Northwestern Architect and Building Budget (1892).

Comparison with an engraving published shortly after the building was completed (Fig. 3.18) shows that it had survived unaltered except for the addition of some discreet lettering. An addition, which was essentially an extension of the original building, had been added at a later date. The city building certificate showed that it was indeed of pure mill construction with bays about 12′ square and posts 14″ in section on the first floor. Oak and pine were used throughout. At the time of inspection the structure continued to give good service as a paper box factory and warehouse.

In order to obtain an idea of what the building meant to the city in the years immediately after it was opened, it is necessary to quote at length from the newspaper article:

A trip through the big structure is at once instructive and suggestive. There is an unusual quantity of light during the hours of sun, and dark corners are unknown, even the basement being different from the caves of gloom one generally sees beneath our large blocks. There are two elevators, run by electric motors, which also supply the artificial light needed. The shipping is done from a half floor in the south half of the building opening directly on to the court leading to Rosabel Street. In the basement proper (which is enlarged by taking in the width of sidewalk) are stored such heavy materials as nails, fencing wire, sheet iron, tin plates and the like. The first floor, entered from Fourth Street, is particularly light, commodious, and well arranged. Along the Rosabel Street side are ranged the offices (and there is plenty of clerical work, as the company employs eighty persons, including fifteen travelling men), President Hackett's office being in the corner fronting Fourth. The city sales are conducted on this floor, and here, too, is stored the stock of shotguns, rifles, fishing tackle, ammunition and sporting goods in general. Cutlery and samples, here find place also, and the arrangements are all as complete as they are convenient and simple. On the second floor are shelf goods in long lines, and here the outside orders are packed for shipment. On the third floor are found tinware and general house furnishing hardware, the idea being to put the heavier articles on the lower floors and the lighter ones on those above. On the fourth floor are hand agricultural improvements such as shovels, spades, hoes, rakes, axes, tinners tools, etc. and on the fifth the lighter wooden wares, such as wheelbarrows, churns, fancy tools, and the like.

To give an extended list of all the articles found in the huge stock would be to publish a hardware and sporting goods calendar. Suffice it to say that the arrangement made possible by the admirable facilities afforded by the new building is as perfect and convenient as could be desired, and in the transaction of business the maximum of results is obtained with the minimum expense of labor and worry. The entire plant is a credit to the Northwest in general and to St. Paul in particular, and a visit there is at once profitable and interesting.[16]

Clearly a notice of this quality is indicative of a strong community interest in the building itself and in the wholesale trade during the 1890s. Indeed, until fairly recent years it would have been unusual to find a similar article in a major daily newspaper in Gateway City. One of my pleasures during the last decade has been to note the increasing attention given to architecture by such papers as the *Milwaukee Journal*, the *St. Paul Pioneer Press Dispatch*, and the *Minneapolis Star Journal*. Unhappily the *Omaha World Herald* has, as I am writing, not yet engaged a qualified reporter to cover this beat.

Charles W. Hackett, the client responsible for this building, had been in the jobbing business at least since 1873. Gradually his firm's operations expanded; he bought out and in 1885 incorporated the Strong-Hackett Hardware Company with a capital of $500,000. In 1889 he bought out the interest of Mr. Strong and became sole proprietor. Hackett was the second president of the Jobbers Union and also president of the Chamber of Commerce. Like Noyes and Gotzian he was prominent in business and civic affairs for many years.

His architect, Clarence H. Johnston was born in Waseca, Minnesota in 1859 and must have been one of the first men from the state to attend MIT, from which he graduated in 1881. He also worked in the office of Edward P. Bassford, the grand old man of the profession in St. Paul, and supplemented his formal education with travel in Europe. In later years Johnston was retained as architect by the Minnesota State Board of Control and designed the State Prison at Stillwater, for many years regarded as a model of its kind. He also did a number of buildings at the university and many other structures in St. Paul, including Miller Hospital, the Park Congregational Church, and the Lowry Medical Building. In addition, he was architect for St. Mary's Hospital at Rochester.[17] It is this writer's opinion, however, that Johnston never did anything better than the Hackett Block. Its loss by fire a few years ago was a great misfortune. Nonetheless, it should be reported that the slow-burning construction proved itself. The blaze smoldered for several days and had to be carefully watched by the fire department. The addition remains in use as a framers' shop and artist studios.

MERCHANTS NATIONAL BANK
(Edward P. Bassford, 1889)

The wholesale trade inevitably requires the services of bankers. The jobber, after all, handled the products of many manufacturers in distant parts of the country and abroad, and he was always dealing with a variety of bills of exchange. As the country prospered, he might very well become an importer on a substantial scale.

From its early days St. Paul had a customs house, a collector, and bonded warehouses. Customs officials did not, however, do any significant amount of business until the 1880s when dutiable goods went up from $62,783 in 1881 to $538,754 in 1888. For the jobbers this expansion was both an opportunity and a problem. It meant that they had a chance to make more money but that they had to deal with unfamiliar financial instruments.

The aptly named Merchants National Bank (Figs. 3.19, 3.20) was founded in 1872 in a good location in the wholesale district, and jobbers were well represented on its board of directors. Both Daniel Noyes and Conrad Gotzian were members. The first president was Maurice Auerbach, but the leading spirit of the institution at the time this building was erected was William Rush Merriam, who became president in 1882 and held the job until 1896, meanwhile serving as governor of the state for four years. In addition to his political duties Merriam was also president of the Shenandoah Coal and Iron Company. He well exemplifies the combination of business and political activity which is so characteristic of the late nineteenth century.

That the bank flourished is indicated in a Chamber of Commerce publication of 1900. At that time it did a general banking business, receiving accounts of banks, bankers, corporations, partnerships, and individuals. The bank bought and sold foreign exchange. Among its correspondents were the American Exchange, the Gallatin National and the Chase National banks of New York, the First National and Union banks of Chicago, the National Exchange Bank of Boston, and the Philadelphia National Bank of Philadelphia. Perhaps its proudest advertisement was that its depositors and stockholders included James J. Hill. A few years later the Merchants National would be absorbed in Hills' banking consolidations.[18]

The program of this bank was fairly simple. It had to contain vaults, small public spaces, and a certain amount of rentable space.

Fig. 3.19. Edward P. Bassford. Merchants National Bank, 1889. Photo: Phillip James.

Fig. 3.20. Merchants National Bank. Photo: Minnesota Historical Society.

There was a stairway at the front, and because there were only four stories it lacked elevators. It was, however, well built (it was budgeted at $80,000) and beautifully finished. Today it is occupied mostly by lawyers; there is also an excellent tavern in the basement. Architecturally the most outstanding attributes of the Merchants National (now the McColl Building) are its color and texture. The architect, Edward P. Bassford, chose to use red Kasota sandstone combining a rough surface with intricately carved decoration. The columns of polished grey granite are an interesting variation in texture. On the interior the wainscotting, a remnant of the original trim, is pink marble. Though small in size in comparison with the neighboring Galtier Plaza, it holds its own very well indeed.

Edward P. Bassford, the designer of this bank, is an important but somewhat problematical character in the architectural history of St. Paul. Born in Calais, Maine, in 1837, Bassford attended a local academy and apparently received some architectural training in Boston. This experience could not have been at MIT since that institution did not open its doors until 1867 but was more likely in one or two of the good Boston offices. At the outbreak of the Civil War he enlisted with the 44th Massachusetts Volunteers and served until the conflict was over. After Appomattox he returned to Portland and opened a partnership there. Within a few months he dissolved it and headed west; one guesses that, as with many young men, the war had made him restless, and he certainly sensed the great opportunities available in the Mississippi Valley. He walked the last stage of his journey from Hastings, Minnesota, arriving at St. Paul in the fall of 1866.

His first work in the new country was as a carpenter and machinist, and it is important that most of his structures were exceedingly well built. Like William LeBaron Jenney in Chicago, he had a deep respect for the facts and problems of construction, and he passed on this feeling to the young men who worked in his office. These included Cass Gilbert, J. H. Stevens, and Clarence H. Johnston.

From the middle 1870s and for almost twenty years thereafter Bassford was the acknowledged leader of the profession in the city. Among his most important works were the Post Office, the Court House, the Germania Life, and the original building for Schuneman and Evans Department Store. He was also a local supervising architect for the U.S. Treasury, an appointment which would argue good political connections.

On the basis of his extant buildings and those now vanished and known only through photographs, I would say that Bassford was in touch with the most progressive architectural thought of his day but that he was closer to Richardson than to Sullivan. He was, after all, almost the same age, and the great designs of Richardson's maturity would have come to him as a revelation, as they did to most of his contemporaries. About 1895 he began to retire from the active practice of architecture, though he continued as a consulting expert. The obituary in a local newspaper remarks that until this date he was the acknowledged master builder in St. Paul, and that he was content to step aside for the younger men because he had trained many of them himself.

Aside from the foregoing, we know little about Bassford. According to the testimony of his friends, he had a great sense of humor and in the manner of his time, was a notable raconteur. Like certain other shrewd architects, he accumulated a good deal of real property in and around St. Paul. (One thinks immediately of the Greene brothers and Bernard Maybeck in California.) He married twice and had several children, one of whom was an architect. He died in 1912 at his summer cottage in Osakis, Minnesota. In short, we have a picture of a successful designer without much formal education who nevertheless was an exceedingly sound builder and who was extremely influential on the architecture of his city.

Fig. 3.21. James J. Hill and Nelson D. Miller. Great Northern Railroad Headquarters, 1885–1887. Photo: Burlington Northern Railroad.

GREAT NORTHERN RAILROAD HEADQUARTERS NUMBER 1
(James J. Hill and Nelson D. Miller, 1885–1887 and 1887–1889)

In 1885 James J. Hill was ready to build a headquarters for the St. Paul, Milwaukee, and Manitoba Railroad. This was the line that Hill, with Norman Kittson, George Stephen, and Donald Smith had taken over in 1878 and built into the extraordinary railroad which was to become the nucleus of the Great Northern. Our photographs show the building at completion, when the addition of 1887–1889 was in process, and as it is today (Figs. 3.21–3.24).

Fig. 3.22. Great Northern Railroad Headquarters, with addition in construction, 1887–1889. Photo: Burlington Northern Railroad.

Fig. 3.23. Great Northern Railroad Headquarters (Hill Building). Photo: Phillip James.

In early photographs the structure which Hill put up has a distinct resemblance to a Florentine palazzo, an altogether appropriate seat of power for one of the economic titans of the age. It might also be described as stripped Richardsonian; certainly the great entrance, with its enormous blocks of rough cut ashlar, owes much to Richardson (Fig. 3.25). About it there is also much of the power and severity we associate with the Empire Builder himself. Unhappily the designer is not known, but the building falls within the tenure of Nelson D. Miller as chief engineer of the railroad (1885–1895). We know that

57

Col. C. C. Smith designed the famous stone arch bridge across the Mississippi at Minneapolis, and we know that Hill himself took a close personal interest in the project. He was, in fact, always fascinated with problems of construction. His first biographer, Joseph Pyle, remarked that in the second headquarters for the Great Northern (1914) there was no detail of plan or construction with which he was not familiar and that many of them were his own suggestions. It is safe, I think, to assume that the building shown here is the result of a collaboration between the railroad magnate and his chief engineer. For his mansion on Summit Avenue Hill imported the Boston firm of Peabody and Stearns, but in the headquarters Hill probably played as active a role as Abbot Suger at St. Denis.

The structural system of the building, in fact, suggests that Hill was as interested in arches as a Roman emperor. It is a framework of 12″ steel I beams spanning 5′ bays covered by segmental vaults of sand mould brick. These vaults are overlaid with a thin slab of concrete; on this layer the wooden floors are superimposed. Resting on a base of regularly cut ashlar, the exterior is brick over a stone foundation. The entire structure gives the feeling that it was built for the ages, or at least with the same solidity that Hill obtained in the roadbed of the Great Northern.

Fig. 3.25. Great Northern Railroad Headquarters, interior vault. Photo: Phillip James.

Fig. 3.24. Great Northern Railroad Headquarters, entrance. Photo: Phillip James.

58

Unhappily the excellent proportions of the original building were spoiled by an addition of two floors in 1889–1890. The construction photograph is valuable in showing us how the building went together, but the remodeled structure is much clumsier than its predecessor. These shallow brick vaults are, of course, by no means uncommon in smaller structures of the 1880s and 1890s, but I know of no other instance where they were used throughout a major building. This construction was certainly more fireproof than cast iron, and it was definitely much more conservative than the newly invented steel frame. Somehow the system is entirely in keeping with the character of Jim Hill.

As to program, the building was from the very beginning an office structure, although at a later date it housed the food catering operations of the Great Northern. In plan it is U-shaped around an open court to allow for the maximum number of windows and adequate light for all offices. The Empire Builder originally intended to light it with gas, but electricity came into practical use before it was finished, so the switch was made. It has had electric light ever since its first occupancy. Hill's own office, a huge room with two fireplaces, was on the second floor overlooking the yards. One can easily picture him checking his pocketwatch to see that the trains were running on time. The office was finished with elaborate woodwork, and there is also a wealth of fine detailing elsewhere in the building, notably in the stair rails. Today the building is on the National Register of Historic Places and has quite properly been renamed the Hill Building. Ironically the same structural system which gave it such remarkable solidity in its early years will undoubtedly be a substantial problem for the developer who wants to return it to active use.

As one who knew and liked St. Paul in his early years, I was delighted to return to it in 1987 and to find so many of the fine old buildings which were of particular interest to me saved by adaptive reuse. After much cogitation, reading, and conversation with a variety of individuals, I can offer the following possible reasons for the success of this particular Gateway City:

1. Philanthropic foundations with a deep interest in the city. The whole development would have been impossible without consistent support from the Ordway, McKnight, and Wilder Foundations.

2. A high-risk, high-reward attitude toward creative financing. St. Paul is a city where Industrial Revenue Bonds and Urban Development Action Grants (UDAG) have been important. Another popular development method is tax increment financing (TIF), through which the city issues bonds to acquire and prepare a site and then recovers its money through increased property taxes on the developed site.

3. A vigorous and enlightened leadership at City Hall. All writers agree on the significant role which Mayor George Latimer has played in the entire story.

How long these three bases for successful redevelopment will remain in place is anybody's guess. Happily, the foundations will be on hand for the indefinite future, and they are not likely to lose their interest in the city. On the other hand, the Revenue Act of 1985 made the adaptive reuse of old buildings somewhat less attractive to developers. According to Ian D. Spatz, legislative counsel for the National Trust, applications to the National Park Service to qualify for the 20 percent tax credit for rehabilitation on certified historic buildings have dropped from 270 a month in mid-1986 to about 150 a month at present.[19] The problem is the disappearance of 19-year tax depreciation and a limitation on the maximum amount of credit that an investor can apply against his income.

Furthermore one can easily imagine that the supply of money for UDAG grants might dry up or that a state law might make tax increment financing difficult for the city. Still, the developers who have been attracted to St. Paul are obviously the sort of people who are accustomed to dealing with obstacles. And by now the Lowertown phenomenon has a momentum of its own. Most important of all is the career of Mayor George Latimer. He is unlikely to stay where he is for the indefinite future. A few years ago a writer for the *Milwaukee Journal* remarked, "No one here doubts that within a few years he [Latimer] will seek higher office, and hardly any one believes that he won't win what he goes after."[20] Minnesota politics have always been interesting, and there is also the prospect of a federal appointment. In the meantime St. Paul is an exciting example of a Gateway City renewing itself.

4

Omaha

The Transcontinental Railroad and the Wholesale District

"Omaha, Nebraska," wrote Rudyard Kipling, "was but a halting place on the road to Chicago, but it revealed to me horrors that I would not have willingly missed. The city to casual investigation seemed to be populated entirely by Germans, Poles, Slavs, Hungarians, Croats, Magyars, and all the scum of the Eastern European States, but it must have been laid out by Americans. No other people would cut the traffic of a main street with two streams of railway lines, each some eight or nine tracks wide, and cheerfully drive tram cars across the metals. Every now and again they have horrible railway-crossing accidents at Omaha, but nobody seems to think of building an overhead bridge. That would interfere with the vested interests of the undertakers."[1]

Thus did the famous English novelist and apologist for imperialism comment on Omaha in 1889 when the city was at the height of one of its numerous booms. While his remarks seem today notable chiefly for their ethnic snobbery, he did make one observation of substantial importance for this narrative: the primacy of the railroad.

While wholesaling in every Gateway City is heavily dependent on the railroad, in none is this dependence exhibited more clearly than in Omaha. James Vance has convincingly demonstrated that long distance trade by rail and river was the father of cities of this type, and in Omaha the relationship of steamboat landing, railroad, and warehouse district is particularly clear. The city came to prominence in the middle 1860s and its rise would have been impossible without the possibility of transportation on the river. While the Union Pacific was under construction, there was no rail line into Council Bluffs or Omaha from the east. All goods had to be moved by river boat from the railroad at St. Joseph or fully up river from St. Louis. Hence there is a direct relationship between river landing and warehouse district. Once this connection had been established, changes in the means of transportation did not shift the location of the hub.

The site of Omaha is a large bend in the Missouri River, with flat bottom land gradually rolling up to a series of hills which are now prime residential districts. As early as the 1820s a few shrewd fur traders settled there, among them a Spaniard, Manuel Lisa, and a Frenchman, Jean Pierre Cabanne. The urban history of the place, however, does not begin until 1852, when land sharks, speculators, and potential settlers began to gather across the river at Council Bluffs, Iowa. They were awaiting a treaty between the government and the Indians which would open Nebraska for settlement, and so impatient did they become that some of them crossed the river and staked claims, even though the land still belonged to the Omaha tribe. Finally, they had to retreat to Council Bluffs and wait for the treaty before they could take possession.

This early foray was repelled, but the Council Bluffs and Nebraska Ferry Company continued to be important in the affairs of the city for several years. The company owned a townsite on the west bank of the river which, several leading Council Bluffs businessmen were convinced, had a great future. These gentlemen included Milton Tootle, later to make his mark in St. Joseph, and a certain Dr. Enos Lowe. They formed a company to develop the site and sent Dr. Lowe down the river to St. Louis with funds to purchase a steam ferryboat. As soon as the treaty was concluded and the government officially organized the territory, the company employed Alfred D. James (later territorial postmaster), with assistance from an army officer, Capt. Charles H. Downs, to survey the land. A recent writer has noted that James made all streets 100' wide except Capitol and Nebraska (now Twenty-first Street) Avenues which measured 120'. It is this distinctive breadth, together with the contours of the terrain, which give the city its characteristic quality. It is a place which calls upon a person to stretch ones legs in long strides.[2]

In St. Paul one can easily walk from the eastern edge of Lowertown to the Civic Center area in twenty minutes. Omaha, in contrast, seems to have been laid out for people on horseback, or in carriages. The main streets, named after army officers—Dodge, Farnham, and Harney, among others—run straight and true due west from the steamboat landing where the early commercial activity was centered. The land itself rose gently to a low ridge running north and south around Twentieth Street; here are situated the present central business district and the major civic institutions such as the Douglas County Courthouse, City Hall, the convention center, and the Joslyn Art Museum. Here also, until 1867, was the state capitol, now replaced by Omaha Central High School. From this ridge the gridiron pattern was extended toward the beckoning horizon and the Platte River valley. All this is clearly visible in Edward Austin's painting of 1905 commissioned by the *Omaha Bee* and now hanging in the Joslyn Art Museum, but an engraving of 1892 makes the impact of the railroads even clearer (Figs. 4.1 and 4.2).

The Union Pacific came across the bridge which is the central feature of the picture, and its major terminal is shown at the left in Fig. 4.2. The Burlington, financed by Boston capital and built much more conservatively, crawled across northern Iowa at a snail's pace and arrived over the other bridge only in 1882. As might be expected, other lines followed the easy grades of the river valley up from the south. Thus the area between the river's edge and Twelfth Street became the archetype of the warehouse district in Gateway City, its streets lined with powerful buildings in which the jobbing trades were housed. As the railroads built spurs to accommodate their business partners, it became crisscrossed with tracks. The development probably reached a peak in 1907–1908, at which time the great branch warehouse of the John Deere Plow Company was built at Ninth and Howard on the site of the old Roman Catholic Cathedral (the church is clearly visible in the engraving). Commerce displaced religion in both fact and symbol.

In comparison with St. Paul, then, the site of Omaha is more western in character. One senses in these early overviews that the settled area comes to an end somewhere on the edge of the prairie. Beyond the last white frame houses there will be only two tracks of steel stretching westward towards the horizon. In St. Paul, on the other hand, the growth of the city is constricted by the river valley and by a series of hills. Of the two places Omaha is much the more typical of the Middle-American Gateway City. Such a town, as we have seen, is essentially the result of a frontier settlement on a river with the subsequent imposition of the facilities of a transcontinental railroad. The railroad is the key in the development of the warehouse district.

The idea of a transcontinental line had, of course, been much discussed wherever men of affairs gathered to discuss business and politics during the 1850s—but the slavery issue made its actual construction impossible. One westerner particularly interested in the project of a transcontinental route was a prominent railroad lawyer from Illinois named Abraham Lincoln. Realizing that the Missouri River crossing was crucial for any prospective road, he toured the valley twice in 1859, visited St. Joseph, and on a second trip went up the river to Council Bluffs. There he met a wiry and intense young civil engineer named Grenville M. Dodge, who convinced him that the most logical route for the line was the broad valley of the Platte with its gentle grades. Although no one was aware of it at the time, their meeting was of historic significance. Lincoln ran for the presidency in 1860 on a platform which committed him to the building of a trans-

Fig. 4.1. Omaha As Seen from the Bluffs East of the Missouri River.
From Pen and Ink Sketches of Omaha *(1892).*

continental line. Other great issues, of course, claimed his attention, and the Pacific Railroad Act of July 1, 1862, which provided for the construction of the railway, was vague as to the eastern terminus. Lincoln evidently had an early inclination for Omaha, not out of any deep preference for the town but because he did not wish to be accused of capitalizing on his real estate interests in Council Bluffs. He did not make his final decision until the fall of 1863.[3]

It should be noted that until Lincoln's action the future of Omaha was not particularly bright. In 1854 J. Sterling Morton, an ambitious young man from Michigan, chose to settle at Bellevue and removed to Nebraska City the following year, where he became editor of the newspaper, a power to be reckoned with in state Democratic politics for many years, and ultimately secretary of agriculture in the cabinet of President Cleveland from 1892 to 1896. Nebraska City was

Fig. 4.2. Edward J. Austen. Aerial View of Omaha, 1905. *Oil on canvas, 59⅝" × 118". Commissioned by Edward Rosewater for a special edition of the* Omaha Bee News *Photo: Joslyn Art Museum.*

already important as a freight station for the wagon trade across the plains, whereas there was not a single cabin at Omaha until July 4, 1854. On that date a party got together in Council Bluffs, crossed the river, and put a log cabin on the townsite, though they were unable to roof it. The town was therefore essentially the creation of the ferry company, whose proprietors laid it out and then offered inducements for people to settle there. In September 1854 the proprietors were of-

fering lots to people who would improve them. These tactics were not unusual during this period in the nation's development. Morton later remarked on the amount of time spent,

> talking and meditating upon the prospective value of city property. Young Chicagos, Increscent New Yorks, Precocious Philadelphias, and Infant Londons were daily staked out, lithographed, divided into shares, and puffed with becoming unction and complaisance.[4]

The inhabitants of Omaha were evidently distinguished from those of other towns along the river by their greater aggressiveness and proclivity for violence.

For the first few years after 1854, the town indulged in what can only be called an orgy of speculation. A comprehensive map appeared showing the existence of a newspaper and a brick building suitable for a territorial legislature. Although no capital had been selected, the first legislature met in Omaha, January 16, 1855 (in later years the capitol and the state university were the only institutions which the city lost to its rival, Lincoln). The early inhabitants were known as "boomers" and with excellent reason. They were a rough-and-ready crowd having no acquaintance with federal land laws and less desire to know them. A good example of their tactics was the Omaha Claim Club, which was organized to secure an allowance of 320 acres per person as against the government's allotted 160. A chronicler relates:

> In the beginning, when each man was required to improve his claim and to live upon it, the members of the Claim Club built a house on wheels and moved it from one claim to another, so that each might say that he resided upon his claim. When a part of the claim of Postmaster A. D. Jones was staked by a Frenchman, Cam Reeves, a Missourian, was induced to come across the river forcibly to eject the offender. Such crowds came to witness the fight that it took three trips of Browne's ferry boat to transport them. The battle was long but the Frenchman finally fled to Iowa. The performance of Cam Reeves in this fight was so satisfactory that he was soon afterward elected sheriff.[5]

The psychology of the Claim Club and the enthusiasm for the fight are typical of the early days of Omaha. There were several other notable local instances of violence and even of lynch law. By comparison the early history of our other cities looks almost sedate and well mannered. Something of the atmosphere of this final period seems to linger on. In *Inside U.S.A.* John Gunther wrote that Omaha was "one of the most masculine cities in America . . . full of dust, guts, noise and pith."[6]

So much for topography and civic character. The crucial event for the warehouse district in this rowdy town was the coming of the first transcontinental railroad, the Union Pacific. As we have already noted, the question of its eastern terminus was not one to which Abraham Lincoln gave much study. He sent an ambiguous message to the railroad's chief promoter, Thomas C. Durant, and the latter, shrewdly interpreting it to mean Omaha, not a point on the *east* side of the river, proceeded with the ground breaking. The spot was on the Missouri River bottoms near the old ferry landing, and the ceremonies were memorable. Guns boomed on either side of the river, horns blared, and messages of congratulations were read by the silver-tongued orator of the day, George Francis Train, who was almost as fantastic a promoter as Durant. Subsequently Durant kept the order in his private possession, "lost" it, and some of the Union Pacific authorities, becoming apprehensive, asked Lincoln for a second order, which was given on March 7, 1865. This document placed the point at Council Bluffs *opposite Omaha.*

Durant's chicanery started a legal tangle which went on for years, since it eventuated in a long and bitter lawsuit as to which company, the Union Pacific or one of the Iowa railroads entering Council Bluffs, was to bear the entire cost of bridging the Missouri River, the most difficult engineering problem that the builders of the Union Pacific had to solve. Durant also obtained city donations to the Union Pacific of extensive areas within the limits of Omaha, and large quantities of land in adjoining counties. Included in the donations were 4360 acres in Douglas County, valued at the time of conveyance at between $200,000 and $300,000, which were taken in the name of "T. C. Durant, Trustee," without any language describing the beneficiary of the trust. Ultimately his maneuvers were too much even for the Gilded Age, and he was forced out of his directorship of the railroad in 1869. These details are, of course, only a small part of an immensely complicated story. They are related only to suggest the wild atmosphere which surrounded the beginnings of the line in Omaha and its importance to the city.[7]

The impact of the Burlington was equally great but considerably different in character. The Burlington system can be understood as essentially an extension of the Michigan Central, a railroad built slowly and carefully under the leadership of a cautious group of Boston capitalists whose outstanding figure was John Murray Forbes. As it proceeded across the Midwest it inevitably absorbed large numbers of smaller lines. By 1870 the Burlington was at Council Bluffs and the following year took over the crucial Omaha and South Western, which gave it control of the rich territory south of the Platte. From that time onward expansion in Nebraska was a major theme in the company's policy. This decision meant a steady increase in the road's construction program at Omaha: the building of yards, stations, repair shops, administrative headquarters, and numerous other edifices.

The impact of construction by the railroads on the physical development of Omaha was, then, overwhelming. Linked to these building programs was the development of the wholesale district. Large-scale jobbing began in the city about 1880 and grew rapidly for the next decade as the farm economy flourished. In the 1890s, however, agriculture suffered from extended drought, grasshoppers, and record low prices. Disillusioned farmers abandoned their homesteads and the Union Pacific Railroad, so important for the wholesale trade, went into bankruptcy. It lost control of all but 2000 miles of its 8000-mile system. The drummers found no market for their wares. Mari Sandoz caught the grimness of the period in a fine biography of her father, *Old Jules* (Boston 1935).

The Populist convention of 1892, which met in Omaha, represented agrarian discontent throughout the entire region, and profoundly shocked conservative business elements in the city. Prosperity did not really return until just before the turn of the century. The Trans-Mississippi Exposition of 1898 helped convince Omahans that the depression was over, as did a good wheat crop in 1897. Finally, the Union Pacific regained control of its branch lines, improved its roadbeds, and purchased larger locomotives with greater hauling capacities. Once again the Omaha jobbers were ready for business.

And business came. The jobbing trade grew with the economy during the first two decades of the twentieth century. In 1890, before the depression, jobbing sales in Omaha were $47,200,000. They were below this level for the next few years, but by 1900 had climbed to $62,500,000, and in 1916 reached $188,000,000. With this growth of the wholesaling trade came a demand for space. Said a writer for the *Omaha World Herald* in 1903:

> I am told by several of the best informed businessmen in the city that buildings suitable for jobbing purposes are now very scarce; that houses recently organized and being organized here are waiting somewhat impatiently for an opportunity to spread their wings in larger quarters and are meantime chafing under the necessity of renting warehouses, more or less scattered and unsatisfactory as well as expensive and unhandy . . . it would cause general chagrin if some important addition to the houses now here could be prevented for lack of floor space, yet such would seem a contingency.[8]

A related article remarked that the problem also affected the city's acquisition of new businesses. Several concerns wished to locate in Omaha but could find no space suitable for the jobbing trade.

The result of this situation was a second building boom in the area already staked out by the jobbers during the 1880s. It was adjacent to an earlier market area and quickly became known as "Jobbers Canyon." The nickname comes from the fact that the buildings are generally six or seven stories in height, display almost a wall-to-wall density, and are altogether of brick with a minimal amount of trim in stone and terra-cotta. Visually it has a remarkable unity. A 1976 photo (Fig. 4.3) shows a portion of the area at a time when it was somewhat more active than it is today. Deere & Co. was still using its huge warehouse on Ninth and Howard, and Lindsay Brothers were jobbing hardware out of the New Idea Building.

I may note in passing that one of the interests of this warehouse study has been that I have dealt *both* with buildings used as they were originally intended *and* with buildings converted to other functions. This has forced me to consider questions of adaptability which do not usually come within the purview of the historian. While increasingly impressed with the potentialities of mill construction, I have also become convinced of the wisdom of a maxim usually attributed to Lord Melbourne: "If a thing is doing well enough, leave it alone."

As this essay shows, I like Omaha. I was fortunate to learn to know it under the guidance of author Carl Jonas. Omaha was his native city. He knew it deeply and loved it well. In his novels it was always Gateway City, and his sense of place was so strong that he caught its flavor exactly. Carl was a visual person. He was a trustee of the Joslyn Museum, had an excellent collection of Netsuke and some fine graphics. He was a carver himself and created huge and ferocious Missouri River catfish, which floated on poles in his backyard. (Perhaps they were some kind of totem.) Carl lived in an architect-designed house, and when I told him about my project, he was immediately sympathetic. In his youth he had known John Latenser. He recalled that Latenser had been especially proud of some of the work he had done in the warehouse district. Still, as with many perceptive people who have never thought of warehouses as architecture, it was a bit difficult for him to understand some of my enthusiasms. I hope that the following pages will explain to Carl, wherever he is, the sources of my feelings.

Fig. 4.3. The warehouse district of Omaha, 1976. Photo: Phillip James.

G. W. SMITH BUILDING
(Mendelsohn and Lawrie, 1887)

This fine structure was constructed for a certain George W. Smith who is listed in Omaha city directories of the period as a carpenter. In our view it is likely that he was a substantial contractor and that the building was his headquarters and storage warehouse for building materials. He may, in fact, have built it himself. It was square, 66′ × 66′, six stories high, and almost a perfect cube. At grade level the framing was cast iron; mill construction starts at the second floor and continues through the sixth level. As the photographs show, the building was rich in molded brick and terra-cotta (Figs. 4.4 and 4.5).

Fig. 4.4. Mendelsohn and Lawrie. G. W. Smith Building, 1887. Photo: Phillip James.

Fig. 4.5. G. W. Smith Building, detail of terra-cotta. Photo: Steve Slater.

Its early usage is somewhat uncertain, but after 1945 it was owned by the Northwestern School of Taxidermy for more than three decades. Unhappily, I must report that in an act of civic vandalism it was destroyed to make way for a parking lot. In today's era of heightened preservation consciousness and federal tax credits, a developer would undoubtedly have been found for the building. As architecture its merits were considerable, and it was typical of a great deal of other Omaha commercial work now lost.

On the basis of engravings I would say that it strongly resembled the Paxton Block (by Eckel and Mann), which was described by contemporaries as the finest structure between Chicago and Denver. The recently demolished United States National Bank Building (Hodgson and Son, 1887) was in the same Richardsonian vein. I should add that while the bank was indeed an extremely handsome edifice, it probably had to go in order to make way for the Central Park Mall.[9]

The architects for the Smith Building were Louis Mendelsohn and Harry Lawrie, two prominent Omaha designers who were associated for only a single year. Louis Mendelsohn was born in Berlin in 1842, studied in New York City, and practiced for nine years in Detroit, Michigan, prior to his arrival in Omaha in February, 1880. From that date until 1885 he was in business with A. R. Defrene. After Defrene departed, Mendelsohn worked with George L. Fisher for two additional years and was in various partnerships in Omaha until the mid–1890s.

Harry Lawrie was a Scotsman who had worked nine years in offices in Edinburgh and Glasgow before emigrating to the United States in 1883. He settled in Chicago and spent four more years with Burnham and Root before coming to Omaha in 1887. Ultimately Lawrie associated in business with Fisher, a civil engineer from Michigan, and together the firm made a major contribution to the warehouse district.

WRIGHT AND WILHELMY WHOLESALE HARDWARE
(Fowler and Beindorff, 1889; remodelled by John Latenser, 1906)

The history of this concern is particularly well documented. Here we can see very clearly the relationship between business enterprise and the problem of building. The records of the company

67

have been beautifully preserved, and its history shows an extremely flexible response to the changing conditions it has encountered in its existence of over a century.

In 1871 John F. Wilhelmy and H. Larson formed a partnership and opened a wholesale and retail hardware store in Nebraska City. The products they handled were those usually associated with the sodbuster: hand tools, pitchforks, harnesses, small farm implements, wooden buckets, oil lanterns, rifles and revolvers, ranges and stoves, and cooking utensils. The firm outfitted westward-bound wagon trains, supplied general stores and other hardware dealers in the smaller towns of eastern Nebraska and southwestern Iowa, and also furnished goods to peddlers who went from homestead to homestead. In their first year of business Larson and Wilhelmy grossed $16,000—a very respectable sum for that time and place—but five years later Larson sold his interest and moved to Syracuse, Nebraska. W. S. Rector took his place, and the concern became Rector and Wilhelmy. J. J. Hochstetter, a Nebraska City real estate and insurance man also bought into the firm, and his son, Frank B. Hochstetter, became one of its first travelling salesmen.

The company's centennial brochure notes that the 1870s were an era of great upheaval and rapid change on the western plains, and this, if anything, is an understatement. Barbed wire, an essential element in the transition from open range to agricultural land, was invented in 1875, and soon Rector and Wilhelmy were distributing large quantities to the dealers in their growing territory. In 1876 General Custer met disaster at the Battle of the Little Big Horn. The United States Army immediately moved troops and horses to the prairies, and Rector and Wilhelmy, as an army supplier, shipped blasting powder, nails, crowbars, and sledge hammers to the garrisons on the Niobrara and at Fort Robinson. As the Indian problem was overcome, more immigrants poured into the new country, some to farm and ranch, others to work in the growing cities and villages. Often Rector and Wilhelmy helped these young families start their own hardware and general merchandise businesses. Their salesmen, Hochstetter and John H. Harberg, carried patched-up catalogues and a few samples from town to town, and returned to Nebraska City to pack their own orders for shipment.

By 1880 most of the company's business was at the wholesale level, and it had six employees. Three years later the owners decided to move to Omaha, which had surpassed Nebraska City as a trading center. The major reason for this growth was Omaha's strategic position with regard to the railroads. By this date the development of the wholesale district, which is shown so dramatically in the illustration of 1893, was well under way, and the firm joined other companies locating there. In 1884 it was strengthened by consolidation with the wholesale division of DeVol and Wright in Council Bluffs, and since that year the firm has carried its present title. Wright moved across the river to devote full time to its affairs, became a civic leader in Omaha and three times president of the National Wholesale Hardware Association—the only person ever to be so honored. Wright and Wilhelmy seem, in fact, to have enjoyed a generally high quality of management which has enabled

Fig. 4.6. Fowler and Beindorff. Original Wright and Wilhelmy Building, 1889. Photo: Wright and Wilhelmy.

them to survive depressions, droughts, and various other business vicissitudes in the midlands.

At first the company rented space, and then in 1889 began construction of its own building at the corner of Tenth and Jackson by local architects Fowler and Beindorff. This first structure was greatly enlarged by John Latenser in 1906, but as the photographs demonstrate (Figs. 4.6 and 4.7) Latenser retained the essential design of his predecessors. He simply added additional bays all the way around so that the floor area was almost quadrupled. With the flexibility of mill construction this was easy to do. The expansion could hardly have been more tastefully handled. There is, of course, no hint of historicism in the structure. It is direct, forceful, and beautifully adapted to its purposes, which have changed interestingly over the long span of its existence. Although the company is no longer engaged in jobbing major appliances, it has enlarged its operations in general hardware, housewares, sporting goods, and electrical and plumbing supplies. In these areas, it proudly declares, it maintains an inventory that is second to none in its seven state trading area.[10]

Fig. 4.7. John Latenser. Remodelled Wright and Wilhelmy Building, 1906. Photo: Photographers Associated, Omaha.

CHICAGO, BURLINGTON, AND QUINCY HEADQUARTERS
(Original building, 1879; remodelled by Thomas Kimball, 1889)

As we have noted previously, the Burlington railroad played a major role in the development of Nebraska. By the year 1887 it operated nearly 1956 miles of track from its Omaha headquarters, and by 1901 it ran nearly 8000 miles of road and had built its lines to Denver, Minneapolis, and St. Paul, and from Lincoln northwest to a connection with the Northern Pacific at Billings, Montana. Its lines in Nebraska covered the most fertile portion of the state, and it was natural for the road to want a building of civic importance in Omaha. It was, in fact, one of the outstanding railroads of its day, so well built and managed that even the great railway magnate James J. Hill admired its operation.

When John Wellborn Root designed the Burlington's Chicago offices in 1882, he deliberately sought a building which would be "a suitable architectural expression for a great, powerful, and stable railway corporation."[11] (See Fig. 4.8.) It was the first of his office buildings in which he aimed at a strong corporate image, and the Omaha headquarters, on the edge of the warehouse district, can be thought of in the same terms (Fig. 4.9). Root achieved his end by strictly architectonic means, as did Thomas R. Kimball, who was responsible for a major remodelling of the Omaha building in 1889. Strong local tradition has it that Kimball's design was intended to resemble the Chicago building by Root.

Originally constructed in 1879, the Omaha headquarters of the Burlington and Missouri River lines occupied three lots on the northwest corner of Tenth and Farnham Streets. It was a three-story structure and cost about $40,000 to build; the company spent another $13,000 on the interior and furnishings. The first floor was divided into retail stores with cast-iron fronts and plate glass windows, while the upper stories were used as offices by the railroad. Each floor was provided with fireproof and burglar proof vaults. The stone basement was used for storage and housed the furnace which steam-heated the entire structure. Evidently the office space was insufficient for the company, since an additional story was added in 1886, and another lot was purchased to give the building a total frontage of 88' on Farnham Street. The additional floor was supported by cast-iron columns rather than interior bearing walls as in the floors below. A massive cornice, scaled to the whole length of the building, covered the entire structure. The railroad company now took over the second, third, and fourth floors, while a wholesale grocer and a wholesale notion dealer were on the first.

On the night of January 1, 1887, a fire started in the quarters of Sloan, Johnson, and Company, the wholesale grocers. Their stock, valued at $75,000 was entirely destroyed, but the damage was fortunately confined to the first and second floors. In the railroad offices, however, the treasurer's office was almost ruined, and the telegraph department also fared badly. The general manager's office was totally flooded with water, which also wetted the stock of notions stored by Vineyard and Schuster, the other wholesaling firm in the building. Evidently temporary measures were taken at that time, because a major remodelling was postponed until 1889, when Thomas R. Kimball, the city's best known architect, received the commission.

Externally Kimball made very few changes. The railroad now wanted the first floor for offices; so brick pillars were put in to replace the cast-iron store fronts for additional support, and enlarged windows were added for illumination. On the interior, however, Kimball developed a vertical core of space culminating in a pyramidal skylight (Figs. 4.10 and 4.11). The skylight required a pair of steel trusses and galleries and all staircases were cast iron and were enlivened by the handsomely designed initial of the Burlington (Fig. 4.12). The sharply cut fenestration opening to the light court was defined by dark brick, while the walls were faced with light glazed brick. The floor between court and basement was fitted with glass blocks for effective lighting of the storage area and furnace room. On the first floor were the general offices; the second contained a conference room, mail room, and paymaster's quarters, while the third and fourth held spaces for the master carpenter, roadmaster, division superintendent, master mechanic, and various other important personages. The company used the building until it moved to new headquarters in 1956.

While the exterior of this structure is certainly not prepossessing, the light court is an elegantly handled design of glass and cast-iron, a type of space of which the nineteenth century was especially fond. Perhaps its earliest expression is in train sheds; one thinks immediately of the great work of Barlow at St. Pancras, London, in 1867 and of the obvious fascination which the Gare St. Lazare in Paris had

for Claude Monet, who painted several versions of the shed there. Such a construction was, of course, impossible without the new materials provided in abundance by industrial technology, and architects and engineers were quick to use steel, glass, and cast iron in new and dramatic ways. In the United States John Root was probably the greatest master of these towering interior spaces. A huge light court was a major feature of the Burlington's Chicago headquarters. The interior of the Rookery (Chicago, 1884–85) is an excellent surviving example of his work, much admired by architects and historians everywhere.

Kimball's light court in Omaha, then, belongs to a great tradition. Its space is magnificently unified and interpenetrated by the staircases and balconies, which disclose every motion and activity within the structure. The solidity of the brick walls provides a superb contrast to the lightness and airiness one feels in the cast iron and glass. Everywhere there is a feeling of movement and tension. The whole court is, in fact, like a great stage on which the drama of the railroads' business activities is played out; it is comparable to the setting for arrival and departure given by the great train sheds. It should be noted that this kind of vertical space remains a persistent theme in twentieth-century architecture. Frank Lloyd Wright used it in his famous headquarters for the Larkin Company (Buffalo, 1904), and more recently Kevin Roche has done the same thing in his widely publicized office building for the Ford Foundation (New York, 1970). John Portman's Regency Hyatt hotels, which expose the movement of elevators, offer a rather flamboyant variation of the idea. The design persists because it is basically sound. People like to watch a show and the vertical core gives them a chance to do so.

When I first saw the structure, it was filled with automobile tires, and its future was in doubt. It has now been converted into first-class office space and is occupied mostly by attorneys and accountants.

Fig. 4.8. Burnham and Root. Chicago, Burlington, and Quincy Railroad, General Office Building, Chicago, 1882–1883. Photo: Chicago Historical Society.

Fig. 4.9. Burlington Railroad Headquarters. Remodeled by Thomas Kimball, 1889. Photo: Phillip James.

Fig. 4.10. *Chicago, Burlington, and Quincy Railroad General Office Building, interior light court. Photo: A. M. Rung and Burlington Northern Railroad.*

Fig. 4.11. *Burlington Railroad Headquarters, interior. Photo: Steve Slater.*

Fig. 4.12. *Burlington Railroad Headquarters, interior detail. Photo: Steve Slater.*

RICHARDSON WHOLESALE DRUG COMPANY
(Henry Voss, 1890)

Among the most reliable and successful wholesale drug firms of the city, said a writer in 1892, was the house of J. C. Richardson. Founded in St. Louis by an enterprising businessman who was also president of the Chemical National Bank in that city, it established an Omaha branch in 1887 with Charles F. Weller as manager. Weller, who was vice president of the company, bought out the Richardson interests in 1889 at the time of the latter's death, but retained the firm name. Under his leadership the Omaha branch flourished, employing fifty to sixty clerks in the home office and numerous salesmen on the road in Arizona, New Mexico, Iowa, Kansas, Nebraska, Wyoming, and British Columbia. An interesting J. C. Richardson specialty was the stocking of complete drug stores.[12] In 1890 the firm put up the building shown here (Figs. 4.13–4.15).

Fig. 4.13. *Henry Voss. Richardson Wholesale Drug Warehouse, 1890. Photo: Steve Slater.*

73

Fig. 4.14. Richardson Wholesale Drug Warehouse, interior. Photo: Lindsay Bros. Hardware.

Fig. 4.15. Richardson Wholesale Drug Warehouse, interior. Photo: Lindsay Bros. Hardware.

In 1927 Richardson merged with the Churchill Drug Company and moved to larger quarters. The building was sold to the New Idea Spreader Company (later the New Idea Farm Equipment Company), an Ohio-based manufacturer of farm implements. In 1958 the structure was purchased by Lindsay Brothers of Minneapolis, a successful wholesale distributor of hardware and plumbing and heating supplies. This history certainly shows a wonderful flexibility: pharmaceuticals, agricultural implements, and, finally, hardware. The building accommodated them all.

In 1985 a local developer purchased the building and began conversion to a combination of commercial and residential use. It will contain 24 loft-style apartments and 6000 square feet of office or commercial space at grade level. Since it is a certified historic rehabilitation, the exterior character of the building will be maintained.

Henry Voss, architect for the building, was born in Germany and was particularly noted for his designs of Omaha's largest breweries. These included the Anheuser-Busch Beer Depot and the Krug (Falstaff) brewery as well as a large number of civic, commercial, and industrial buildings in both Nebraska and Iowa. Originally Voss's project for this building was even more Richardsonian than what was actually built. The drawings show decorative tourelles, a quarry-faced limestone base, and a powerful, broad, round entry arch. Early photographs show that the structure was modified in execution, though the arched entryway was retained. It is, nonetheless, a strongly articulated building very much in the tradition of H. H. Richardson's Cheney Block (1877) in Hartford, Connecticut, and Marshall Field Wholesale Store (1885) in Chicago.

Indeed, as one surveys the history of the American warehouse in the 1880s, one has the feeling that a very large number of the architects who tackled the problem in that decade found the Richardsonian solution so compelling that there was simply no way around it. This, of course, does not in any way detract from the excellent quality of the Omaha building and the similar structures in St. Paul and Winnipeg. It is simply an attempt to explain them and set them in their historical context.

The south and east facades of the Richardson Drug Building are divided into five and six bays with each bay defined by piers supporting a series of arches which culminate in large, round-arched windows at the fourth floor. A dressed-stone, segmentally arched doorway has replaced the original quarry-faced entryway. Large, tripartite, double-hung sash is used throughout the first three floors of the building. At the top level narrow, double-hung windows are grouped in threes. The entry solution resembles the Hackett and Powers blocks in St. Paul of almost the same date. Structurally the building is a standard mill frame throughout with graduated masonry bearing walls. Overall it has a basic dignity which makes it a worthy companion to its neighbors, the warehouses for Deere & Co. and Wright and Wilhelmy.

M. E. SMITH COMPANY
(Thomas Kimball, 1906)

Founded in Council Bluffs in 1884, the M. E. Smith Company moved to Omaha in 1886 and shortly thereafter began importing dry goods from Europe. So successful were they that within a few years the firm was ranked as one of the most important houses in the city, and in 1906 they commissioned the pair of warehouses shown here from Thomas R. Kimball (Figs. 4.16 and 4.17). Like Wright and Wilhelmy, the Smith Company was essentially a family firm. Its leading figure was Monroe E. Smith, a native of Iowa; two brothers, Arthur C. and Walter D. Smith, were also active in the business, which employed more than forty clerks in its headquarters and numerous salesmen who travelled in Nebraska, Iowa, Kansas, the Dakotas, Colorado, and Wyoming. Although the company also manufactured work clothes, its major success was in the wholesaling of imported dry goods, an interesting commentary on midwestern taste of the time.

Fig. 4.17. Smith Warehouses, exterior details. Photo: Phillip James.

Fig. 4.16. Thomas R. Kimball. Warehouses for the M. E. Smith Company, 1906. Photo: Phillip James.

By 1906 the Smith business had grown to the point where it required additional space, and the brothers turned to Omaha's best known architect Thomas R. Kimball. He produced a pair of powerful, majestic buildings, extremely restrained in detail except at the doorways and on the eighth level, where he allowed himself a rather extravagant treatment. On the basis of the detail it could be argued that the buildings were in the style of the Renaissance Revival; unquestionably Kimball used this manner for his City Library of 1891. More important than any question of style, however, is the beautifully proportioned grid of pier and spandrel and the clear expression of the heavy timber frame. The corners are resolved into powerful towers reminiscent of those in the nearby Deere & Co. warehouse but not so severe as in that building. By the first decade of the century warehouse architects were no longer committed to the image of Richardson's wholesale store for Marshall Field and were moving in several different directions. Kimball's treatment of the problem is excellent and will bear comparison with the best in this building type.

The double warehouse was, of course, not a Kimball invention. Similar examples can be found in Chicago. The idea makes excellent sense because it allows the introduction of a sheltered railway spur between the two structures. Loading platforms are thus easily available. Each warehouse was 132' x 132'. The total floor area was tremendous, and all of it was equipped with state of the art technology for fire safety: brick enclosed stairways and elevators, standard fire doors, standpipes, an automatic sprinkler system, and outlet scuppers on each floor. For the mill frame the capitals on cast iron fittings were a common but very handsome type.

When I studied these buildings in 1975–1976, one of them was occupied by the Pendleton Woolen Mills of Oregon, while the other was used by McKesson-Robbins for the jobbing of drugs. Since that time one has been lost to make way for the Central Park Mall. Happily its counterpart has been saved and at this writing is scheduled for conversion into condominiums. Professor Robert Darvas, the structural designer and a valued colleague, has remarked to me on the pleasures of working with the heavy timber frame.

BEMIS BAG BUILDING
(Mendelsohn and Lawrie, 1887; Lockwood, Greene & Co., 1898; C. A. Tripp, 1902)

This structure, which has a somewhat complicated history, grew from a relatively small edifice, five stories in height and standing about seventy feet above ground. This original section is on the right in the photograph (Fig. 4.18). The detail in the exterior masonry and the fenestration seem somewhat finicky in detail. The interior structure is a hybrid of light joist and heavy timber construction with two levels of posts on each floor producing bays approximately 12' × 22' in dimension. Vertical circulation was obtained by two centrally located service elevators and two open stairways on the east and south elevations. The building provided factory and warehouse space by floors: basement—storage; first—bag-making and bailing; second—business office and print shop; third—cutting and sewing; fourth—overall factory, stove; fifth—tin shop.

Fig. 4.18. Bemis Bag Building. Harte and Lindsay, 1887; Lockwood, Greene, 1898; C. A. Tripp, 1902. Photo: Lynn Meyer.

Because this first structure did not provide adequate space, an adjacent lot was purchased and a three story plus raised basement addition in the same red brick as the original was constructed on the site. The designers were the noted engineering firm of Lockwood and Greene in Boston, who were responsible for an immense amount of industrial construction all over the country. This addition had a frontage of 66' on Jones Street and is on the left in the photograph. It cleverly uses the original proportions and massing—a nice exercise in contextual design—but is considerably simpler in detail. A significant departure from the detailing in the original building was the substitution of white limestone lintels above the window openings to replace the older segmental arches. The fenestration also varies somewhat in the handling of the mullions, and the top row of round arches is enlarged. On the interior, wood floors and joists were supported by steel pipe columns to secure a 12' × 26' grid with steel beams. When the addition was finished, the company put the sewing and cutting operations on the second floor of the addition and established a lunch room and gymnasium on the third. Part of the newly created space was then leased to King and Smead, manufacturers of shirts, overalls, and pants.

In May 1902 the Bemis Company again expanded. This time it entrusted the building to the local firm of C. A. Tripp, which produced an addition at the rear of the warehouse identical in detailing to the work of Lockwood and Greene. Tripp, however, reverted to mill construction and produced a somewhat smaller 10' × 20' bay. The handsome white limestone sills and lintels were maintained, as was a stone stringcourse with brick details at the sill level of the third floor. Hence both the Jones Street and the Eleventh Street elevations display a pleasing unity.[13]

The company occupied the building until March, 1978, when it moved to a new location. In the same year the structure was designated a local landmark by the City of Omaha, and in 1985 it was nominated for the National Register. At present the tenants are an art gallery, artists studios, and the Mercer Management Company.

Judson Moss Bemis (1833–1921), whose company was responsible for the building, was one of the relatively unknown American industrial pioneers of the nineteenth century. In 1858 he established his first bag factory in St. Louis to produce cotton bags for flour. At this time flour was commonly contained in wooden barrels, and bag manufacturers were few and far between. Over the next few decades, however, wooden barrels became increasingly costly, and bags and sacks became more popular. They were less expensive and easier to handle. An additional factor which worked in Bemis' favor was the shift in the milling industry to chilled steel rollers for grinding wheat in the 1880s. Minneapolis was the headquarters of this development. Bemis opened his first branch factory there in 1882. Previously he had moved the firm's offices to Boston where he personally handled financial matters and the purchase of raw materials for his factories (cotton, burlap, jute, etc.) from markets in the U.S., India, and Scotland.[14]

The Omaha branch factory and warehouse was his second. Though the city was not a milling center, it did possess railroad connections and favorable rates for economical and prompt shipment of goods to the West. (It was also built to counter a competitor's factory in Kansas City.) Originally the branch manufactured burlap and cotton bags and dealt in grain sacks and twine. Initially sixty persons were employed in the manufacturing and printing of flour sacks. Its success can be gauged by its expansions. This growth of the company was, of course, closely tied to the expansion of American agriculture during the pre–World War I decades. By the end of the century Bemis had built six additional factories at strategic points and was the largest concern of its kind in the world. The company continued to expand in the early twentieth century with new factories, overseas investments, and the establishment of a factory and company town at Bemis, Tennessee. I have discussed one of the Canadian buildings in a separate essay.

Architecturally the Bemis Bag Building is a good representative of a type familiar in many cities in the United States: the strictly utilitarian industrial building. It is large in scale, simple and direct in statement. In the Ruskinian sense ("Ornament is the principle part of architecture.") it is hardly architecture at all. Yet it makes a distinguished contribution to an important section of the city.

FAIRBANKS-MORSE BUILDING
(Fisher and Lawrie, 1907)
Thaddeus Fairbanks was a clever Yankee. In 1830 at St. Johns-

77

bury, Vermont, he devised a platform scale. The invention was immediately popular, and by the Civil War E. & T. Fairbanks dominated the weighing field with a variety of devices which ranged from scales that measured in ounces to others that weighed boats of more than five hundred tons. By the end of the war the company employed more than one thousand people, had offices in New York and Boston, and traded in Europe, the Far East, the Caribbean, and Latin America. And that was only the beginning of the story. Charles Morse, nephew of an early Fairbanks salesman, apprenticed himself to the firm in 1850 at age seventeen and by 1866 had moved to Cincinnati to open up a branch house under the name of Fairbanks, Morse & Co. Under his leadership the firm dominated the market for scales in the Midwest. Morse was a gifted businessman, and he soon added a number of new products to his inventory. These included windmills, pumps, and various kinds of farm equipment. And gradually he bought up factories so that he was not only jobbing but also manufacturing. Morse's business ability far overshadowed that of the Fairbanks sons, and in 1916 he took control of the corporation.

Fairbanks-Morse came to Omaha in 1889 at the end of the first boom. The house survived the depression of the 1890s and by 1907 was ready to move to a location in Jobber's Canyon, where it remained for fifty-four years. To give it suitable accommodation the company called on the Omaha architectural partnership of Fisher and Lawrie in 1907, who were responsible for several of the best warehouses in the city. Obviously happy with this kind of architectural problem, Fisher and Lawrie adhered to the functionalism of Louis Sullivan and the Chicago School. In the Fairbanks-Morse Building they produced a structure which is, in fact, so plain and so severe that its qualities may easily be overlooked on the first visit (Fig. 4.19). It is, in fact, a second glance building if ever there was one.

The building can be easily described. It is six stories in height and in plan is a rectangle measuring 66′ × 132′. These dimensions are typical of many structures in the area. The exterior walls are of graduated brick masonry, 24″ at base and 16″ at top. The frame is mill construction with 14″ square posts producing a series of loft spaces four bays wide by 7½ bays deep. The ceilings are approximately 14′ high (on the top floor the ceilings are somewhat higher and the posts smaller, 11″ square). The posts are joined to split wood

beams by steel castings with double bolts. Windows are 4′3″ square and arranged in pairs. Floors are 2″ × 4″ boards set side by side and covered with a flooring capable of carrying the heavy machinery purveyed by Fairbanks-Morse. An early automatic sprinkler system has been repaired in recent years. When the company was using the building, the plan was very much like those of the other warehouses we have studied, with the offices and salesrooms on the first and second floors. The fourth floor was used as a scale service shop.

Fig. 4.19. Fisher and Lawrie. Fairbanks-Morse Building, 1907 (demolished). Photo: Lynn Meyer.

At street level the building is dramatized with an arched entrance, ornament, and large paired windows, sills, and spandrels recessed behind piers. This assortment of forms, materials, and planes contrasts with the simplicity of the upper floors. At the second floor the fenestration is narrower, and the windows above that level are compressed further into squares so that the scale alters as the building rises. All windows above the first level and without spandrels are in the same plane as the surrounding wall with the result that the visual forces are in balance. Narrow sills and shadows cast from the recesses are the building's only "decoration" at the upper stories. The brown brick has a distinct purplish hue which differentiates Fairbanks-Morse from the structures surrounding it. Altogether there is a maximum effect with a minimum of means. It would be hard to improve on the analysis of Judith Timberg:

> Fairbanks-Morse reflects its functions in the design of both interior and exterior. Inside, the relatively small windows are sufficient for the amount of light required; loft spaces provide expanses of open area; heavy timber construction and a sprinkler system help reduce fire danger; floors, posts, and ceilings in storage areas are of unpainted brick; a large open elevator can transport bulky loads; reinforced floors support heavy machinery. Outside, the regular, unadorned rhythms of windows on the top four floors suggest the interior sameness, simplicity, and utilitarian purpose of these floors; pairing of windows indicates the size of the bays inside; different exterior treatment of windows on the two lower floors signifies that they have different functions; it also provides the exterior with a visually graduated scale in a manner appropriate to graduated masonry wall construction, where the walls are thickest at the base and gradually become narrower as the building rises; the heaviness and forthrightness of the street level forms communicate strength, both of the building and the company; and even the ornament at the entrance has a functional purpose—it identifies the business concerns of Fairbanks, Morse & Co.[15]

One may also note the dramatic contrast of the richness of the entryway, and its ornament, with the overall plainness of the elevation. The ornament is very much in the Louis Sullivan tradition. It features a series of stone cherubs showing how machinery is made.

Even though eroded, these cherubs are provocative figures. They show minerals coming from the land, transported, weighed, melted, formed, and made into gears, finally producing money for the society that uses machines. Larger stone figures are at the ends of the stringcourse above. They include a man with a wheel, a man with a hammer and anvil, and a man with a scroll, each rising out of the ornament. The entire design and its iconography foreshadow the work of Sullivan and Elmslie at Owatonna a year later, though, of course, this ornament is much less elaborate. A simple, rhythmic arrangement of flowers borders the arch (Figs. 4.20 and 4.21).

Fig. 4.20. Fairbanks-Morse Building, entryway. Photo: Lynn Meyer.

Fig. 4.21. Fairbanks-Morse Building, detail of ornament. Photo: Lynn Meyer.

It is pleasant to report that the interior and exterior of the structure are in good condition. As the signage indicates, it is still in use as a warehouse. It should give good service in this capacity for many years to come.

To bring matters up to date we should note that in August 1986 the city nominated a Jobber's Canyon Historic District comprising twenty buildings for the National Register of Historic Places. It is clear that the City Planner's Office in Omaha and the preservationist community in the city have become aware of this resource, as it was only beginning to do when I first visited in 1975–1976. At that time I frequently encountered astonishment at my argument that these buildings were an architectural heritage worth saving and a potential civic resource of great value.

Today the Old Market Historic District is a thriving collection of small shops, cafes, and restaurants. Two of the buildings which were in use as warehouses when I first studied them are being converted to dwelling units. Obviously Omahans are beginning to think about the virtues of living downtown, but the process has not gone so

far as in St. Paul. Although the city owes much to the enlightened leadership of the Mercer family, who led the way in the reclamation of the Old Market, it lacks the foundations which have been so important in St. Paul. Political leadership on the level of Mayor Latimer is also missing. Nonetheless the warehouse district of Omaha is an impressive place. With luck and effort it could be developed as affectively as St. Paul's Lowertown. The city has already accomplished an exceptional piece of urban design in the landscaping of the Central Park Mall. It may realize the potentialities of its warehouse district in time. As one might suspect from the record of boom and bust, the warehouses of Omaha are not as cohesive in style as those of St. Paul (or Winnipeg). The earlier series from the 1880s are generally Richardsonian in character, but the later group, like the Deere warehouse of 1908, which I have discussed elsewhere, often owe something to the Chicago School. The architects and their clients generally shared an interest in fire safety and technological innovation. Mill construction was used well into the twentieth century (the Fairbanks-Morse Building of 1907) with thick solid masses of timber replacing the flimsy joists and thin flooring of the early warehouses. The Crane Company Building of 1905 by Fisher and Lawrie was the first to use concrete for its fireproofing qualities, but it had a hybrid structural system which combined exterior brick bearing walls with concrete floors supported by steel columns and beams. Nonetheless the building is classified as noncombustible rather than fireproof because the steel is unprotected. The Deere Building, of course, is one of the early triumphs of the concrete flat slab.

The nomination of the Jobber's Canyon Historic District for the National Register states:

> Environmentally, the "Jobber's Canyon" is a unique and cohesive concentration of late nineteenth- and early twentieth-century warehouse buildings. The canyon-like space created by the massive brick walls of the structures that line brick-surfaced Ninth Street is an important urban streetscape in the city. Brick and cobblestone streets, railroad spur lines, and loading docks and dock-canopies all contribute to the special character of the area.[16]

In this study I have added certain buildings away from Ninth Street which seem to me to be important for the somewhat larger warehouse district of Omaha. And I think I should remark that the buildings of the city's central business district suffer greatly in architectural quality when compared with those of the warehouse district. The reasons for this failure are deep-seated and perhaps not an appropriate subject for discussion here. The fact remains that since 1945 not a single structure in the central business district has received national recognition.

POSTSCRIPT

This essay has a melancholy conclusion. As the foregoing paragraphs show, in February 1987 when I revisited Omaha, I saw that the warehouse district still maintained architectural integrity and some economic life of its own. It appeared to me that it would, in time, again become a vital part of the urban fabric. I continued to hold to this belief through the following summer when I wrote the body of the chapter. During this period the executives of Con Agra Inc. must have been at work on plans for their new headquarters, to make room for which a large number of the buildings shown on the preceding pages have been obliterated.

"Con Agra," says the opening sentence of its *Fiscal 1987 Annual Report*, "is a diversified family of companies operating across the entire food chain—from farm to table." This statement is corporate jargon. Con Agra is a holding company (an agribusiness, if you will) that owns a large number of other businesses which actually produce or process everything from fertilizers to flour to sausages. By itself it makes nothing—except money for its stockholders, who, it must be admitted, have, over the last decade, done very well indeed. The figures are impressive. For twelve straight years Con Agra has met or exceeded its financial objectives, and in 1987 it reported record sales and earnings for the seventh straight year. It increased its dividend to 15.5 percent and split common stock two for one. It also acquired companies which added major strength in red meats and seafood. Con Agra ranked fourth among *Fortune 500* companies in ten years' average annual return to investors at 41 percent.

Con Agra has been, in fact, one of the most amazing success stories in American business of the last decade, and that success is largely the work of Charles M. Harper, now the company's chairman. He joined the company in 1974, sold off marginal operations, cut

debt, and developed a long-range plan for expansion throughout the food industry (*New York Times*, May 29, 1988). So successful has the company become that certain agricultural economists have become concerned about the concentration of ownership in the beef-packing industry among Con Agra, Excel (a Cargill subsidiary), and IBP. There is at least a possibility of market manipulation, if not now then at some point in the future. In an interview at his Omaha office, Chairman Charles M. ("Mike") Harper scoffed at his critics' fears of a meat-packing cartel. Consumers, however, can only hope that the spirited competition of the present will continue. In any event, it is clear that the company is making a great deal of money.

One might hope that an organization with such an excellent financial record would display a sensitivity to the urban quality of the city in which it makes its home. Unfortunately there is no such feeling in the leadership of Con Agra. With high-handed brutality, Con Agra is going to build a new headquarters/laboratory complex which will effectively destroy the warehouse district.

The origins of this decision are difficult to untangle. During the winter of 1986–1987 the Omaha City Council and the administration of Mayor Simon supported the successful nomination of the Jobbers' Canyon Historic District to the National Register of Historic Places. This nomination was, of course, no protection against corporate greed. Newspaper accounts (*Omaha World Herald*, December 6, 1987; *Des Moines Register*, January 10, 1988) seem to indicate that in late summer the city and Con Agra were actively considering the warehouse district as the site for a new company headquarters. In an August newspaper interview Chairman Harper declared that the district contained only "some big ugly red brick buildings." One suspects that at that point a firm decision had already been made and that, from the company's point of view, it was only a question of swinging the appropriate local authorities into line and overriding the opposition. Leonard Sommer, president of Landmarks Inc., a local group of preservationists, tried to persuade the corporation to preserve at least some of the outstanding structures; he correctly noted that the city had flip-flopped on the preservation issue within a single year.

Aside from this, certain other aspects of the struggle are noteworthy. Clark Strickland, regional director of the National Trust for Historic Preservation in Denver called the razing of Jobbers Canyon "the largest demolition of a nationally registered district in the history of the National Register—one of the best collections of such buildings in the U.S." (*Omaha Sunday Journal Star*, May 1, 1988). On the other hand, Bruce Lauritzen, President of the Omaha First National Bank and President Elect of the Greater Omaha Chamber of Commerce said that the disappearance of Jobbers Canyon will help pave the way for "one of the greatest redevelopment projects that the city of Omaha, or any city close to its size, has ever seen." The battle drew the attention of newspaper editorial writers in Lincoln, Nebraska City, and elsewhere. Reporters were as interested in the *Omaha World Herald*'s coverage of the story as they were in the project itself. PROUD (People for Responsible Omaha Urban Development) argued that their side of the story was not told because Harold Anderson, publisher of the *Omaha World Herald* is a member of the Omaha Development Foundation and one of the riverfront plan's strongest backers. The Lincoln *Journal* said that the *World Herald*'s pattern of coverage was indeed "interesting." The *Nebraska City News Press* went further and remarked editorially that the *World Herald* had paid "scant attention" to preserving Jobbers' Canyon and added, "It's a shame that this slash-and-burn corporate mentality is endorsed by the state's largest newspaper." To summarize a sad story, all efforts were to no avail.

Here let it be noted that the city of Omaha, and especially planning director Martin Shukert, were in an extremely difficult situation. In a letter to me of January 13, 1988, Mr. Shukert pointed out that the city's role as a regional economic center had been threatened by certain trends in American business. Omaha had been jolted by the move of Enron Corporation to Houston, Texas. The effects of this move spread through the economy affecting retail sales, home buying, and charitable giving. "In contrast," he wrote, "Con Agra is a growing company which will add 500 jobs immediately in Omaha, with up to 3,000 jobs over the next ten years. An economic force of this size is vitally important to our city. I believe that the full economic development potential for Omaha of a Con Agra project can only be realized at the riverfront site."

Mr. Shukert and Mayor Simon were between a rock and a hard place. Con Agra made it perfectly clear that if it did not get what it wanted in Omaha, it was quite prepared to move its headquarters to another location. The city would then lose the much-needed jobs. Mr. Shukert noted that the city had worked on several other possibilities, but none of these were satisfactory. "We then," he said, "had to decide whether the benefits of a Con Agra location in downtown Omaha outweighed the costs of the redevelopment of the Jobbers' Canyon. I believe that the answer to this question is yes." And so, as this is written (June 1988), the Fairbanks-Morse Building and several other fine structures have been demolished. The John Deere Warehouse is scheduled to go. Brute corporate power is eliminating an important part of the city's heritage. My esteemed colleague Professor Kingsbury Marzolf once remarked that historic preservation is like a war in which there are a few victories, many defeats, and numerous drawn battles. In my view the loss of Jobbers' Canyon is a major disaster for the city and the region.

Let us grant, then, the absolute necessity of the riverfront site for a new corporate headquarters for Con Agra so the company may continue to contribute to the economic well-being of Omaha. What, we may well ask, is the civic responsibility of the company which caused so many fine buildings to be torn down? The *Fiscal 1987 Annual Report* declares: "Con Agra is committed to responsible corporate citizenship. We give financial support to a long list of organizations for educational, civic, cultural, health, and welfare programs in our communities." I argue that in this case corporate responsibility should go beyond encouraging member companies to donate to food banks. A company which has caused the loss of excellent structures has an obligation to replace them with something at least equally good if not better. The obvious way to achieve this objective is with an architectural competition having strict rules, ample prize money, and a blue ribbon jury. But Con Agra has not chosen this method. It has entrusted its new buildings to the Opus Corporation of Minneapolis, Minnesota. Mr. Gerald Rauenhorst, chairman of the board and chief executive officer of Opus Corporation, has been a director of Con Agra since 1982. Obviously his organization enjoys the confidence of Chairman Harper, and from the inquiries I have made, it appears to be an excellent construction company. But I cannot help wondering whether we have here a situation which will result in buildings of true architectural distinction. The *Fiscal 1988 Third Quarter Report* notes only that: "Con Agra will soon begin construction of a new headquarters and food laboratory complex on the Missouri River in downtown

Omaha." The first phase of the project is to be completed by the summer of 1989.

I cannot help contrasting the corporate behavior of Con Agra with that of Humana, Inc., a company I came to know reasonably well during a few months as a visiting professor at the University of Louisville in 1985. Humana, an extremely successful company in the health care field, needed a corporate headquarters in the early 1980s and chose a site on a key location in downtown Louisville. As with Con Agra, a historic building of substantial importance had to be destroyed before this new structure could be built. But Humana *did* hold a competition. Michael Graves won it, and an office tower of great architectural merit was built. Moreover, Humana took care to preserve an adjoining bank, a fine structure in the old neoclassic tradition, and reconditioned it into a health maintenance facility for its employees. It seemed to me that Humana had contributed something of great value to the urban culture of Louisville—beyond jobs and charitable donations (of which, by the way, there were a great many).

Con Agra, on the other hand, has contributed substantially to the destruction of Omaha's architectural heritage. The situation is particularly regrettable because the city does not have any other important body of civic architecture to commemorate one of the great moments in its past. As I have remarked elsewhere in this volume, the men and the companies who built the Gateway City warehouses played a large and honorable role in the settlement of the West. In Omaha the evidence of that achievement is now gone. A chunk of history has been destroyed. A colleague who is a native Philadelphian remarks that it is as if greedy businessmen had torn down Carpenter's Hall and Independence Hall. We would then have no physical record of the tremendous role which eighteenth-century Philadelphia played in the American Revolution. In Omaha many of the buildings which were key monuments in the city of 1895–1914 have already disappeared. The excellent United States Courthouse and Post Office, a powerful Richardsonian structure, was demolished in 1966. The U.S. National Bank by Isaac Hodgson, Jr. (1889) is gone. So is the Paxton Hotel by Eckel and Mann. So is the *Omaha Bee* building of 1887–1888. Unhappily, the list could be extended. At one time Omaha had a public architecture which gave substantial distinction to the city. Con Agra has levelled the only set of buildings in the city which were a

record of that interesting period and a reminder of this distinction. And it has given no indication that it will put up anything of the same architectural quality.

On September 22, 1988, I attended the stockholders meeting of Con Agra in Omaha. I met both Chairman Harper, who announced a dividend increase, and Mr. John Phillips, who is project manager for the new headquarters and laboratory buildings. I also spoke briefly with Mr. Gerald Rauenhorst of the Opus Corportion. During management's presentation of its record for the last year, several site plans and renderings of the new structures were shown. They will be low-rise buildings, of three or four stories, clad in brick with a good deal of copper trim. The construction budget is $60 million. The project architect is Mr. John Albers of Opus Corp.

In conversation with Chairman Harper and Mr. Phillips, and in response to my questions from the floor, it became clear that Con Agra had deliberately not sought an architect of national reputation. Mr. Phillips stated, "Your company is unique among large companies. We didn't want an architectural competition. We didn't like what we saw. It would not have served our needs to go to a competition."

He therefore screened a panel of about fourteen companies, mostly developer with design/build capabilities, and Con Agra chose Opus, the organization of Mr. Rauenhorst, who was already on the board. Major requirements were that the selected firms have a large body of accomplished work and participate in the financing. Leo Daly, Inc., architects in Omaha, will do the interiors.

To date there appears to have been remarkably little coordination with the city planner's office. Several urban design aspects of the project are unresolved. For example, how the Con Agra "campus" will relate to the existing street grid above Tenth Street and to the successful Old Market area is not at all clear. In view of the controversy surrounding the entire project, I was somewhat startled to hear Chairman Harper remark that, after much consideration, they concluded that "it would be better for the community if we moved downtown."

Later that afternoon I called at the Wright and Wilhelmy Building on Jackson Street. The firm continues to do well, but with some regret will move to new quarters in March 1989. Its building is scheduled for demolition in June.

5

Winnipeg
The Northern Anchor of the Wholesale Trade

The Michelin Green Guide for Canada awards the city of Winnipeg a three star rating. It is therefore a distinguished place which is "worth the journey." While I cannot comment on the whole gamut of Winnipeg's attractions, I will agree that it has much to offer the tourist, and after a visit in the summer of 1987, I will reiterate my previously published opinion that in most respects its warehouse district is architecturally the finest on the North American continent. The splendor it displays within a rather concentrated urban area has its roots in Winnipeg's economic and cultural situation in the late nineteenth century. The beginnings were somewhat unpromising.

While Winnipeg dates its incorporation from 1873, its origins go back to the Selkirk Colony of 1811–1812. This was the project of a Scottish nobleman who was able to buy into the Hudson's Bay Company, and it combined philanthropy and commercial ambition in equal degrees. The Earl of Selkirk wanted to relieve the distress of Scottish crofters, who were being driven from their homes by the Enclosure Movement, and to resettle them in the fertile valleys of the Assiniboine and the Red River of the North. The difficulties of the enterprise were enormous. The first settlers had to come down the Nelson River from York Factory on Hudson's Bay, and they were separated from their fellow countrymen in Ontario by hundreds of miles of wilderness. Furthermore, they had to endure an exceptionally harsh climate

and the hostility of the North West Company of Montreal, which actually staged a massacre at Seven Oaks in 1816. Subsequently a defensive position and trading post were built by the Hudson's Bay Company at Fort Garry. The new settlement survived, but it did not grow rapidly.

During the first half of the nineteenth century Manitoba can be understood as a region equally devoted to hunting and to farming. Its historian, W. L. Morton, speaks of a few centers of culture such as the Red River library, but adds "around them washed the dull waves of an essentially primitive life, an economy founded on the hunt and the trapline, a society based on the union of the nomad and the trader."[1] In 1869, the year in which Manitoba joined the confederation, the entire province had a population of approximately 12,000 persons of European descent. Of these about 5000 were French half-breeds, 5000 were English half-breeds, and the balance were immigrants from eastern Canada and the United States. The frontier was still very close. Lynn Frank's *Dakota Boat*, painted in 1872, conveys the atmosphere of the Winnipeg Settlement (Fig. 5.1).

When, after intense political maneuvering, the city of Winnipeg was incorporated in December 1873, it united a series of communities near the juncture of the Red River of the North and the Assiniboine. With the act of incorporation secured, a number of urban institutions emerged during the next decade. A hospital, a legal society, and a College of Physicians and Surgeons were perhaps the most noteworthy. A city hall and market were built, board sidewalks were constructed to give pedestrians some relief from the pervasive mud, and the streets were surveyed. The most important, Portage and Main, followed the routes of the old Red River trails and were given sufficient width to accommodate the famous carts, which travelled in echelon in order to avoid being mired in the mud. For the builder, the soil conditions of Winnipeg were hideous.

Winnipeg differed from its counterparts in the United States in one important respect: The riverfront was of lesser importance in the economic life of the settlement. Because of navigational difficulties, steamboating on the Red River was never as significant as it was on

Fig. 5.1. Lynn Frank. The Dakota Boat, ca. 1872. Oil on canvas, 26½" × 36". Photo: The Winnipeg Art Gallery.

the Mississippi and the Missouri. For about fifteen years, sternwheelers ran between the Red River settlement and St. Paul but the traffic was uncertain and expensive. Because steamboating was so unreliable, a railroad connection with the outside world was essential. When the first council took as a civic coat of arms three golden wheat sheaves and a locomotive, they chose well. Manitoba wheat was to become world famous, and when the Canadian Pacific Railroad selected Winnipeg as its western headquarters, the city's future was assured. The decision meant that Winnipeg would become the primary wholesaling center of a vast and fertile agricultural area encompassing the present provinces of Manitoba and Saskatchewan and stretching westward into Alberta. This was truly an imperial domain.

In order to understand the full impact of the railroad's action one must take into account the traditional extent of government intervention in the large construction projects of Canadian history. The country is enormous; it is thinly settled and rarely has there been private enterprise large enough and daring enough to take the risks of opening and populating virgin lands. The Rideau Canal connecting Ottawa and Lake Ontario was financed in 1832 by the British government, and the opening of Upper Canada was aided by roads built by the British army. In the 1860s the Royal Engineers built the first Cariboo Road into the interior of British Columbia.

As for railroads, the Grand Trunk, the first important Canadian line, was constructed to connect the centers of the St. Lawrence valley, partly with private money, but also with substantial contributions from colonial treasuries and from cities that wanted to be served. From the very beginning, railroads were part of the politics of confederation. Strategic considerations made them imperative; these were readily illustrated in 1863, when there was a threat of war with the United States and 15,000 British troops had to travel by sleigh from Fredericton to Quebec. In 1871, following the American example, the House of Commons resolved that the Pacific railroad should be operated as well as built by private enterprise, but there was never any thought that the job could be done without subsidies. There does not seem to have been any true realization of just how large those subsidies would become.

It was not, however, until 1880 that the Canadian Pacific Railway Syndicate was formed and undertook to complete the line. With the complicated story of the politics which brought the road to Winnipeg we need not deal here; it is sufficient to note that, as in the United States, there was tremendous competition from neighboring municipalities, particularly the town of Selkirk. Winnipeg secured the prize but at great cost: exemption in perpetuity from municipal taxation for the railroad, together with right-of-way and land for station and yards. Selkirk survived only as the river port on Lake Winnipeg.

Also extremely important at this time was the protective tariff policy of the recently elected Conservative government under Sir John A. McDonald. Combined with the building of the transcontinental railway, it diverted trade from its former flow north and south to an east-west direction which still exists today. An exuberant writer in the Winnipeg *Telegram* of September 18, 1906, proclaimed that the city was the key to the whole West and that all business east and west must pass through the Gateway City. Numerous writers used exactly the same imagery.

The excitement of the crucial years 1880–1882, when the town was essentially a staging area for the building of the Canadian Pacific Railroad across the prairies, resulted in a frenzied boom. Real estate values soared, and within these two years the population almost doubled. A bird's-eye view of Winnipeg in 1884 shows a town in which the population was about 16,700. The impact of the railroad is clear (Fig. 5.2). Its tracks and roundhouses dominate Point Douglas Common. Industry is beginning to move in (Ogilvie Flour Mills), and log booms are visible next to some of the sawmills. Portage Avenue, then called Queen Street, leads off to the northwest, and its intersection with Main Street, which will become the commercial center of the city, has already developed a moderate density. Housing is expensive, and most dwellings are modest structures; as yet the costly homes along the Assiniboine have not been built. The insets show some startling contrasts with the straggling village and trading post of *Dakota Boat*. The Hudson's Bay Store has become a three-story structure (shown at lower left) and J. H. Ashdown's hardware enterprise (lower right) has also done very well. The wholesale district will develop in a roughly rectangular shape on both sides of Main Street just to the east of the intersection with Portage.[2]

The coming of the railroads, then, launched the city on a period of sustained but uneven growth. The boom years of 1880–1882, however, were not repeated. In fact, after the completion of the transcontinental railroad in 1885, development seems to have proceeded at a slow and steady pace until the late 1890s, when the population reached 42,000. Several factors were undoubtedly responsible for this relatively slow growth. The second Riel rebellion (an armed uprising of the militia against the established government) in Saskatchewan of 1885 made people hesitant. Then, too, the difficulties of farming on the open plains were substantial; the Mennonites, who were accustomed to the Russian steppes, showed the way, and it took time for the lessons they taught to be absorbed. Perhaps most important of all, good farm land in the United States was available for homesteading until 1900 when the best that country could offer had been taken up.

At the end of the century, a series of events combined to stimulate interest in the Canadian west. Among these were the discovery of gold in South Africa and the great strike in the Yukon in 1897. These discoveries meant increased gold backing for the world's currencies and additional money available for investment in railway stocks, government bonds, and farm mortgages. Also important were a series of bumper crop years which called the Prairie Provinces, last of the great agricultural frontiers, to the world's notice. Until the eve of the First World War immigrants poured in—from eastern Canada, from the United States, and from Europe.

At the federal level this movement was furthered by the forceful policies of Clifford Sifton, an attorney from Brandon, Manitoba, who became a minister of immigration in the Laurier government. Sifton reformed what had been a rather haphazard operation. He set up effective offices in Europe and the United States, and his policies met with great success. By 1912 Winnipeg had a population of 160,000 and was often referred to in the press as a Canadian Chicago.

This spectacular growth meant enormously increased opportunities in the jobbing trade. Most of the businessmen who led the way had come in the Ontario migration of the 1880s. Now they expanded and consolidated their operations. They established branches in towns like Brandon, Saskatoon, Regina, Calgary, and Edmonton, and they made additions to their buildings in Winnipeg. The physical growth of the city is immediately apparent in a rare print of the city in 1912 (Fig. 5.3). By this time the wholesale district is shown as a

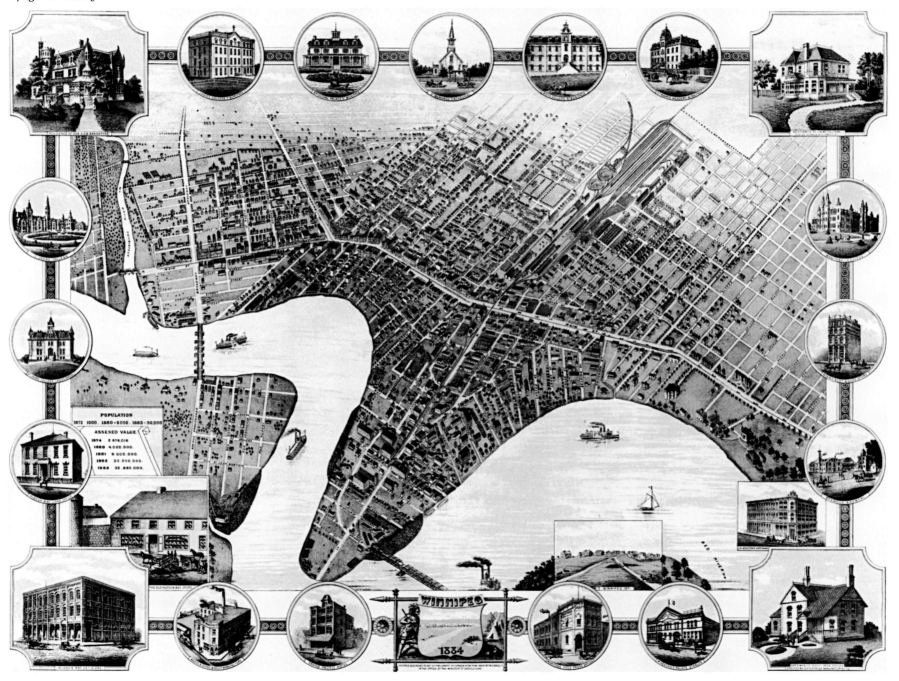

Fig. 5.2. City of Winnipeg, 1884. Photo: Ernest Mayer, The Winnipeg Art Gallery.

series of large buildings on both sides of Main Street. It is laced with railway spurs, the most important of which runs parallel to Princess Street. On the left side of the picture can be seen the imposing passenger terminal of the Canadian Pacific Railroad, and a few blocks away the conical towers of the Fort Garry Hotel. The North End, a polyglot district of recent immigrants and industrial workers stretches away at the top of the picture. Not shown is the recently finished Wellington Crescent with the mansions of the wholesaling magnates.

Today this central area is known as "The Exchange District," a name officially conferred in 1985. Its heart was the Grain Exchange, which remained here until 1980, when it moved to a nearby office tower. About twenty blocks square, it was a place where every major bank, trust company, insurance firm, farm implement dealer, and wholesaler wanted to locate in order to cash in on what popular historian James Gray has called "an unparalleled economic debauch." The drygoods business alone grew so rapidly that by 1890 more than

eighty wholesalers had established warehouses in the district and were doing $15 million worth of business per year. Manufacturing followed with seven clothing factories in operation by 1914. As more than one observer has noted, there was much display of this new wealth. Winnipeg was a city built by businessmen, and business ran it, not always with an eye to the general welfare. Still, the generation which built the district between 1890 and 1914 left a remarkable legacy of excellent buildings.[3]

The commercial elite put little on record concerning their views on matters of architecture. Indeed, no substantial analysis has ever been made of the character of the men who have commissioned industrial buildings. It is probable that the Winnipeg wholesalers displayed the same split in architectural taste as the men who commissioned the famous automobile factories of Albert Kahn. Whether or not Henry Ford, Walter P. Chrysler, or Henry B. Joy cared about their plants as architecture we do not know. We *do* know that the automobile manu-

Fig. 5.3. Winnipeg in 1912. Photo: Randy Rostecki.

facturers wanted their buildings to be supremely efficient containers for the industrial process and that they turned to the Kahn office because of its ability to solve the problem of function. Their residences, only a few of which were done by Kahn, did not show any predilection for advanced architecture. A biographer remarks that Kahn himself liked pre-1870 music and impressionist painting, felt that Duchamp deserved ridicule, and rejected the important European architecture of the 1920s. He adds that Kahn's clients would have agreed with his preferences.[4]

In one respect the warehouse client was in a different position from the builder of automobiles. The structure he erected was essentially a more *public* building type than a factory. Contemporary descriptions make clear that the warehouse was at least in part a civic monument. Time and time again the phrase recurs that a building is "a credit to the city." Furthermore the jobbing trade was fiercely competitive and highly concentrated in area, so it was desirable for the building to present an image of strength and stability. These were qualities which were required in the buildings themselves. Finally, many of the wholesale concerns were family enterprises. The merchants hoped that their sons would take over when they themselves passed from the scene. The warehouse therefore had something of the quality of an emblem or a coat of arms. Their owners were in all probability conservative in their tastes in music and art, but their architectural programs were well defined and they built some magnificent structures. The buildings which are illustrated in this essay are simply the finest of an exceptional group.

The Architects

The men who designed the Winnipeg warehouses were almost entirely local practitioners. While the financial community sometimes called in outside architects for important commissions, the wholesalers generally relied on firms within the city. Thus J. Wilson Gray, a prominent Toronto designer, did the Confederation Life Building on Main Street in 1912, and McKim, Mead, and White did the original building of the Bank of Montreal, but J. H. Ashdown relied on Winnipeg designers, not only for work in the city, but also for branch houses in other prairie towns. It seems appropriate to give some attention to the

biographies of these provincial worthies who created a style of remarkable unity and distinction. It is, so far as I can determine, impossible to say exactly who was responsible for each particular innovation.

An abundance of good building materials in the region is certainly important. The quarries at Tyndall were known earlier, but were opened for large scale production only in the 1890s. Thereafter the architects developed the habit of using several courses of quarry-faced granite as bases for their buildings. Customarily these courses are about shoulder high. Walking through the warehouse district is therefore curiously like walking through an actual quarry—a primal experience. Above these powerful blocks of granite the exterior cladding was the common local brick, made from a yellow clay. It is an excellent building material. The warehouses are entirely bearing wall structures, and the walls are treated in a highly abstracted Richardsonian manner. Ornament is held to a minimum. There are none of the tourelles or terra-cotta details which one finds in St. Joseph. The buildings derive their quality from proportion, scale, and the beautifully integrated relationship of arches, spandrels, and mullions. It is an extremely severe architecture, and to this observer it appears very northern. A parallel might be drawn with some of the Arctic landscapes of Lawren Harris a generation later. He shared with the Winnipeg warehouse designers an interest in the reduction of his subject matter to its bare essentials. Perhaps we have here a distinctively Canadian idea. At any rate, the warehouses are an enormously impressive body of work.

The first architect who made a major contribution to the district was Charles H. Wheeler. Born at Lutterworth, north Leicestershire, in 1838, Wheeler received his first education at the local grammar school and from the vicar of his parish. Almost equally talented in architecture and music, he decided on architecture, and gained practical experience in carpentry, bricklaying, and stone masonry. He also learned pattern-making at the Coventry Engine and Art Metal Works. Wheeler practiced architecture first in Birmingham and later in London. Some of his work took him to the continent.

Having read newspaper accounts of life in Canada, Wheeler decided to emigrate and arrived in Winnipeg with his wife and six children in February 1882. His first major work was Holy Trinity

Church, which he won in a competition against more than sixty other entries in 1884. Holy Trinity is done in a very free Perpendicular Gothic manner with tracery windows of the kind seen in Gloucestershire. (His wife came from Fairford, a village with an exquisite fifteenth-century church.) Thereafter his practice flourished. By 1897 he had designed over 270 buildings in Manitoba and the North West Territories.

In 1895 he did Dalnavert, a large house for Sir Hugh John Macdonald who was a figure of considerable importance, and it was a significant commission. For an American observer Dalnavert is a High Victorian dwelling, vaguely reminiscent of Frank Furness. It has much corbelled brick, the paired round arches which Wheeler evidently liked, and richly detailed interior woodwork.

For the government of Manitoba, Wheeler did the Home for Incurables (originally a mental hospital and later a tuberculosis sanatorium) at Portage La Prairie in 1890. His correspondence about this building with the Minister of Public Works reveals him to be extremely exacting in supervision. Concerning the plumbing he wrote, "I have not passed the work yet, and shall not do so until I have a full report that there is no leakage in the large tank."[5] Part of Wheeler's importance lies in the fact that he brought the high standards of British professionalism to Winnipeg. Prior to his arrival, practice in the city had been, to put it mildly, rather careless. By example, and through a series of articles in *The Canadian Architect and Builder*, he raised the level of professionalism substantially.

After 1901 Wheeler gradually turned away from architecture and devoted himself to music. He became the choir director at Zion Church and Knox Church and music critic for the *Winnipeg Tribune*. He died in January 1919 after a fall suffered while on his way to review a play.[6]

Also important in establishing sound building practice in the warehouse district was the contractor-architect James Henry Cadham, who was born near London, Ontario, in 1850. Cadham left school at sixteen to learn the carpenter's trade. At twenty he moved west to settle in Manitoba. Like most men of his age in Winnipeg, he enlisted for service under General Wolseley in the 1870–1871 rebellion of Louis Riel, receiving his discharge with the rank of sergeant. From that time he was active in the building field in Winnipeg, at first as a contractor and after 1895 mostly as an architect. His obituary in the *Manitoba Free Press* of December 11, 1907, remarked that his operations had been confined principally to stores and warehouses and that he was responsible for many of the edifices in the warehouse district. Particularly notable was his work for J. H. Ashdown and R. J. Whitla.

Newspaper obituaries are almost always fulsome, but certain phrases in Cadham's are impressive. The most impressive feature of his character, said the writer, was his professional integrity. "He was," said an associate, "the straightest man I ever knew." He never advised a client to put up a building unless he could show that it would pay, and he never allowed a contractor to skimp. His own buildings were exceptionally well constructed, and he obviously enjoyed handling the massive timbers of the mill frame. In short, he was the typical honest builder of the old school. Otherwise Cadham appears to have been an unremarkable personality. He liked to hunt, was a Mason and an Oddfellow, and left behind him a wife and five children.

In terms of style the most significant of the warehouse architects was unquestionably John Hamilton Gordon Russell. Born in 1862 in Toronto, Russell was educated in that city and received his first architectural experience in the office of H. B. Gordon. In 1882 he came to Winnipeg with his family, but remained in the city only a few months. Evidently feeling the need for additional training, he went south and for the next decade worked in various offices in Chicago, Spokane, Tacoma, and Sioux City. These were the years of the enormous American enthusiasm for H. H. Richardson and the advent of the steel frame for office structures. Russell undoubtedly saw Richardson's great Marshall Field Wholesale Store in Chicago and innumerable Richardsonian buildings elsewhere. Russell returned to Winnipeg in 1893, and when he opened his own office in 1895, was immediately successful. In addition to his work in the Exchange District, he did numerous buildings throughout the city, including the excellent Knox Presbyterian Church on Edmonton Street, the Child's (McArthur) Building on the corner of Portage and Main, and the enormous J. H. Ashdown residence of 1912. He was the first Manitoba architect to become president of the Royal Architectural Institute of Canada.[7]

GALT BROTHERS WHOLESALE GROCERY WAREHOUSE
(Charles H. Wheeler, 1887)

With its distinctive pattern of economic development, it is not surprising that the best buildings in Winnipeg's warehouse district were built within a limited time span, approximately 1897–1912. The Galt Building (Fig. 5.4), which was finished in 1887, is a foreshadowing of the type which was to flourish in the great years after 1900. It was recognized as a landmark by a column in *The Morning Call* of August 22, which was entitled "A Splendid Structure." Like American cities, Winnipeg was always conscious of the symbolic value of solid, well-built structures in brick and stone, and the article emphasized its excellent construction. The era of log cabins and mud huts was, after all, well within the memory of a great many citizens. It is, then, the earliest of the important wholesale houses.

The exterior is done in the local yellow brick but the yellow has been painted red. Its most notable feature is the fine series of interrelated arches, which, as in H. H. Richardson's Marshall Field Building (1885–1886) have a profoundly musical quality. Nonetheless, I do not believe that this is a Richardsonian building. It is rather an example of the Romanesque revival which was important in several European countries in the late nineteenth century, especially in Germany. The style was less common in England, but there are some notable examples in the warehouse area of Bristol.

Wheeler was, indeed, a medievalizing architect, as his other work shows, but there is nothing Richardsonian about either Holy Trinity or Dalnavert. The Galt warehouse might be called "castellated." *The Morning Call* termed the building "English baronial," a probable reference to the elaborate corbelling and the arches. The granite trim was Bedford stone from Indiana; the quarries at Tyndall, which were to supply so much fine material for the district, were not opened until 1895. The corner was rounded with two entrances which form a single porch; shipping and receiving doors are placed at the side, opening onto a block paved courtyard. A view of Princess Street in 1900 (Fig. 5.5) shows the building and also the neighboring Sanford Block by Wheeler of which only a portion remains.

Many pains were taken with this building. The basement was done in stone and was well lighted and drained, unusual qualities in Winnipeg at that time. An interesting feature was the butter vault, which was connected with the ice house above. The structure was framed in heavy timber, and the ground floor was divided up into general and private offices, a large sample room, fireproof vault, liquor store, bonded warehouse, and packer's office. Wide stairways and an elevator gave access to the second and third floors, which were fitted up to meet the needs of a large and increasing business.

The clients were John and George Galt, members of a prominent Ontario family. John was the son of Sir Alexander Tulloch Galt, one of the fathers of confederation and for a time Canadian high commissioner in London. After an education which included study with a private tutor in Germany, he was private secretary to his father for a brief period and then spent five years with the Bank of Montreal. By

5.4. *Charles H. Wheeler The G. F. and J. Galt ...lding, 1887. Photo: Manitoba Archives.*

Fig. 5.5. *Princess Street, 1900. Photo: Manitoba Archives.*

Fig. 5.6. *The G. F. and J. Galt Building in 1977. Photo: Henry Kalen.*

the early 1880s, western Canada was beginning to appeal to young men with an independent turn of mind, and so, in 1882, he came to Winnipeg with his cousin George, the son of Sir Thomas Galt, the chief justice of Ontario. In that year the Canadian Pacific was at the height of its construction activity, employing thousands of men and hundreds of teams. This fact evidently suggested to the Galts that they might do well in the wholesale grocery business.

The Galts specialized in imported groceries such as teas, coffees, and spices. In 1907 they formed the Blue Ribbon Company, which was devoted exclusively to this line of trade. It was so successful that they wound up the grocery side of their business in 1910, and from that time onward concentrated on specialty imports. They also gave much time to civic affairs, other industrial interests, banking, and insurance. John Galt was a director of numerous companies and president of the Union Bank of Canada and the Canadian Indemnity Company, and was closely identified with the Board of Trade and the Industrial Bureau. George Galt had an equal number of directorships, was president of the Northern Trust Company, and served for thirty-one years on the board of the Winnipeg General Hospital.

In 1904 the grocery trade had so expanded that they asked J. H. Cadham to add an additional story to their building. A recent photograph (Fig. 5.6) indicates that he did so in excellent taste, showing that respect for the work of his predecessor which was so common among the architects of his generation in Winnipeg. It may be noted that the jobbing trade expanded so rapidly that an addition was a common problem for architects working in the district. At this writing the Galt Building is occupied by a discount furniture business, the Lutheran Goodwill Society, and the Highbrow Book Store.

Fig. 5.7. J. H. Cadham. George D. Wood Warehouse, 1896. Photo: Manitoba Archives.

GEORGE D. WOOD WAREHOUSE
(J. H. Cadham, 1898)

In all probability the George D. Wood Warehouse of 1898 was the first major work of J. H. Cadham after he withdrew from contracting and turned to architecture. It was perhaps the first of the real giants among the Winnipeg warehouses (Fig. 5.7). The Wood Warehouse (Fig. 5.7) has four stories, a basement, and a street frontage of 73' × 132', giving it adequate floor space for a really immense stock of shelf and heavy hardware. The layout is ingenious. The ground was treated as a single space and was used for storage of heavy merchandise. The older photograph reveals a large receiving dock on the south side, and two additional arched openings which ran straight through the building to make shipping possible in all sorts of weather conditions. The offices were on the second floor; particular attention was paid to the problem of visibility for the management so that customers could be greeted as they entered. The third and fourth levels were devoted to the storage of lighter goods. The building was steam heated, and the elevators were electrically powered. The roof pitch was calculated to carry the rain water away in two 4" pipes. In terms of practicality, the George D. Wood Warehouse, like most of its neighbors, was a success.

Fig. 5.8. George D. Wood Warehouse. Photo: Henry Kalen.

The structure of the building, as is the case with most of the Winnipeg warehouses, is an extremely heavy timber frame with massive impost blocks at the meeting of post and beam. This frame is expressed in the nicely proportioned grid of pier and spandrel. The base of the walls to a height of 7' above ground is rough cut stone from the quarries at Tyndall, but as in the Galt Building, the trim is Bedford limestone. Above this strong base the walling is the local common brick. The building survives intact with the addition of another entrance on the corner (Fig. 5.8). Today it is known as the Merchants Building and houses several garment manufacturers and a shoe store.

Fig. 5.9. J. H. Cadham. F. W. Stobart Warehouse, 1903. Photo: Manitoba Archives.

F. W. STOBART, SONS & COMPANY
(J. H. Cadham, 1903 and 1907)

The early years of the century witnessed a spectacular increase in the jobbing trade of Winnipeg. Aided by favorable rates from the Canadian Pacific, which were also soon granted by other railroads, the wholesalers expanded their operations enormously. At the height of its prosperity, nineteen lines connected the city to the rest of Canada and the United States. Thus the Grand Trunk, ultimately a part of the Canadian National, ran north through the fertile valley of the Assiniboine to Saskatoon, and the Duluth and Winnipeg, one of the manifold enterprises under the control of James J. Hill, gave the city a connection to the foremost American port on Lake Superior. Contemporary observers noted that the long freights rolled into the yards day and night; the city was the supply point for the settlement of all of western Canada. In these circumstances it is not surprising that the warehouse district underwent a construction boom. Among the finest of the new warehouses was that of F. W. Stobart, Sons & Company, Ltd. on the corner of King and McDermott Streets (Figs. 5.9–5.11).

Fig. 5.10. Stobart Warehouse, with addition. Photo: Henry Kalen.

Fig. 5.11. Stobart Warehouse, detail. Photo: Henry Kalen.

Its description in *The Commercial* for November 1903 is given here in order to show the thoroughness with which the press reported on the architecture in Winnipeg. This thoroughness surely indicates an awareness of the importance of new buildings of excellence for the city. It is noteworthy that for most of the period 1900–1912 each paper produced a special issue which reviewed the activity of the city's building industry for the past year. In the *Winnipeg Telegram* for September 18, 1906, a reporter discussed the achievements of the city's leading architects, their fees, and their role in making the city into a

distinctive and beautiful place. We may well conclude that the level of consciousness of architecture was high. In a rather sneering way, the English poet Rupert Brooke made this point on a visit in 1913 when he wrote that the citizens had "a sort of gauche pride" in their architecture.[8] In contrast, the reporter for the *Commercial*, in an article dated November 21, 1908, had nothing but admiration for the Stobarts and their building. He wrote:

A FINE WAREHOUSE

Among the many fine warehouses which have been erected in Winnipeg this year, perhaps the most conspicuous as regards size, appearance and location is the handsome building erected by Stobart, Sons & Company, Ltd. The warehouse is not fully completed yet, but the work has so far progressed as to allow occupancy of the building. This warehouse is located on the corner of Mcdermott and King streets, which is about as central a position in the wholesale quarter as could be secured. The frontage on Mcdermott is 91½ by 132 on King. There are six floors, including the basement, giving in all 70,200 feet of floor space. The basement floor is well lighted as this part of the building has been carried up well above ground. In fact good light throughout is one of the features of the building, light being obtained on three sides, from the public lane in the rear as well as the two street frontages. The main entrance at the corner, through the immense oak doors which swing on ballbearing hinges, is particularly striking. The two doors are each ten feet high, nearly four feet wide and four inches thick, and handsomely panelled.

The ground floor is especially attractive in appearance. The offices extend along the Mcdermott street front, and are finished in oak, with panels of bevelled plate glass. There are two private offices and the general office. Also two vaults. The main portion of this floor is filled with great piles of staple goods, such as prints, flannelettes, shirtings, etc. The shipping room is cut off by partition wall. There are separate doors for receiving and shipping goods. Also a separate room for cloak and wash room, etc.

The second floor is filled with woolens, dress goods, and house furnishings, including carpets.

The third floor is one of the most interesting sections of the building. The fancy goods and small ware departments are located here, including a great variety of goods. Ladies ready-to-wear lines are also carried here.

The fourth floor is given up to men's furnishings entirely. There is a division wall across this floor, dividing the fancy from the more staple lines. Shirts, neckwear, etc., are carried on one side and underwear, overalls, smocks, etc., on the other. The latter goods are stored in racks. The company has recently established a factory for making overalls and smocks, so that their own make of goods in this line is now carried. The factory is in a separate building on King street adjoining the warehouse.

The fifth or top floor is divided into two apartments. One side is the entry and packing room, where goods are packed and carried by the elevator to the shipping room. The remaining portion of this floor is used for storing surplus stock of the lighter kinds and for travellers sample room, etc.

This fine warehouse throughout is fitted up in the most modern style. The lighting is by gas. It is one of the most up-to-date warehouses to be found anywhere in Canada, and is in every sense a credit to the company who owns and occupies it. The illustration herewith gives a very fair idea of the appearance of the structure.

In planning, construction, and design this warehouse is typical of J. H. Cadham, to whom it was credited in another contemporary account, which remarked that the exterior of the building was plain and dignified and that the interior was designed especially for the purpose for which it was used. Half of the main floor was for offices and all the rest of the building groaned beneath the weight of general dry goods.

Like many of the important Winnipeg warehouses the Stobart Block was quite frankly not a symmetrical building. The site was more extensive on King than on McDermott, so Cadham designed three additional bays on the long side. He later added two more stories. As in the George D. Wood Building the base consists of rough-faced ashlar about 7' high. The same material is used for window trim, but the rest of the walling is brick. The Stobart Block has a corner site, and Cadham handled the entrance in much the same way as John Root in his headquarters for McCormick-Harvester in Chicago (Fig. 3.4). His elevation differs in that the second tier of arches is omitted. The fenestration above the second floor is essentially the

same as in the Wood Building. In neither structure is there a trace of historicism. They are simple, direct, almost brutal solutions to the warehouse problem. If buildings reflect the personalities of the architects and their clients, then Frederick W. Stobart and James H. Cadham must have been memorable men. It is also closely related to the Gotzian Building of St. Paul (Fig. 3.3).

Frederick W. Stobart was born in 1859 in Durham, England, where his father was prominent in the coal and iron trade. His mother was the daughter of Gen. William Wylde of the Royal Horse Artillery; the general was for several years attached to the personal bodyguard of the prince consort. Stobart's family was able to give him an excellent education: private tutors, four years at Wellington, and two years at Cambridge. Young Stobart travelled for a time on the Continent, and then decided to take up marine engineering. This was a sensible choice, since his father owned and operated a fleet of steamships. For a year he worked in engine rooms and machine shops, and then, unexpectedly, was sent out to Canada in 1880 to take over the family interest in a trading partnership based in Winnipeg which had evolved into a wholesale drygoods firm. So successfully did he adapt himself to this new work that in 1884 he was ready to take it over. His business judgment was sufficiently good so that the house became one of the largest in the country with shipments from Port Arthur to British Columbia. Clearly an astute businessman, Stobart branched out into manufacturing in 1903. Under the trademark "No. 1 hard" (referring to grades of wheat and certainly suggesting durability) the firm produced overalls and workshirts in a factory on King Street adjacent to the warehouse. In 1910 a second large warehouse was erected to accommodate further expansion of the drygoods business.

In 1914 Stobart, who had retired to England, was appointed a purchasing agent for the British Army. German blockades and the diversion of production to the war effort left Britain dependent on North America for food and clothing. Stobart, with more than thirty years experience in Canada, was an ideal selection for the job. In recognition for his nation he was awarded an O.B.E., the British crown's highest civilian honor.

At present the building is known as the Bedford Block, after Stobart's home in England. It houses Reiss Furs and several garment manufacturers.

THE GAULT BLOCK
(George Brown, 1900; J. H. Cadham, 1903)

In the spring of 1899, Mr. Alexander F. Gault, a senior partner in the firm of Gault Bros. Ltd. in Montreal, travelled to the West Coast on an American railroad and returned east on the Canadian Pacific. While in British Columbia he and his companion, an executive named Rodgers, visited the Kootenay country, where the Gaults had mining investments. The real purpose of the trip, however, was to select a location somewhere in the west for a branch. With this object in mind, they visited Vancouver and Victoria, but wrote a reporter for *The Commercial*, in an obviously exuberant bit of journalism for June 6, 1899, they were particularly pleased with the business outlook in Winnipeg. They had, in fact, decided to recommend it as the location for the proposed western branch, showing their confidence by purchasing a site in the heart of the wholesale district between King, Albert, and Bannatyne Streets. The reporter for *The Commercial* wrote that the house of Gault Bros. Co., Ltd. was one of the oldest and best known wholesale concerns in Canada and that the establishment of a branch of such a house in Winnipeg would do much toward adding to the importance of this city as a jobbing center. The firm had for years worked to improve its western business and now it was taking a major step forward.

After this auspicious beginning events moved rapidly. A little more than a year later, *The Manitoba Free Press* carried a substantial article on the completion of the Gault Building. It included the usual extensive description of the interior and called particular attention to the greatly increased choice of goods which would be available to retailers. The stock of the Winnipeg house would be almost a duplicate of the holdings of the parent company in Montreal. Hence the retailers would soon be convinced of the advantages of obtaining goods from a source close at hand and would make Winnipeg their buying headquarters. The city's claim to be considered the wholesale center of Manitoba and the entire northwest would then be stronger than ever.

Gault's was a good example of the Anglo-Canadian corporation. With headquarters in Montreal, it imported textiles from its own mills in Manchester; these were brought to Winnipeg by rail where the shipments were broken up and distributed. Twelve or fifteen agents travelled the circuit for Gaults between Winnipeg and the Rocky Mountains. West of the Rockies business was handled by a Vancouver branch. We can obtain an idea of the importance of the wholesale trade to the Manitoba city by an analysis of the employment structure of 1911, in which year the population of Winnipeg was 136,035. It had a high percentage of the population in the work force (45.7), a relatively low percentage of the labor force in manufacturing (17.8), a high percentage in trade (24.9), transport (13.7), and construction (17.2). The peak of its power and influence was probably reached in 1912, when it controlled grain marketing, wholesaling, and finance from the Great Lakes to the Rockies. Like many other observers, the English novelist Edgar Wallace thought that it was destined to become a Canadian Chicago.

Fig. 5.12. George Brown. The Gault Block, 1900; J. H. Cadham, 1906. Photo: Henry Kalen.

For their architect the Gaults selected George Brown of Toronto. The first four stories of the present building are his design, and they are thoroughly Richardsonian (Fig. 5.12). (Richardson's influence was strong in Toronto, as can be seen in the old City Hall by Edward Lenox. It is clearly based on Richardson's Allegheny County Building of 1884–1886.)

A recent discussion of the building by the Winnipeg Historic Preservation Committee remarks:

The original four story facade expresses the nature of masonry construction as a "stacking up" process, and indicates the varying wall thicknesses required at each level to support the weight of the floors above. Within the structure a simple wooden post and beam system is used. The large window openings which provide daylighting to the interior were made possible by the advanced state of masonry construction and foreshadow the even larger openings to be offered by steel frame construction.

When in 1903 Gaults' expanded their facilities by building a six-story addition onto the south wall and adding two stories to the original structure, architect James H. Cadham approached the project in a manner sympathetic to the original building. For the first four floors of the new building he repeated the order of the original facade, with the addition of a driveway through the building which sheltered the loading docks. For the top two floors required over both buildings he repeated the order of the top floor of the original building. It is virtually impossible to tell that the Gault Building is in fact two separate buildings.[9]

Once again one is impressed with the deftness with which the expansion was handled—and with the growth of business which required it.

In 1985 the building was renamed Artspace and converted into quarters for twenty-four literary, performing, media, and visual arts organizations, eighteen of which are nonprofit. It now contains: eight studios for visual artists, one of which is a residential studio; four studios for playwrights and writers; three exhibition galleries and a retail craft gallery; literary and visual art resource center; workshop spaces; cinemateque; production studios for film, video, and photography; meeting rooms; and a publishing company, a lithographic print shop, and an intaglio print co-op.

Says a brochure:

There are also administrative offices, all occupied by artist-run organizations who fight an ongoing battle to educate the general public and the whole cultural infra-structure of government on the necessity of recognizing and supporting the people who actually paint the paintings, throw the pots, write the plays and the poems and the books—the people who make possible the galleries, the theatres, and the large cultural institutions on which we pride ourselves.

On the basis of a visit in July 1987, I would judge that the conversion is a substantial success. For many years I have observed that artists are fond of warehouses. Here a number of them have obtained what they want.

R. J. WHITLA BLOCK
(J. H. Cadham, 1899 and 1906; J. H. G. Russell, 1911)

The success of R. J. Whitla in jobbing dry goods can be gauged by the fact that the building shown here of 1899 was the third he constructed in the wholesale district. The first was on Main Street and probably resembled the pioneer store of J. H. Ashdown. The second was on Albert Street and was later used by *The Winnipeg Telegram* in 1882–1884. For the third he turned to J. H. Cadham, the warehouse specialist, and that designer gave him another structure in his abstracted Richardsonian manner (Fig. 5.13).

Cadham, of course, retained the vocabulary of heavy base courses and window sills in Manitoba granite which were important constituent elements of the style. Slabs of Tyndall stone emphasize the grid of pier and spandrel which is such an excellent expression of the heavy timber frame (Fig. 5.14). Cadham added a substantial addition in 1906, and J. H. G. Russell built an adjoining structure in 1911 so that the entire block is about 185' × 100'. In this last portion, cast iron framing was used, but the expression is the same. Thus the building does not have the same unity as the Woods and Stobart blocks, but it is nonetheless extraordinarily fine. At present it is known as the Silpit Building and is occupied by several garment manufacturers.

Fig. 5.13. J. H. Cadham. The R. J. Whitla Block, 1899. Photo: Manitoba Archives.

Fig. 5.14. The R. J. Whitla Block. J. H. Cadham, 1899 and 1906; J. H. G. Russell, 1911. Photo: Henry Kalen.

The client for the building was one of the most colorful businessmen of his generation in Winnipeg. One of ten children, Robert J. Whitla was born in Ulster in 1846 and emigrated to Canada at age twenty-one. At first he settled in Ontario, where he ran a retail store at Arnprior on the upper Ottawa River for nine years. He came to Winnipeg in 1878 just before the great boom, and by 1882 was concentrating his energies on the wholesale trade. These talents were formidable. Like many Ulstermen he had unbounded energy, strong convictions, and great moral fervor. He was converted to Methodism by the great evangelist Caughey at the old Richmond Street Church in Toronto, and this experience stayed with him all his life. A devout churchgoer, he was noted for his kindness to his employees, and he was a strong supporter of the YMCA, YWCA, Salvation Army, and other kindred organizations. At the same time there was nothing blue-nosed about Whitla. A few years after his death in 1905, one of his contemporaries remembered that he loved guns and dogs and was known for his ability to tell a good story. Whitla was also a major in one of the local army reserve units. After the Louis Riel rebellion of 1884–1885 these formations seemed to be of considerable importance for the community.

Whitla's civic activities deserve comment because they were so characteristic of him and of the merchant aristocracy to which he belonged. Although he was a member of the Conservative party, he joined those who fought Prime Minister Sir John A. McDonald over the disallowance question and ultimately drove him from office. This controversy involved an effort by the federal government to disallow provincial railroad charters. In the view of most Canadian historians, McDonald was often insensitive to the needs of the West, and he ended up on the wrong side of this fight. A few years later came the "Manitoba School Question" (a local dispute over school financing), which finally resulted in the abolition of the dual school system in the province. As a loyal Orangeman, Whitla took to the stump. Tradition has it that his speeches were so vigorous that he several times had to pay damages for tables smashed up during his orations. One feels that whatever Whitla did, he did with energy, and this energy was characteristic of the entire mercantile elite.

FAIRCHILD BLOCK
(Herbert Rugh and John D. Atchison, 1907)

This building shows a sharp break with the type developed so successfully by J. H. Cadham, and it is, in fact, the work of an architect who came directly out of the Chicago tradition. Instead of the heavy rustication at grade level, we have ample fenestration; farm machinery, unlike drygoods, was a public attraction. Instead of the unornamented elevation so common elsewhere, we have dramatic swatches of terra-cotta, very much in the manner of Louis Sullivan. Instead of the local white brick, we have a pressed brick in a soft shade of buff imported from the Twin Cities. Rugh, a graduate of Armour Tech in Chicago, seems to have been the designer, but John D. Atchison, another American architect practicing in Winnipeg, signed the working drawings. In any case, the building's antecedents are clear.

The architect(s) took advantage of the metal frame to open up the rear of the building in a manner which would become conventional twenty years later. (This is one of those startling architectural experiences which reward those who take the trouble to walk all the way around buildings.) The section and the plans show that the structure had six floors and a basement and that the entire first floor was given over to machinery display. The building is a good expression of its metal framing, and it represents something entirely new in the wholesale district. Once again the decision of the agricultural implement makers and their jobbers to build a handsome show case for their wares was a decisive factor for the architectural design (Figs. 5.15–5.17).

Although the building is properly known as the Fairchild Block, the client was Hodgson W. Hutchinson, yet another native of Ontario. Born at Durham in 1862, he came to Winnipeg at age twenty and found employment as a bookkeeper with David Maxwell, a jobber of agricultural implements. By 1884 he was a manager, and he held that post until 1888 when he moved over to the firm of F. A. Fairchild and Company in the same job, which he held until 1895 when it was reorganized as a limited liability corporation and he became secretary-treasurer. Fairchild's had begun as a partnership of two brothers from Oakland in Mount Pleasant County, Ontario. They undertook to job a variety of farm machinery, particularly the John Deere Plow and the

Moline and Milner wagons. The business did well, though it must have been somewhat cramped in the Grain Exchange.

Frank Fairchild died in 1898, and Hutchinson was appointed general manager, succeeding to the presidency in 1900. Four years later he purchased a controlling interest in the firm but left the name unchanged, probably for reasons of business good will. There can be no doubt, then, that it was Hutchinson who, in 1907, was the client for the handsome building on Princess Street. In December of that year he sold the business and building to the John Deere Plow Company, a concern which he had come to know well. From that year until 1918, when he moved east to become general manager of Sawyer-Massey Ltd., he was prominent in Deere's Canadian operations and a director of the company. Deere used the building until 1954. The present tenants include a wholesaler of fabrics and three manufacturers of sportswear.

Fig. 5.15. Herbert Rugh and John D. Atchison. The Fairchild Block, 1907. Photo: Henry Kalen.

Fig. 5.16 Fairchild Block, rear elevation. Photo: Henry Kalen.

100

Fig. 5.17. Fairchild Block, ornamental detail. Photo: Henry Kalen.

J. H. ASHDOWN BLOCK
(S. F. Peters, 1896, and J. H. G. Russell, 1906 and 1911)

This remarkable structure (Fig. 5.20) was the culminating effort of James H. Ashdown, perhaps the leading Canadian merchant prince of his generation. Its story is inseparable from his career.

Ashdown was born in London, England, in 1844 and came to Canada with his family in 1852. They first settled at Etobicoke, Ontario, and later moved to Weston where he was a clerk in his father's store at age eleven. Subsequently he walked to what is now the city of

Guelph and thence to Hespeler, where he apprenticed himself to the local tinsmith. For the next three years he earned very little more than his board but supplemented this pittance by keeping the books for the town's blacksmith. In the evenings he read law and English literature. Self-educated, he was both a thoroughly literate man and an extremely convincing public speaker. It was remarked of him that when he finished with a question, there was nothing left to be said.

At age twenty Ashdown decided to see the United States and, by way of Chicago and St. Louis, went to western Kansas where he worked in the building trades at Fort Zarah. With good wages and thrift he accumulated a small stake which enabled him to make his way to the Red River country from St. Cloud, Minnesota, then the end of steel. There he joined a brigade of carts for the nineteen-day trek to Winnipeg. Enroute he met the Methodist missionary George Young who was also to play a great part in the development of western Canada. They struck up a friendship which was to have important consequences.

Ashdown could hardly have picked a less propitious time to arrive in Manitoba. In the summer of 1868 the grasshoppers had utterly destroyed the cereal crop and all pasturage for the cattle. The buffalo hunt was a failure in the fall, and if it had not been for supplies sent by the Dominion government, the public of England, the United States, and eastern Canada, the Red River community would have starved that winter. The prospects of the place could hardly have been considered glowing, and yet Ashdown rejected the appeals of his family to return to Ontario, thereby affirming his faith in western Canada.

The next year, 1869, was marked by economic opportunity and political turbulence. Ashdown was able to purchase the tinsmithing business of George Moser, whose anti-British, pro-American sentiments had been expressed too vigorously. Always one to see an opportunity, Ashdown soon added lines of hardware to the business and thus became the only dealer in the field between the Great Lakes and the Rocky Mountains. He knew how to press his advantage. At the same time the government of the country was in negotiation between the Hudson's Bay Company, the new Dominion of Canada, and the British government. This unsettled condition was the essential reason for the Red River Rebellion in which Ashdown was among those imprisoned by Louis Riel in the winter of 1869–1870. In later years he described the shooting of Thomas Scott, which gave the Orangemen a martyr, as "worse than a crime, it was a blunder." Within a few months after his release his business had grown so much that he had to leave his quarters at the rear of a saloon and move to Post Office Street (now Lombard Street) and thence to the site which the company occupied for almost a century at the corner of Bannatyne and Main. A sketch of the premises is so descriptive that it does not require comment (Fig. 5.18).

Fig. 5.19. S. F. Peters. J. H. Ashdown Block, 1896. Photo: Manitoba Archives.

Fig. 5.18. J. H. Ashdown Building, Bannatyne and Main Streets, in the 1870s. Photo: Manitoba Archives.

From the early 1870s, Ashdown's business grew steadily and his need for better facilities expanded accordingly. His second building, probably of the early 1880s, is shown in an inset of the bird's-eye view of 1884. The third, of 1896, was a really large building and represents the leap in urban scale which was very common in the late nineteenth century (Fig. 5.19). It was the work of S. F. Peters, another Winnipeg architect who was an admirer of H. H. Richardson (see his building for Wesley College on Portage Avenue; it is now part of the University of Winnipeg).

The structure remained as shown here for only five years. On the night of October 11, 1904, the wholesale district suffered the worst fire in its history, and Ashdown's losses amounted to over $400,000, the entire stock of goods for the Christmas trade. Immediately rebuilding and expansion began, this time under the direction of J. H. G. Russell, who was also responsible for further additions in 1906 and 1911, when the structure reached its present 207' × 140' and height of seven stories (Fig 5.20).

In view of this complicated building history the continuity of the design is remarkable. The same structural system, a heavy timber frame, is used throughout the complex, and the different parts relate to each other so handsomely that the additions can hardly be distinguished from each other. The architectural vocabulary is the same throughout: a heavy granite base, common brick walling, and sills and window mullions of Tyndall stone. The detailing of the brick around the arches is especially fine. In its dignity and monumental scale the building is among the very best works of industrial architec-

Fig. 5.20. S. F. Peters and J. H. G. Russell. J. H. Ashdown Block, 1896–1911. Photo: City of Winnipeg.

ture produced in the nineteenth and twentieth centuries. It is noteworthy that its completion came at the very moment when Winnipeg's commercial dominance was at its height and when Ashdown himself was at the summit of his power.

As a man Ashdown was as interesting as his buildings. In business he had a tremendous flair for legitimate publicity. In 1878 he inaugurated the custom of an annual staff gathering which featured dinner, entertainment, and the distribution of cash gifts to his employees. In 1900 he created another novelty in Canadian business organization when he shipped an entire trainload of forty cars of hardware to his customers in western cities; this was termed "the Ashdown special" and received notice in every newspaper in the country. Appreciating

his business genius, Alexander Begg, a historian who was a witness to his achievements, expressed the sentiments of the community when he wrote, "No wonder Ashdown grew rich."

Business activity was only one facet of his character. He took an active part in the political life of Winnipeg. In the early days he fought hard for its incorporation as a city, expressing the idea that if it were going to become an important place, it should not start as a village or a town. This was an exceptionally hard battle, since many property owners who would become tax payers upon incorporation resisted to the bitter end. In later years he served the public as an alderman, a member of the school board, and as mayor in 1906–1907, at a time when the city's finances were in chaos. Ashdown straightened the situation out, though he was regarded by many as a radical for his advocacy of municipal ownership of the utilities. He also worked hard and effectively to bring the Canadian Pacific Railroad to the city and, like R. J. Whitla, was in the midst of the disallowance question. He also fought the railroad monopoly and played a major role in securing the favorable rates which were so essential to the expansion of the jobbing trade. It would be hard to find a better example of the independent civic-minded businessman anywhere.

He took the responsibilities of his wealth with utmost seriousness. With Whitla, he contributed largely to the support of Wesley College, the YMCA, and the Winnipeg General Hospital. And he was not content to simply give money, but also contributed generously of his time to the conduct of affairs of these institutions. At his death in 1924 his estate was the second largest in the history of the province, and approximately one-quarter of it was distributed to charitable and educational institutions. In Ashdown, the ancient doctrine of stewardship had a modern exponent.

Finally Ashdown seems to have been one of those businessmen with a genuine feeling for style in building. In whatever wholesale district one visits between Winnipeg and the Rockies, the Ashdown Building will be outstanding for architectural quality. The store in Edmonton has recently been successfully recycled as "The Boardwalk." The others, in Calgary (still visible from the railroad), Regina, and Saskatoon continue to give useful service as warehouses. Among his other qualities, James H. Ashdown was a remarkable patron of architecture.

CAMPBELL BROTHERS AND WILSON WAREHOUSE
(J. H. G. Russell, 1903 and 1912)

Among Winnipeg jobbers Campbell Brothers and Wilson were outstanding in the wholesale grocery trade. R. J. Campbell was a native of Toronto with experience in the grocery business. He came to Winnipeg in 1881 and in 1885 went into partnership with his brother W. J. In 1900 R. R. Wilson joined the firm, which then became Campbell Brothers and Wilson. It was, however, clearly R. J. Campbell who was the dominant partner. A man of great civic consciousness, he was also chairman of the city's Sinking Fund for several years and a member of the administrative board of Winnipeg. The grocery business did

so well that in 1903 J. H. G. Russell was commissioned to do the first unit of the building shown here (Figs. 5.21 and 5.22). It is one of Russell's finest works. With the customary rough granite base and lintels, it has uncommon dignity. Russell undertook a striking innovation when he brought out the surrounds of his bays and maintained the same excellence of design when he added two stories in 1912.

Grocery jobbing was carried on in essentially the same manner as the trade in drygoods and pharmaceuticals. The jobbers purchased goods in quantity, broke them down into lots, then packaged and distributed them. Small town grocers in western Canada purchased teas, coffee, spices, mustards, jelly powders, extracts, dried fruit, and tobacco from Campbell Brothers and Wilson. The brand name was Royal Shield, but they offered a number of other lines as well.

Fig. 5.21. J. H. G. Russell. Campbell Brothers and Wilson Block, 1903 and 1912. Photo: City of Winnipeg.

Fig. 5.22. Campbell Brothers and Wilson Block, detail. Photo: City of Winnipeg.

At the Princess Street front a driveway has been constructed into the building, near the centre, for receiving or shipping goods by horse vehicle. Three doors open into this passage, giving facilities for loading and unloading under cover. In all, this gives six shipping and receiving doors, which makes first class facilities for handling goods.[10]

Today this driveway and receiving section have been closed off and the area converted into a showroom for the furniture company which occupies the structure. It is known as the Adelman Building, and the owners have taken advantage of a Heritage grant to clean it, greatly improving the appearance.

For this building, as for certain others in the Exchange District, cost figures are available. The original structure cost about fifty thousand dollars, and the addition another thirty-four thousand dollars. I believe, however, that building costs varied so widely from city to city in the United States and Canada that such figures are not in themselves of any great significance. What *does* matter is that the wholesalers in every Gateway City were willing to spend money to obtain buildings which would be a credit to themselves, to their families, and to their cities. Further, they were men of conviction with carefully thought out programs. These are the essential points. Whether the client is an individual, a government, or a corporation, it requires more than money to secure truly distinguished architecture. In the United States, Canada, and Europe we have had in the last generation too many instances where major buildings, public and private, have simply been occasions for conspicuous display. In contrast the Winnipeg jobbers look like an extremely lucky or intelligent group of patrons.

MERRICK-ANDERSON BLOCK; NICHOLSON AND BAIN BLOCK
(John J. McDiarmid, 1899)

These two buildings, today known as "The Brokerage," were built in the same year and share a common wall (Figs. 5.23 and 5.24). Merrick-Anderson, on the left, were manufacturers' agents for several lines of stoves and furnaces. Established in 1883, the firm also carried heavy hardware, tin shop supplies, building paper, and bags of cotton and jute for the milling industry.[11] By 1899 the wholesale business had

With goods coming and going on a grand scale, loading facilities and access to transportation were critical for the business of the grocery wholesaler. Like so many others in this study, the Campbell Brothers and Wilson Warehouse was located adjacent to the Princess Street spur of the Canadian Pacific Railroad. A contemporary account remarks:

105

grown to such an extent that they asked John J. McDiarmid for a new structure on a site on Bannatyne Street east of Main near the Ashdown Block.

In the same year McDiarmid also, in all probability, erected the adjoining three story building for Edward Nicholson, an Ottawa-born merchant who had come to Winnipeg in 1882, married into the wealthy and influential Bawlff family, and had done well in the wholesale grocery business. The Nicholsons were socially prominent, and Edward Nicholson was an avid curler. In 1905 Nicholson made a partner out of his young accountant, Donald Bain, and the firm was thereafter known as Nicholson and Bain.

Born in Belleville, Ontario, Bain had come west as a child. He, too, was an accomplished amateur athlete—a hockey player, cyclist, and figure skater of great ability. This athletic partnership did well as brokers and commission agents for specialized grocery items. The firm expanded to Edmonton and Calgary in 1909 and by 1930 had added branches in Vancouver, Regina, Saskatoon, Fort William (Thunder Bay), and Montreal. In 1917 Bain became the sole owner of the business. For many years the smaller building was known as the Bain Block.

Fig. 5.24. The Brokerage. Photo: City of Winnipeg.

Fig. 5.23. J. J. McDiarmid. Merrick-Anderson and Nicholson Bain Buildings, 1899. Photo: Manitoba Archives.

About John J. McDiarmid we know very little except that his firm at one time owned a lumber yard. Obviously he adhered to the prevailing Winnipeg warehouse style, but here enlivened it with some handsome straw basket brick work. There is also elaborate ornamentation at the cornice level and a carved panel dated 1899. These are perhaps the most fanciful of the city's warehouses. It should be noted that another spur line of the Canadian Pacific Railroad gave Merrick-Anderson, Nicholson and Bain, and the other wholesalers in the area access to transportation which they required.

In 1976 developer Tom Dixon purchased the two buildings, powder-blasted the exteriors, and recycled them into attractive office space within 1200' of the corner of Portage and Main. He renamed the complex "The Brokerage." Both were designated as Heritage buildings by Council in 1980. Although the adaptive reuse has been, on the whole, successful one wonders whether it would have been executed in its present form if it had been carried through after the passage of the ordinance of 1978. The by-law seems to require the maintenance of fenestration in its original form. Here it has been much altered. A comparison of the two photographs makes one understand the importance of the heavy window mullion for the integrity of the warehouse style. On the other hand, the buildings have been saved, and as the Historical Buildings Commission remarks, they provide "office and commercial space to lovers of brick, massive wood beams and history."[12]

BEMIS BAG PLANT
(W. H. Lester, 1906)

An important shift in construction technology occurred when the Bemis Bag Company came to the city in 1906. Bemis was attracted to Winnipeg by the convenient access to railroad transportation and the rapidly growing requirements of jobbers and other industries, particularly milling. Wholesalers and millers required large quantities of containers, notably bags made from paper, cotton, and jute. Ogilvie Mills, for example, was a particularly good customer.

The move to Winnipeg by the Bemis organization was a natural action in a program of expansion heavily influenced by the boom on the prairies. Founded in 1858 and incorporated in Missouri in 1885, Bemis was already a large corporation by 1906. It owned cotton mills

in St. Louis, Indianapolis, and Beaver, Tennessee, as well as factories in Boston, St. Louis, Minneapolis, Indianapolis, Omaha, New Orleans, San Francisco, Seattle, Memphis, Galveston, Houston, and Jackson, Tennessee.

Bemis Bag Company's structural requirements were entirely different from those of the Winnipeg wholesalers: A reinforced concrete frame was necessary to support the heavy machines required for manufacturing its products.

In the early 1900s Bemis had a company architect, W. H. Lester, about whom practically nothing is known. In all probability, however, he was one of those all-but-anonymous professionals like Oscar Eckerman, who designed a great many structures for Deere & Co. but received little historical notice. In any event, Bemis entrusted the design of its new building to Lester and the construction to him and Mr. Stenerwall, supervisory assistant. This decision was undoubtedly conditioned by the fact that Winnipeg builders were unfamiliar with the technology that was to be employed (Fig. 5.25).

Fig. 5.25. W. H. Lester. Bemis Bag Factory, 1906. Photo: Henry Kalen.

107

The building was to be six floors and these had to support the heavy loads of the machines which fabricated bags and printed the labels. These presses were variants of the printing presses of the time. The first installation could turn out seventy-five thousand bags daily and two hundred thousand bags with additional machinery. Light and power were generated from the firm's own boilers on the premises. The plans (Fig. 5.26) show that the structure was almost entirely loft space except for offices on the first floor and the boiler room. According to the local paper, the manager was George C. Watson, who had been employed at Bemis for twenty-five years and shortly would become a Canadian citizen. The company had 132' (40 m), of trackage on the much-used Princess Street spur at the rear of the building.[13]

Fig. 5.26. Bemis Bag Factory, plan. Redrawn from the original by Robert Daverman.

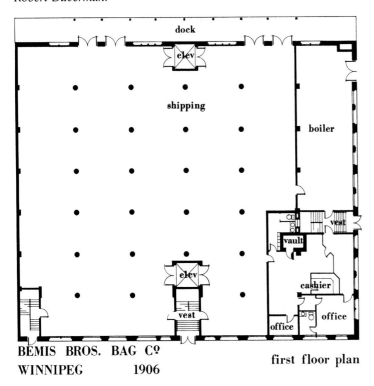

BEMIS BROS. BAG Cº
WINNIPEG   1906
first floor plan

Of course, there was nothing new about using reinforced concrete for industrial construction in North America in the first decade of the twentieth century, but there were a number of places where it had not been tried, and Winnipeg was one of them. In the United States, the pioneer was the engineer Ernest L. Ransome, who had a thriving practice and was granted several patents for his contributions to the technology of the material. Among his major contributions was the factory of the Pacific Coast Borax Co. in Bayonne, New Jersey, built in 1897–1898.

The Borax factory, according to Ransome, marked the end of the traditional concrete building constructed in imitation brick or stone with comparatively small windows set in the walls. It should be noted, however, that the structural frame comprised columns and beams, a technique that went back to the work of Francois Hennebique in France in the 1860s and 1870s. The section (Fig. 5.27) shows that the same technology was used by Lester in Winnipeg in 1906. The original drawings, still preserved by the company, indicate that beams were generally 18″ × 24″ (45.7 cm × 61 cm) in section and that the recently invented Kahn reinforcing bar was used.[14]

In elevation, the Bemis Building presents an absolutely unadorned grid of pier, mullion, and spandrel; comparison with an old linocut in the *Winnipeg Commercial* (Fig. 5.28) shows that there have been some changes in the building. It continues, however, to function very much as it did when it was opened for production. The exterior is protected from weathering only by a coat of white stucco. It would be hard to find a more severe application of the engineering aesthetic. In view of the supposed rapid obsolescence of industrial buildings, the most surprising aspect of the structure is that it is still used for the same purposes for which it was originally intended.

The old presses have been replaced by newer models, while modern equipment makes possible the manufacture of many types of plastic containers. Nonetheless, the plant still uses large quantities of jute imported from Bangladesh, and the flour mills are still good customers for bags. Little deterioration is visible in the concrete, and weathering has been minimal.[15]

After the building's success, the Winnipeg warehouse district witnessed the erection of several smaller structures in reinforced concrete, notably the Great West Saddlery of 1910 by William Wallis

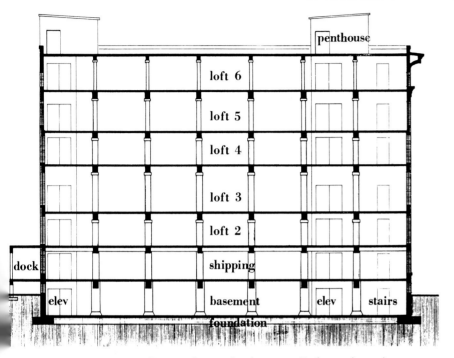

Fig. 5.27. *Bemis Bag Factory, longitudinal section. Redrawn from the original by Robert Daverman.*

Fig. 5.28. *Bemis Bag Factory. Engraving: Manitoba Archives.*

Blair for Elisha Hitchings, but many others remain to be explored. Almost no research has been done further west.

In 1910 an unknown designer, probably from Winnipeg, put up a handsome warehouse in Calgary for J. H. Ashdown, but it was an extremely curious structure framed partly in timber and partly in flat slab concrete. The reason for the change in structural system is unknown.

Two years later, Hill and Woltersdorf of Chicago built a magnificent warehouse in Saskatoon for the Rumely Tractor Co., done altogether in flat slab concrete. Today it is used as a wholesale furniture store. The owners of Simpson's department stores were also quite interested in the flat slab; their branch in Regina in 1915 was built from this material. The discovery of the Bemis Building points to the

need for further work on the history of reinforced concrete in western Canada.

In July 1987 I revisited this building and was delighted to find it in good condition and in active use for the manufacture of bags. The only difference is in the ownership. Subsequent to my first inspection Bemis sold its Canadian business to Bowmar Ltd., a multinational corporation with headquarters in Scotland. However, local management seems happy with the structure and there is no disposition to seek another facility. There is, to be sure, more emphasis now on plastics, since the shipment of jute from Bangladesh has become unreliable. Still, if production continues for another twenty years it will have endured for an entire century. The structure may be a classic among industrial buildings.

The Future of the Warehouse District

In the winter of 1977 I spent January and February working in Winnipeg. I recall clearly that my colleagues took it as evidence of my devotion to scholarship that I would spend part of my sabbatical leave there at that time of year, but having grown up in Minnesota, I was certain that the climate would be familiar. It was. In any event, the visit was successful. I stayed in a good hotel on the edge of the district, walked its streets almost every day, and did a lot of work at the Provincial Archives and Library. I did not do much work at the City Archives because these were not at that time readily accessible, but I did make the acquaintance of an engaging young city planner named Charles Brook. He was almost as enamored of warehouses as I was. Brook had already published, in 1974, a pioneering study of what was then called the Historic Winnipeg Restoration Area. It is almost identical with the Exchange District.

It was Brook who pushed hard to obtain an ordinance from the City Council establishing the area as an historic district in August 1978. It was extended to include several important blocks east of Main Street in August 1984. Co-coordinated with the by-law setting out the district was another ordinance establishing an Historic Winnipeg Advisory Committee and giving it an annual budget and powers of review. With the publication in January 1983 of an excellent set of design guidelines, also mostly written by Brook, the mechanism for the entire preservation process was thus put in place. This young man deserves great credit.

Canadian preservation practice generally resembles American custom, but there are some interesting differences. As in most cities in the United States, in Winnipeg it involves a system of listing (i.e., rank ordering) in terms of architectural and historical merit. The criteria will be familiar to American readers:

1. Significance in illustrating or interpreting history in the city
2. Association with important historic persons or events
3. Illustration of the architectural history of the city
4. Distinguishing architectural characteristics of a style or method of construction.

There are three categories for Heritage buildings. GRADE I buildings are those of outstanding architectural or historic merit which are to be preserved in perpetuity. This would apply to the entire building, both interior and exterior. A Grade I listing ensures that all repairs or alterations are appropriate.

A GRADE II listing preserves the exterior of a building and may include a significant interior element such as a handsome marble staircase, a particularly significant room, etc. Alterations to the exterior and such interior elements are monitored to ensure compatibility.

A GRADE III listing prevents the demolition of a building where the demolition is deemed by the Community Committee and Committee on Environment to be "unnecessary," based on individual circumstances. Where a demolition is approved, a Grade III listing may regulate the manner in which the building is dismantled, and record or preserve, where possible, building components of interest.

So far so good. The inquiring American architectural historian naturally has two major questions: How much actual preservation has been accomplished under this ordinance? And is there any equivalent to the federal tax credit, which has been such a help to preservation in the United States? The answers to these questions are closely related.

Each year the Winnipeg Historical Buildings Committee brings to Council from its total municipal inventory a carefully selected series of recommendations on buildings to be listed. There are ordinarily about fifteen or twenty nominations, and they are mostly in Grades II and III. Each is carefully studied, and ordinarily no recommendation is made without owner consent. The committee publishes a handsome brochure yearly. This brochure includes pictures of the buildings listed and a well-written commentary. Thus the public consciousness of preservation is raised. If an owner of a warehouse or other structure has a building listed, the owner becomes eligible for a grant from Council which can be used to clean the structure, spruce it up, and improve the signage within design guidelines. As in the United States one is generally free to do what one wishes with the interior, unless, as the ordinance indicates, the building contains some outstanding feature.

There is no system of tax credits. Many Canadian preservationists apparently wish that one existed. Still, a great deal has been done with municipal grants to enhance the appearance of buildings in the warehouse district. The signage portion of the design guidelines has wrought a substantial improvement. Indeed, a number of owners have been shamed into taking advantage of the ordinance to improve the appearance of their buildings. Overall, then, the Canadian tendency has been to do with government grants what the United States has tried to do with the system of tax credits. This brings us to the Core Area Initiative.

In briefest terms the Winnipeg Core Area Initiative is a $96 million effort funded jointly by the Government of Canada, the Province of Manitoba, and the City of Winnipeg. It was undertaken in 1981 to revitalize the central core of the City of Winnipeg through a broad range of programs. These include areas such as employment, job training, housing community services, and the development of key sites in the inner city. It was the Core Area Initiative which supplied the major part of the funding for the transformation of the Gault Block into Artspace. In my mind the Core Area Initiative may be roughly compared with the Lowertown Redevelopment Corporation in St. Paul with the reservation that it does not work so closely with commercial developers. As Andrew Malcolm has brilliantly pointed out, Canadians are accustomed to government intervention in many spheres of life.[16] The redevelopment of inner cities is no exception to this generalization. I believe that further action can be expected from the Core Initiative as opportunities arise.

One surprise on my visit to Winnipeg was that not a single one of the warehouses which had impressed me a decade earlier had been lost to the wrecking ball. The area displayed remarkable stability. I believe that the chief reason for the survival of so much good architecture is that most of it was, in a sense, recycled probably forty or fifty years ago when the warehouses were, in effect, turned into small factories for the garment industry. If one penetrates into an upper level of one of these buildings, he will find that, typically, it is filled with large cutting tables and row-upon-row of sewing machines. At these machines will be working large numbers of women, most of them new Canadians. Some are Philippinos, many are Latin Americans. On their breaks they chatter away in Spanish. Working conditions are not particularly good, but these are not sweatshops. With the installation of automatic sprinkler systems there is little chance of a Triangle Shirtwaist fire. Wages are low, as they are generally in the needle trades everywhere, but these are jobs which offer the possibility of employment to people who might otherwise be on welfare. On balance I hope that the garment industry will stay in these buildings. If it

moves out, another use must be sought, and this is always a problem. One might argue that a function of the Core Area Initiative could be to give design assistance to these small entrepreneurs. In the contemporary world of fashion, market share depends to a considerable extent upon design quality. There is a chance here for improvement and retention of the industry at small expense.

What about the possibility of converting some of these buildings into housing, luxury or otherwise? Here the great question is the Ashdown Block, a wonderful piece of architecture which is at the same time a large reservoir of usable urban space. At first glance the location would appear to be superb. It is only a few minutes walking distance to the financial district, to the theatre which is the home of the Royal Winnipeg Ballet, and to several excellent restaurants. With properly dramatic architectural treatment for the interior of this excellent building, first-class condominiums or apartments could be a resounding success. I am told that the developer on North Portage Avenue has been able to presell most of his proposed condominiums, thereby securing highly desirable upfront money. But there are problems with the Ashdown Block. Now is the moment to announce a new role, which, like Adolf Loos in one of his essays, I give to a waiting world: The possibility of a vital core in a Mid-American Gateway City depends upon *compactness*. The business district must have the best shops, the art museum, the symphony hall, the theatre, and the fashionable clubs. For the institutions of culture to flourish, they must be within easy walking distance of offices and first class condominiums. The reason is very simple. *The same people support both the essential business life of the city and the institutions of culture.*

It seems to be now generally accepted that first-class living quarters are a necessity in a lively downtown. Cities like San Francisco and Chicago have long boasted elegant residential districts on the edge of downtown. One thinks immediately of Pacific Heights and the Gold Coast on the Near North Shore. In these cities it is perfectly possible to walk to a good restaurant from one's dwelling, eat, and go to a concert or a play with minimum difficulty. In bad weather, one takes a cab, and it is a few minutes' ride. For the most part the residents of Pacific Heights and the Gold Coast are affluent people who have an active concern with the affairs of their cities. They often are refugees from the suburbs, no longer interested in the upkeep of lawns

111

and in schoolboard politics. Their children are grown, and window-boxes may become a substitute for gardens. They do, however, continue active in business, or if they are retired, they want to be able to lunch at "The Club," see their old friends, and perhaps enjoy a game of bridge or backgammon in the afternoon. They also continue to participate in the affairs of the museum, the symphony orchestra, or the ballet. In one sense they are autumn and spring people. They want to be able to enjoy the city when it is at its best and when the social calendar is full. In winter they generally manage a southern vacation. In summer they move to a cottage at the lake. For such people a condominium or apartment in an historic and beautifully reconditioned structure has much to offer. When they go away, they can turn the key, make arrangements for their mail, and forget about it. But—and it is a very large but—for the idea to work the residence has to have a reasonable proximity to the business district and the institutions of culture.

Obviously the idea is working in St. Paul. One of the reasons that it is working is the cramped quality of the downtown, which Montgomery Schuyler noted almost a century ago. It is perfectly possible to walk from one's condominium on Mears Park to the Minnesota Club, have dinner there, and attend a performance at the new Ordway Theatre next door. Indeed, judging by the pre-concert dinner reservations at the Club, this seems to be a popular thing to do. And as we have previously noted, the financial district and first class shopping are within easy range of the new condominiums in the old buildings.

Winnipeg is not so fortunate. The Manitoba Club (founded 1885) is directly across from the Canadian National Railroad Station, the present VIA Rail terminus. It is several blocks away from the Exchange District, as is the Art Museum on Memorial Drive. Still, the location of the Ashdown Block is marvelous. It is only five minutes away from the corner of Portage and Main, where the pressure for development is as intense as at any point in Canada. As this is written, negotiations with a developer for this area are in process. The task will not be easy. It will be a large project and absolutely first-rate architectural talent will be required. There is the advantage that the Ashdown Block has a timber frame—much easier to work with than reinforced concrete. If it is successful, there are likely to be additional similar conversions within the Exchange District, and the entire area will take on new life. Across Canada Winnipeg has the reputation for hard winters, hot summers, and good people. One can only wish the city well.

112

6

Oscar Eckerman
Architect to Deere & Co., 1897–1942

In the years around the turn of the century the John Deere Plow Company undertook a major program of building expansion. Founded by John Deere (1804–1888), the man who made the first effective steel plow in the West, the company enjoyed first class leadership from his son, Charles Deere, an almost equally gifted businessman.

Charles Deere (1837–1907) grasped the necessity of a distribution system which could also service the increasingly complicated farm machinery the firm was producing. His case is parallel to that of George Eastman and several other great businessmen of the age who grasped the importance of the distribution function. He saw that it was not enough to make the best plow in the world; the product must also be distributed and serviced. Furthermore, he formed partnerships with other makers of agricultural equipment. In 1877 Deere and Mansur began to make corn planters at Ottumwa, Iowa, and in the next two decades the company took over distribution of the popular Success Manure Spreader made by Kemp and Burpee and of the J. M. Dain line of sweep rakes. By 1900 Deere & Co. was jobbing the products of four other noncompetitive manufacturers, and its distribution system was the envy of the industry.

The first branch selling houses were opened in St. Louis and Kansas City in the 1870s, and by the time of Charles Deere's death in

1907, there were fifteen, all but two of them west of the Appalachians. Obviously this great program of expansion required buildings to house it, and the man who designed most of them was Oscar A. Eckerman, one of the most important but least known architects in the history of American industry.[1]

Born in Moline, Illinois, on April 19, 1873, Eckerman was the son of John Eckerman, a veteran Deere & Co. employee. After attending Augustana College, he went on to the Chicago Art Institute for the only architectural education he ever received. There, in the fall and spring of 1892–1893, he took courses in cast drawing, perspective, and still life in charcoal, pen and ink, and watercolor. In later years he felt that this training started him off in the right direction. There is no record of his activities during the next three years, but on the basis of his executed buildings, one is inclined to suspect that he stayed in Chicago and worked as a draughtsman in one of the large offices, possibly D. H. Burnham & Company. There is a kind of family resemblance between many of Eckerman's buildings and certain industrial structures by the Burnham firm, notably their enormous warehouse for Butler Brothers of 1912.

In any event, something of the directness of expression which has long been a Chicago characteristic must have rubbed off on him. Returning to Moline, he went to work for Deere & Co. on January 1,

1897, and remained with the firm until his retirement in 1942. His newspaper obituary in 1950 remarks that during this time he personally designed practically all the buildings of the company. Those who knew him agree. In the office he was dignified, stern, and a stickler for detail; even today, old timers in the company will occasionally remark that a building has "the Eckerman touch." His associates recall that he was tall, immaculately dressed, had a passion for neckties, and was a man of strong likes and dislikes. His family life seems to have been unremarkable. He was married once, had two children, was a member of the First Lutheran Church, and was active in the Masons and the Moline Elks. He also served on the local housing authority board during the Second World War. In short we have here a man who fitted nicely into the society of small town midwestern America. His distinction was that he was able to give a great company exactly the buildings it wanted.[2]

When Oscar Eckerman went to work for the John Deere Plow Company, Charles Deere's expansion program was just getting into swing. The large warehouses for Deere in St. Louis, designed by Eckerman, are undoubtedly representative of his early work in mill construction (Fig. 1.4). Equally striking is a dated series of construction photographs showing the erection of the Oklahoma City warehouse in the summer of 1906; of these, five are shown here (Figs. 6.1–6.5). The digging of the foundations by teams of mules, the pouring of the concrete by squads of sweating barrowmen, and the relation of the building to the townscape are vivid commentaries on the determination of Charles Deere to make his products available to the farmers of the territory. In structure, the building is simply a smaller version of the St. Louis warehouses. The planks carry the load to the joists, the joists to the girders, and the girders to the columns. The exterior expression of this system is also substantially the same as in St. Louis. The heavy timber frame required a regular grid of pier and spandrel, a perfectly logical revelation of the structural system. The piers received the beam ends, and the wall, for which no exterior framing was needed, was nothing more than a screen. The only decoration was the famous leaping stag at the entrance. That was all there was to the building.

In 1907–1908 the Deere management and their architect made an important decision: For a large new warehouse to be built at Omaha, Nebraska, they would turn to the reinforced concrete flat slab. For a company accustomed to building in mill construction, this was a daring innovation. Reinforced concrete fascinated industrial architects and engineers in the first decade of the twentieth century, but there were, as Reyner Banham has dryly observed, problems:

> To build in a single material with a single technique would entail less complex specification writing, costing, and site supervision and require far fewer skilled trades, and should thus prove simpler and therefore faster, and therefore cheaper. It did finally prove to have all these qualities, but only after the industry had become more familiar with it. The number of spectacular collapses, some of them repeat performances on the same site, reported in trade and professional magazines of the period force one to conclude that the Age of the Pioneers around 1910 must also have been the Age of Faith.[3]

Fig. 6.1. John Deere Plow Co. Warehouse, Oklahoma City, excavation, June 2, 1906.

Fig. 6.2. John Deere Plow Co. Warehouse, Oklahoma City, concrete process, June 1906.

Fig. 6.3. John Deere Plow Co. Warehouse, Oklahoma City, framing at grade level, July 7, 1906.

Fig. 6.4. John Deere Plow Co. Warehouse, Oklahoma City, Sept. 22, 1906.

Fig. 6.5. John Deere Plow Co. Warehouse, Oklahoma City, Dec. 5, 1906.

The great triumph of the early phase of reinforced concrete in column and beam construction is undoubtedly the series of factories designed and built by Ernest L. Ransome for the United Shoe Machinery Company at Beverly, Massachusetts, in 1903–1906, and as Banham rightly remarks, generally and shamefully omitted from conventional histories of architecture. These factories, and much of Ransome's other important work, were on the East Coast, and Deere was at that time essentially a midwestern company. The management may have been unfamiliar with Ransome's work. In any event, for their building technology, Deere & Company and Eckerman turned to Minneapolis, which was much closer to its headquarters at Moline, Illinois.

In that city there was already a lively interest in reinforced concrete for grain storage bins for the milling industry. The local engineer Charles A. P. Turner had invented in 1905 what Carl Condit has called the first sophisticated system of reinforced concrete construction developed in the United States. It featured a grid of radial reinforcing and columns with mushroom capitals somewhat similar to the contemporary designs of Robert Maillart in Switzerland.[4] Although Turner was not entirely clear about how his system worked, he did know that stress was concentrated around the perimeter of the columns; hence he designed the characteristic flared capital, much as in a Doric column. Far more fire-resistant than the traditional mill construction, it could also take much greater floor loads.

In Deere's Omaha warehouse the panels were 18′ 9″ square, reinforcement was by sixteen ⅜″ rounds diagonally, and fourteen ⅜″ rounds directly from column to column. The building had a measured deflection of ⅜″ and a capacity of 550 pounds per square foot. Equally important, greater spans from column to column were possible with this system. The key dimension here is the width of the standard American railway freight car which was (and is) 10′ 6″. One of the photographs shown here (Fig. 6.13) is particularly interesting because it demonstrated the introduction of the freight car directly into the building. This, of course, meant all-weather loading and unloading.

Finally, the Turner system offered great savings in construction time. The St. Louis branch houses required almost two years to build. For the Omaha building, Leonard Construction Company of Chicago,

who were probably Eckerman's favorite builders, broke ground in June 1908, and the structure was ready for an implement dealers' convention on December 1, 1908. We show a series of nine photographs of the building under construction and at completion (Figs. 6.6–6.14). The sample room, more highly finished than the rest of the building, was on the eighth floor. Perhaps it is hardly necessary to add that it had the lowest fire insurance rate in the United States for some years.

Fig. 6.6. *John Deere Plow Co. Warehouse, Omaha, Aug. 31, 1908.*

Fig. 6.7. John Deere Plow Co. Warehouse, Omaha (corner of the building at Harvard and 9th Street), Sept. 1, 1908. Photo: Joslyn Art Museum.

Fig. 6.8. Basement, first floor, and second floor completed; forms being erected for third floor. Photo: Joslyn Art Museum.

Fig. 6.9. Interior photograph, Nov. 2, 1908.

Fig. 6.10. Exterior photograph, Nov. 2, 1908.

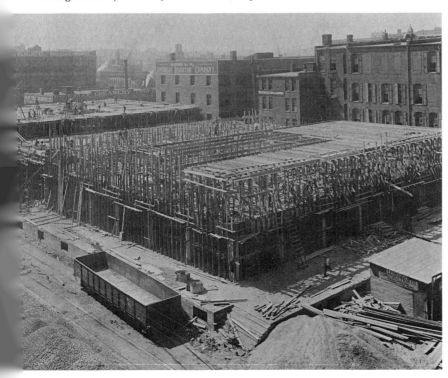

Fig. 6.11. General offices, second story.

Fig. 6.12. Showroom, eighth story.

Fig. 6.13. Completed building, Jan. 1, 1908.

Fig. 6.14. Entrance to Omaha warehouse.

At this point, it is only proper to observe that the Turner system was the center of intense controversy during the next two decades. A recent authoritative discussion remarks, "Because it escaped the imagination of minds trained in the two dimensions of timber and iron, the flat slab was given the treatment of a miracle. While it was endorsed blindly by some engineers, it was resisted savagely by others."[5] Practicing engineers, college professors, and lawyers took part in the debate. The interest of the problem is illustrated dramatically by a comparison made by A. B. MacMillan in 1910 (Fig. 6.15). The bars indicate the amount of reinforcement required by various design procedures in a 20' × 20' interior panel of an 8" thick flat slab intended to carry 200 pounds per square foot. Evidently the material bill for steel could vary by 400 percent depending on the design method chosen. There was obviously room for argument, and indeed so many suits were launched that Turner came to have an almost Dickensian attitude toward lawyers. He made enormous efforts to differentiate his system from the Norcross patent of 1902, which was, "as a mason would understand it," for a slab thick enough to act as an arch, but by 1918 he was under injunction. The best recent discussions tend to uphold his theories stressing the importance of details such as his insistence on very high quality steel in crucial places. While Eckerman was certainly attracted to the Turner system, he was quite willing to use other designs where circumstances warranted it, and he also continued to use mill construction on occasion.

Fig. 6.15. *Weight of steel required in the interior panel of a flats lab by various design methods in 1910.*

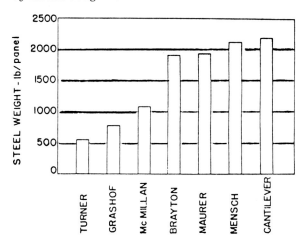

We should also note here the role played by the Leonard Construction Company of Chicago in the development of the flat slab. This extremely successful organization was the creation of Clifford M. Leonard, born in 1879 and educated at MIT, where he took a bachelor's degree in civil engineering in 1900. After a series of jobs as draftsman, estimator, and designer with various engineering and contracting firms in Chicago and St. Louis, he formed the Leonard-Martin Construction Company in 1905. In 1908 its title was changed to the Leonard Construction Company, and he became president, treasurer, and general manager. By 1917 he was acting in the same capacities for a Canadian subsidiary, for the American Steel Window Company, and for the Flat Slab Patents Company. In this same year he had a winter residence on Lakeshore Drive and a summer place in Lake Forest, and was a member of the Chicago, Onwentsia, Indian Hill, and Shore Acres Club—substantial social and economic recognition for a man still under forty.

Leonard seems, in fact, to have been an unusual combination of the gifted engineer and successful businessman. While he perhaps did not grasp the theoretical nuances of the Turner patents, he was quick to see their importance and to form a large organization specializing in flat slab construction. An associate who recalled him well characterized him as "quite a promoter." In addition to the jobs for Deere & Co., he did an immense amount of work for the Quaker Oats Company, most of which also involved concrete construction. It may well be that the Leonard Construction Company was as important for concrete work in the United States as the Starrett Brothers were for skyscrapers framed in steel.[6]

To understand the interaction of structural design, architectural design, and materials handling in the Omaha warehouse, one must begin with the fact that agricultural implements in those days came in bundles. A bundle, according to Nathan Lesser, Eckerman's close friend and collaborator, was a package which could be moved on a handcart by two men. For some reason most of the men who did the moving were Belgian immigrants; when the forklift came in and changed the entire nature of the game, the men in the plants called them "Electric Belgians." The plow, hayrake, corn planter, or whatever, therefore entered the warehouse on a freight car, was moved in bundles by elevator or handcart to its storage quarters, and was dis-

119

tributed in the same series of bundles. With the aid of a set of directions, and perhaps a local representative, the farmer could then assemble the machine. If service was required, the Deere representative would be there, as he still is today.

This, then, was the theory of the distribution system. To make it work within the warehouse several technological innovations were required. Most of these were the contribution of Max Sklovsky (1877–1967), another unnoticed genius in the history of American industrial technology. Given the vast size of these structures it became necessary to devise a means of moving goods through them in addition to the handcarts. Sklovsky solved this problem with an arrangement of overhead conveyers adapted from the stockyards. For vertical circulation it was also desirable to have an auxiliary to the freight elevator, which was always overloaded. Sklovsky therefore invented a helical chute with baffles to slow down the bundles. While Eckerman himself seems to have had very little technological education, it is a matter of record that he was a close friend of Sklovsky. The best explanation for his quick grasp of the new structural system is surely that some of Sklovsky's gadgety-mindedness rubbed off on him.[7]

In addition to these constraints, buildings for the storage and movement of farm machinery had other requirements. Bundles of farm machinery weighed more than equivalent bundles of groceries and dry goods, and the buildings in which they were stored had to be able to take greater floor loads, which, as we have noted, these structures easily accommodated. We have also observed that it was desirable to introduce the freight car directly into the building for ease of all-weather loading, and unloading and this objective, too, was more easily achieved with flat slab concrete. The requirement of fireproof construction was traditional. On the psychological side, the exhibit areas had to be comfortable but show a certain overall plainness. Nathan Lesser writes that there was a saying in the company in those early days. "Don't overspend, for our farmer customers are thrifty souls, and if they see us spend wastefully, they may lose confidence in the farm equipment which we offer for sale."[8] This is certainly a fascinating constraint, and it was the background for the great building that until recently stood in Omaha.

So much for technology, dates, and program. What is particularly striking is the continuation and refinement of the architectural expression of mill construction. Upon analysis it will be seen that both the heavy timber frame and the flat slab systems are basically skeletons. True, they are skeletons with different structural characteristics, load-bearing capacities, and fireproof qualities, but they are still skeletons. In the Oklahoma City warehouse the exterior piers and spandrels correspond to a grid of posts, planks, and girders. The photograph of the Omaha showroom demonstrates conclusively that each pier encased a concrete column and that the spandrel took the edge of the slab.

In essential nature the architectural expression was similar, but in Omaha there was a greater refinement of proportion and detail—the mature Eckerman touch. The sense that the wall was simply a brick screen was much greater, and there was a stronger feeling of resemblance to such masterpieces in steel as Sullivan's Wainwright Building in St. Louis of 1891 and the Prudential Guaranty in Buffalo of 1895. Like these buildings, the Deere Warehouse could be read as base, shaft, and capital. Further, Eckerman resolved the corners into powerfully expressed towers; a strong corner is, after all, in the conservative tradition. A minor dichotomy was at the entryway, where classical pilasters were curiously juxtaposed with light fixtures which look as if they might have been designed by Sullivan or Elmslie (Fig. 6.14). The only ornament was, of course, the famous leaping deer, but the structure itself, like Eero Saarinen's headquarters building for Deere of 1960, was a superb image for the company. It conveyed strength and stability, which was exactly what John Deere himself would have wanted.

Since the buildings were of almost exactly the same date, a comparison of the now demolished Omaha warehouse with the famous turbine factory of 1909 for A.E.G. by Peter Behrens in Berlin is instructive (Fig. 6.16). Behind the Behrens building there was a carefully organized body of theory by which the architect sought to work out a new aesthetic for the industrial age. There was also the highly intellectual patronage of the Rathenau family. By the time of this factory, Behrens (b. 1869) had already gone through a Jugendstil phase, and it is clear that he was in touch with many advanced currents of European thought.

By comparison, Oscar Eckerman was a country boy. His only contact with the great world of architecture was a brief period in Chicago. Within the constraints of program, budget, and structural system, he simply designed a direct, forceful, pragmatic solution to the architectural problem. Many years ago in an important article on "The Chicago Frame," Colin Rowe compared Victor Horta's Maison du Peuple of 1897 in Brussels with Holabird and Roche's McClurg Building in Chicago of 1899-1900. He noted that Holabird and Roche's structure was primarily a building and that Horta's was a polemic.[9] Similarly, on seeing the comparison of Eckerman's Omaha warehouse and the turbine factory, an eminent Dutch art historian remarked to me that the latter appeared, "a little neurotic."

Likewise the Deere warehouse had nothing to do with the imagery of the factory as it developed in the Soviet Union after the Russian Revolution. Adolf Max Vogt has convincingly demonstrated in

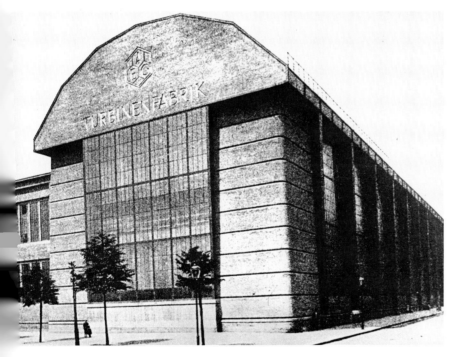

Fig. 6.16. Peter Behrens. Turbine factory for the A. E. G., Berlin, 1909.

his *Russische und Französische Revolutions-Architektur* (Verlag Dumont Schauberg, 1974) that the early Soviet architects thought of the industrial structure as the building type whose form should govern all others. Buildings were deliberately conceived to resemble factories whether they were schools, universities, clubs, or theatres. There was, of course, a great deal of support for this position in Marxist theory, which sanctified the *arbeitsmotiv* as a dominant element in the New World Order which Marx saw emerging in the great conflict between the bourgeoisie and the proletariat. Soviet architects, nonetheless, could not get away from the models of industrial architecture which had already been achieved in capitalistic Western Europe. Vogt shows four projects for the University of Minsk in which one can easily pick out features of Behren's Turbine Factory in Berlin and Gropius' shoe last factory at Alfeld an der Seine of 1911. All are distinguished by large expanses of glass and that 1920s symbol of modernity, the radio antenna. In contrast there was nothing overtly symbolic about Eckerman's Deere Warehouse except the inevitable leaping stag at the corner tower as an emblem of corporate identity. From the Marxist angle the building would probably have been a perfect example of capitalist exploitation. The company, on the other hand, was (and is) very proud of its contribution to American agriculture, especially of the Gilpin plow—"the plow that took the farmer off his feet." Maybe there is, after all, something to the old adage that one of Marx's difficulties was that he was a city boy.

After the triumph at Omaha, the Deere building program went forward with enormous vigor. The distribution system ultimately included facilities in Minneapolis, Kansas City (Missouri), Milwaukee, Dallas, Chicago, Portland, Oklahoma City, San Francisco (an early earthquake resistant structure), St. Louis, New Orleans, Sioux Falls, Baltimore, Bloomington (Illinois), Indianapolis, Atlanta, Spokane, Winnipeg, Regina, Saskatoon, and Calgary. This was in addition to an immense amount of strictly industrial construction such as foundries and factories in the Moline area. The sheer volume of Eckerman's production staggers the imagination. It can only be compared with that of Albert Kahn, who, however, (and it is an immensely significant difference) was never a company architect. In this tremendous output the concrete flat slab was used wherever possible.

A typical example is the Spokane branch house, built by

121

Leonard Construction Company and completed in February 1910 (Fig. 6.17). This building was sited close to a network of railroad tracks and warehouses called the Spokane International Terminal Grounds. The railroad tracks were and still are located exactly adjacent to the north side of the building. The efficient transfer of farm machinery from railroad car to warehouse was obviously an important design determinant. There are, however, other considerations as well. The south elevation has one of the most visually prominent locations in the city, and it had to be designed for maximum impact. Here again Eckerman used a grid of pier and spandrel and relied on a huge sign and the famous logo—a leaping deer—to carry the company's message. On the exterior the columns are entirely surrounded with brick and are therefore expressed as rectangular pilasters. On the interior they are exposed in varying degrees of finish. The ground floor offices and show-rooms have the connections to the wall neatly articulated while at the upper warehouse floors there is rough brick all around. The framing is simply a 16′ × 18′ column grid with flat slab floors and roof. The columns range in diameter from 26″ at the basement floor to 18″ on the fifth floor (Figs. 6.18 and 6.19).

Fig. 6.17. John Deere Plow Co. Warehouse, Spokane, 1910.

Fig. 6.18. Spokane warehouse, interior, June 1910.

Fig. 6.19. Typical wall section. Drawing by Rick Seges.

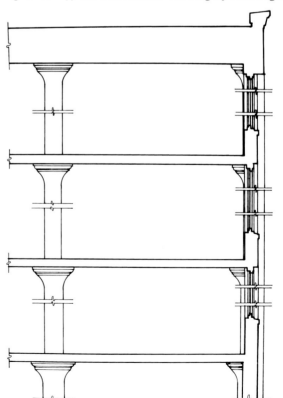

In short, the Spokane building looks exactly like what it is: a large and well-ordered container for heavy industrial goods, a structure which makes a strong but subdued contribution to the city's total environment. It is not oriented to the pedestrian in any way, though it possessed the usual comfortably furnished offices and salesrooms on the first and second floors. Finally it may be noted that the total building cost was just over $100,000 for 100,000 square feet of floor space. This is the kind of statistic that is easily comprehensible. No wonder the company liked Eckerman. The structure remained in use as office and storage space for the Spokane World's Fair until only a few years ago.[10]

The Spokane warehouse, then, may be regarded as typical of the large number of such buildings constructed in the period 1907–1917. Among the most interesting concrete examples were the warehouses at Portland, Oregon (1910) and San Francisco (1911). The Portland building (Figs. 6.20 and 6.21) had a combination of "cantilever flat slab" foundation mat and wooden piles, used because solid foundations could only be obtained at great depth. By floating the building in this way settling was effectively overcome and heavy loads were carried inexpensively.

Fig. 6.20. John Deere Plow Co. Warehouse, Portland, on completion, 1911.

Fig. 6.21. Reinforced concrete skeleton of Portland warehouse, March 2, 1911.

123

Fig. 6.22. *San Francisco warehouse for Deere & Co., 1912.*

Fig. 6.23. *San Francisco warehouse for Deere & Co., 1912.*

The San Francisco earthquake and fire of 1906 had demonstrated the desirability of fireproof structures which could withstand tremors. Here the entire building is concrete without any exterior brick facing whatever (Figs. 6.22 and 6.23).

In his Canadian buildings at Saskatoon, and Calgary (Figs. 6.24 and 6.25) Eckerman preferred mill construction perhaps because of the unavailability of concrete technology in that area or perhaps because no one was entirely sure how the flat slab would behave in extremes of temperature. Construction photographs of 1913 are an interesting commentary on the relationship of the Regina warehouse to its surroundings. It stands isolated in the immensity of the prairie landscape (Figs. 6.26 and 6.27). In general it can be said that the high quality of the brick detailing is the means by which these otherwise undistinguished buildings obtain a degree of architectural interest.

Fig. 6.24. *Saskatoon warehouse for John Deere Ltd., 1910. Modified mill construction.*

Fig. 6.25. Calgary warehouse for John Deere Ltd.

Fig. 6.26. Warehouse for John Deere Ltd., Regina, Saskatchewan, construction photograph, May 1, 1913.

Fig. 6.27. Regina warehouse, construction photograph, May 17, 1913.

In addition to his warehouses Eckerman also did a huge amount of strictly industrial structures, mostly at Moline, where the company greatly expanded its production facilities during the first decade of the century. The agricultural economy was booming, and there was a tremendous demand for Deere's machines. Typical of this side of his work were the manufacturing plant of 1910–1911 (Figs. 6.28 and 6.29) and the "I" building of 1911 (Fig. 6.30). The manufacturing plant was framed in steel, but for the "I" building Eckerman used a cantilever flat slab (Fig 6.31), as he did for the enormous warehouse built in Moline in 1907–1909 (Fig. 6.32). Perhaps the finest of these Moline buildings was the factory for the short-lived Velie Motor Car Company (Figs. 6.33 and 6.34). The interior of the factory is particularly interesting because it shows the system of overhead lines designed by Sklovsky. In my view this factory will easily bear comparison with the contemporary work of Albert Kahn.

125

Fig. 6.28. *Manufacturing plant, Moline, Ill., Jan. 2, 1911.*

Fig. 6.30. *"I" Building, Moline, Ill., Jan. 2, 1911.*

Fig. 6.29. *Manufacturing plant, Moline, Ill., Nov. 7, 1910.*

Fig. 6.31. Cantilever Flat Slab in "I" Building, Dec. 5, 1910.

Fig. 6.32. Deere's implement warehouse, Moline, Ill., 1907 and 1909.

Fig. 6.33. Velie Motor Vehicle Factory, Moline, Ill., 1909.

Fig. 6.34. Velie Motor Vehicle Factory, interior, 1909.

It would be fascinating to know if Eckerman was conscious of his own achievement and the limitations imposed on him by his position with the company. According to his close associates he was a man of fine intelligence, thoroughly conscious of what was going on in the architectural world around him. Undoubtedly he knew the work of the Chicago architects, and he may well have admired such great buildings as Richard Schmidt's superb Chicago warehouse for Montgomery Ward of 1906–1908. In all probability he knew the outstanding buildings of Kahn for the auto industry. In his own work, however, he had to grapple with tight budgets and superiors who knew that he had discovered an inexpensive, sound, and speedy method of putting up the buildings that the company required. The program and specifications varied only a little from job to job, and it was really inevitable that architectural design would be reduced to a formula. The great breakthrough came at Omaha and after its success the formula was simply repeated with variations. This meant a consistency of quality—the Eckerman touch—but a lack of high points.

In a sense Eckerman's situation was in the Deere tradition of anonymity. Far more than with most American corporations of its size, the men responsible for its success are unknown to the public. Sklovsky, for example, never received anything like the recognition given to Steinmetz at General Electric, Kettering at General Motors, or Lee Deforest at R.C.A., and yet he kept Deere & Co. at the forefront of technological change in the agricultural implement industry for over thirty years. So, too, with Eckerman. His contribution is all but unknown, and yet it was vital to the distribution system which made the company great.

Jens Jensen Reconsidered

In 1964 I published a book entitled *Landscape Artist in America: The Life and Work of Jens Jensen*. I welcome this opportunity to return to the work, to appraise it, and to evaluate the impact it had on studies in the history of landscape architecture. It is an exciting challenge to grapple with the interpretation which I first set before the public over twenty years ago.

One of the first questions asked of any writer is, in the elegant words of J. K. Galbraith, "how this good thing came to be done." With regard to the Jensen book, the question is easily answered. In the late 1950s I was engaged in studies of the architecture of the Prairie School. This group comprised the lesser men around Frank Lloyd Wright during the early years of the century: Purcell and Elmslie, Walter Burley Griffin, Hugh Garden, and a variety of others. Together they made a substantial contribution to the great flowering of midwestern culture during the years prior to the First World War.

As I delved into the contemporary literature on the Prairie School, I kept running into references to a Danish immigrant designer named Jensen, who, it was generally believed, had done for landscape architecture what Frank Lloyd Wright had done for building design. A small amount of research established the outlines of his career and that he was indeed a person well worth investigating. I noticed he had

died only in 1951, and I reasoned there must be many people alive who had known him. There were, in fact, a large number, and I was soon launched on a program of fieldwork which took me to most Jensen sites in the Midwest and upper South. The project included interviews with many persons who had known him in various capacities.

Of course there was also a lot of archival research. In the course of the work I acquired the bulk of Jensen's surviving office drawings from his son-in-law, Marshall Johnson, who was keeping them in a woodshed. I also acquired a fair number of Jensen manuscripts. At the archives of the Ford family, which were then housed in the Rotunda at Dearborn I found Jensen's extensive correspondence with Edsel Ford. I was lucky to have looked at it when I did. It was extremely revealing, and it was later destroyed by fire. In short, it was a wonderful period of research, and it culminated in the publication of the book.

In the course of this work I met many forceful and highly intelligent people. There was, for example, Mrs. Abby Longyear Roberts, a matriarch of Michigan's Iron Range. Mrs. Roberts liked her Irish whiskey neat and rode an exercycle. She had come to Jensen through Frank Lloyd Wright, who had designed her house. The conflict between Wright and Jensen at the Roberts place was one of the elements in their final break. There was Mrs. T. J. Knudson of Springfield,

Illinois, who was the moving spirit behind the Lincoln Gardens. Not only was Mrs. Knudson an expert gardener and high in the councils of the Garden Clubs of America, she was also a Republican national committeewoman. Her house was full of elephants. There was Alfred Caldwell, for several years one of Mr. Jensen's best foremen, later a disciple of Frank Lloyd Wright, and when I knew him, just finishing up a distinguished teaching career at the Illinois Institute of Technology. Caldwell, too, was a colorful personality. He had strong ideas on the composition of the Ideal Havana Cigar. Finally there was Mertha Fulkerson, Jensen's longtime secretary, who had come to him during the 1920s, moved to northern Wisconsin with him in 1935, and was running "The Clearing" when I knew it in 1959–1961. I go into this detail partly because these people were dear to me and partly because they all thought Jensen was a genius and a hero. Undoubtedly I absorbed some of their attitudes. Several of my reviewers commented on the hero worship in the book.

Hence I am led to put forward a theory: The first biography of an artist who has been forgotten will inevitably be somewhat hero-worshipping. It will also be imperfect in other ways. When Hugh Morrison published his *Louis Sullivan: Prophet of Modern Architecture* in 1935, Sullivan had been dead eleven years. His reputation among architects and historians was about as shadowy as Jensen's was in 1964. Morrison's work did much to restore him to his proper place in American cultural history. It is still useful. Nonetheless, if a student asks for a reading list on Louis Sullivan, the teacher must supplement it with recommendations of Willard Connely's *Louis Sullivan as he Lived* (1960), John Szarkowski's *The Idea of Louis Sullivan* (1956), and the new biography of Robert Twombly, *Louis Sullivan: His Life and Work* (1986). Much the same thing is true of Arthur Mizener's *The Far Side of Paradise* (1949), the first biography of F. Scott Fitzgerald. It is still a valuable book, but a great deal of important material has been published on Fitzgerald since then. I do not know what the answer to this situation is. I would simply make a plea for understanding of the difficulties of the first biographer. He must necessarily draw the outlines of a picture and hope that others will fill in the details.

By the fall of 1962 I was ready to write, and the question of what form the book ought to take came to the fore. After much cogi-

tation I decided on a chapter dealing with Jensen's years in Denmark and early experience in the United States, a chapter on his public work, a chapter on the private estates, and a concluding essay on the years at "The Clearing." The book was to be copiously illustrated with black and white photographs accompanied by quotations from Jensen himself and from other appropriate writers. On balance I am still happy with this organization. A somewhat amusing note is that when it came out, my now departed and much beloved sister remarked that it was a shame I had not included some color pictures. I had to explain to her that color reproductions were so expensive they could only be used in advertisements by the whiskey companies and seed catalogue people. The irony is that the cost of color reproductions has now dropped sufficiently so that if I were to do the book over again, I could probably include some color plates. I would also include more plans as several reviewers suggested I should have done. In retrospect, one of my best decisions was to leave most of the black and white photography to Bob Fine, who was one of Harry Callahan's best students.

On the whole, the reviews were good. The book was favorably mentioned in several professional journals: *Progressive Architecture* and *Landscape* in the United States, and *Architectural Design* and *The Architectural Review* in Great Britain. Particularly gratifying was an extended review in *Berlingske Tidende*, which in effect declared I had given Jensen back to his native country. Perhaps the most revealing treatment was a brief notice which appeared in *Harvard* magazine in July 1979. My Jensen book was mentioned in conjunction with no less than eighteen other works on the history of landscape architecture which have been published during the last fifteen years. The list indicated that historians of all persuasions have, for some time now, been paying serious attention to garden art. Three titles were devoted to Frederick Law Olmsted, Sr., alone, a measure of the attention now being devoted to this giant figure in American cultural history. Most recently Cynthia Zaitsevsky has published her large and impressive *Frederick Law Olmsted and the Boston Park System* (1982). Since people invariably ask me about the comparison between the two men, I want to say a word about that problem.

Olmsted was born in 1826, thirty-four years before Jensen. So far as I could determine, the two never had any personal contact, though Jensen must have known Olmsted's work in the Chicago area after 1884 when he first came to the city. Alfred Caldwell told me one day that the older Olmsted was about the only American landscape architect for whom Jensen had any respect. A meeting, however, is unlikely. At the time Olmsted was in Chicago meeting the city's business leaders in preparation for the 1893 Columbia Exposition, Jensen had just been promoted to head gardener in Humboldt Park. It is improbable that their paths would have crossed. In certain respects their careers are remarkably similar. In other ways they are radically different. Unquestionably both belonged to the great informal tradition of landscape design represented by Brown, Repton, and Puckler-Muskau. Both were enormously interested in the creation of public parks. Their approach was very similar, though Jensen laid even more stress on the use of natural plant materials. Both were "public men," though Olmsted had a much greater knack for being in the right place at the right time. When one studies his career, one notes that he wrote important books about slavery in the pre–Civil War South at a time when the nation was avid for information on the subject, that he was chairman of the Union Sanitary Commission (ancestor of the Red Cross) during the Civil War, and that he made his name on Central Park in New York, a project which would inevitably attract national attention. All these activities placed him close to the center of what I must call the American cultural establishment. It seems inevitable that he should have worked closely with H. H. Richardson, the greatest architect of his period.

Jensen, too, had a knack for legitimate publicity, but he was nowhere as effective. Perhaps his greatest weapon was the resignation. Undoubtedly he was one of the great quitters in American cultural history. It was front page news when he quit his job with the West Parks. Apparently the profession of landscape architecture watched the progress of his work for Henry Ford with a kind of horrified fascination. He walked off what was generally acknowledged to be the biggest private job in the country at least three times. A fiery temper was a part of his personality. At this point I may say that one of the difficulties in teaching Jensen is that his portrait makes him look like everybody's kindly Danish grandfather. He was a man of strong convictions and powerful passions. If he had been more diplomatic, like Olmsted, he might have achieved more. Their personalities, as nearly

as I can determine, were entirely different, as were their literary styles. Olmsted's collected papers are being published by the Johns Hopkins University Press, and as I dip into them, I am struck by the high quality of the written expression. I have already commented elsewhere on Jensen's difficulties in writing English, which was, after all, his third language. *The Clearing*, a book of his collected meditations, ought to be republished in an annotated edition aimed especially at students of landscape architecture.

Since 1964 a small Jensen literature has emerged—nothing comparable to the overwhelming publication on Olmsted. A major contribution is the doctoral thesis from the University of Wisconsin's Department of Landscape Architecture by Steven Cristy, "The Growth of an Artist: Jens Jensen and Landscape Architecture." Cristy had the benefit of certain sources which were denied to me or of which I was unaware. The most notable of these is unquestionably a collection of four thousand photographs discovered in 1972 at The Clearing by Darrel Morrison, Dean of the School of Environmental Design at the University of Georgia. These pictures were taken almost entirely by Jensen, and they document his entire professional career from about 1903 to 1925. They are at the Morton Arboretum in Chicago, as are his working drawings for The Clearing. At the Wisconsin Historical Society is an excellent collection of twenty years' correspondence between Jensen and William Evjue, founder and editor of the *Capital Times* of Madison. Also included are a number of articles by and about Jensen. Mertha Fulkerson's diary is at The Clearing. I expect that additional Jensen material will turn up for at least the next decade or two. The University of Michigan has just acquired a large number of photographic negatives from the Loeb family in Chicago. How much else there is, nobody knows.

In my mind Cristy's major contribution to Jensen studies is his excellent analysis of three key places executed during Jensen's long and productive career. The first of these is Indianola, the Glencoe estate of the Hermann Paepckes (1901–1902). The second is Columbus Park of 1916. The third is The Clearing, in a series of designs from 1935 to 1940. In my mind Cristy's treatment of Indianola is particularly important because it establishes the Paepcke place as, in all probability, the first moment when Jensen's mature style was manifest. (He had been fired from his job in the West Parks in 1900, was desperately looking for work, and gave the Paepcke job his undivided attention.) Cristy writes:

> There is a nod to the past as seen in the tremendous outpouring of planting design and also a look to the future in the sensitive handling of spaces on the grounds. On the one hand there is Jensen the parks laborer, very knowledgeable about his materials but as yet having little control over them. On the other hand there is Jensen the artist, making the first of many brilliant moves he would make in his treatment of the meadow and bluff.

Cristy was fortunate in obtaining a set of early photographs of the Paepcke place and in interviewing Mrs. Paepcke's surviving daughter, Mrs. Louis Guenzel. My own guess would have been that Jensen's mature style was first visible in the Harry Rubens estate, also in Glencoe, of 1903, but Cristy's contentions must be accepted.

With Columbus Park Cristy amplifies the analysis I made in 1964, but I do not think he says anything essentially new. For The Clearing, on the other hand, he does an admirable job of tracing the development of the idea from its early stages at Jensen's studio in Ravinia to its realization at Ellison Bay. It may have been, as Cristy says, the most complex work of art Jensen ever created. He produced a large number of projects for it, especially after the fire of 1937. Though it was certainly the most complete embodiment of his philosophy, it was not finished during his lifetime, and indeed one wonders if he ever intended it to be finished in the ordinary sense of the word. Cristy does a great job here. The Clearing, like Jefferson's campus at Charlottesville and Olmsted's Fenway, is one of the great American landscapes, and it ought to be so recognized.

A work not entirely devoted to Jensen but in which he plays a major role is J. Ronald Engel, *Sacred Sands: The Struggle for Community in the Indiana Dunes* (1983). This excellent volume chronicles the long struggle which culminated in the establishment of the Indiana Dunes National Lakeshore in 1966—the first element added to the National Park System over the opposition of the congressional district in which it was located. The author sees the struggle as an important manifestation of the American civil religion of democracy which was especially strong in midwestern progressivism at the turn of the century. If there was indeed a civil religion of democracy (and I would

tend to agree with the concept), then Jensen was one of its high priests. Maybe "chief druid" would be a better term. Time and again he mobilized his "Friends of Our Native Landscape" for pilgrimages to the dune country. He was known as an eloquent speaker, and he must have spoken a hundred times in behalf of the Save-the-Dunes Movement. Indeed, it is hard to see how they could have been saved without him. I am happy to have this recognition of Jensen's importance in the conservation movement, an achievement which I could only suggest in my book. I am particularly grateful for the section on Professor Henry Cowles of the University of Chicago, from whom Jensen certainly learned a great deal about plant ecology.

There is a small periodical literature on Jensen. One of the most significant items is Malcolm Collier's "Jens Jensen and Columbus Park," *Chicago History* (1970). Collier reviews Jensen's involvement with the West Parks. She is particularly good on the curious chain of events which enabled Jensen to put together Columbus Park in 1916. It was one of his finest achievements. J. R. Christianson in "Scandinavia and the Prairie School: Chicago Landscape Artist Jens Jensen," *Journal of the Danish American Heritage Society* (1982), stresses the Scandinavian features of his career. Christianson includes material on the folk high schools at Vinding and Tune, where Jensen studied, and points out that many of the same plants he used in his prairie landscapes were actually part of the environment of his youth at Dybbol in Denmark. I neglected this important detail. In Ossian Simonds' "Prairie Spirit in Landscape Gardening," *Prairie School Review* (1975), Mara Gelbloom argues that most of Jensen's ideas for his prairie landscapes came from Simonds and that Jensen's genius for publicity has obscured Simonds unduly. Her contention does not seem to have had wide acceptance.

We are certainly now ready for a new generation of Jensen studies. The work of Robert Grese on the Lincoln Gardens at Springfield, Illinois (1936), is a wonderful beginning. When I was doing my research on this project in the early 1960s, I easily drew two conclusions. One was that the Lincoln Gardens were probably Jensen's masterpiece and that they were worthy of a much more extended analysis than I could give them. The other was that the preservation of the gardens was going to be a substantial problem and that it needed to be studied in depth. I knew Jensen had taken unusual pains with the design. With its extraordinary network of paths and council rings, it was extremely complicated and unlike anything else he ever produced. I also knew that the late works of a great artist are often complicated and little understood in his own generation. Beethoven's contemporaries thought he had gone off the deep end with his late quartets. They are still a challenge for music lovers. Jensen was seventy-six when he did the Lincoln Gardens. I put forward the notion that they were a reworking of the old European idea of the maze, as in Hampton Court. Grese has effectively demonstrated that I was mistaken, and I am delighted to have him put matters right.

The problem of preservation in the naturalistic landscapes of Jensen was also perplexing. In the course of my journeys throughout the Midwest I had seen many places by Jensen which had deteriorated to the point where only traces of his style were visible. At the Lincoln Gardens, in contrast, it was "all Jensen." Much of this happy condition was obviously due to Mrs. Knudson, a woman of remarkable quality who understood his intentions completely. Yet Mrs. Knudson, though vigorous, was well along in years. She would obviously not live to see the maturity of the grove of white oaks Jensen had planted around her beloved Lincoln Council Ring. (I recall that one of my colleagues in the Department of Landscape Architecture was astonished when I remarked that Jensen had specified white oaks in the Lincoln Gardens. Nobody, he declared, had ever done such a thing). What was the answer?

It lies, I believe, in the acceptance of the unique time frame in which Jensen worked and in the development of management principles such as Grese has propounded. The preservation of a naturalistic landscape is, after all, an entirely different problem from that encountered in the gardens of, say, Dumbarton Oaks as planted by Beatrix Farrand. With a garden like Dumbarton Oaks one worries about trimming, edging, mowing, and even topiary work. When Mrs. Farrand and the Blisses finished their work, the design was "set" for all time (or as long as the endowment holds out). With the Lincoln Gardens, the design is much more a framework for change, and that change must be controlled in accordance with Jensen's intentions. This is the essence of Grese's section on "Management Principles," and I concur with it entirely. It is a pleasure to welcome him to the ranks of Jensen scholars.

Finally it remains to be noted that, as with Wright, there is plenty of work for both the scholar and the preservationist. We need more analyses of the kind that Grese has accomplished, and we need to have a number of his landscapes placed on the National Register of Historic Places. We owe Mr. Jensen this effort. His time has come.

The essay reprinted here is my first attempt to bring Jensen to the attention of the public. With minor alterations it is reprinted as it appeared in *Progressive Architecture*, Dec., 1960. There are no footnotes. Exact references and a bibliographical essay can be found in my book on Jensen which is mentioned in the first paragraph.

Today, when landscape design is taking on a new lease on life, is a good time to observe the centennial of Jens Jensen, perhaps America's greatest landscape architect. In addition to being a superb artist in his own right, Jensen was active in Chicago at a time when the architects of that city were in an extremely creative phase, and his career shows a remarkable interaction between the arts of architecture and landscape design. It is no exaggeration to say that Jensen stood for most of the same qualities in landscape architecture that Sullivan and Wright represented in the building art; the relationship between these men is therefore of peculiar interest. Although Jensen deserves to be ranked among the outstanding American artists of his generation, his name is surprisingly little known. A brief biography is in order.

Born into a prosperous farming community in the Danish province of Jutland on September 13, 1860, Jens Jensen was educated at the local agricultural college to take over a property which had been in his family for more than four hundred years. Dissatisfaction with the political conditions in his native province (it was frontier territory and Jensen had to serve in the German army) and personal reasons caused him to emigrate to the United States in 1884. After brief periods working in Florida and Iowa, he began in 1886 as a common laborer for the West Chicago Park System, rising in the course of the next fourteen years to superintendent of Humboldt Park. In 1900 he left the Park System to set up his own practice as a landscape designer, only to return in 1906 as landscape architect and general superintendent. Jensen served in these capacities until 1909, continuing in a consulting relationship until 1920, when political differences with Gov. Len Small forced his resignation. From 1909 until the early thirties he enjoyed a large private practice, doing estates for Julius Rosenwald, Ogden Ar-

133

mour, Henry and Edsel Ford, and many others among the country's financial and industrial leaders. In 1935 Jensen retired to Ellison Bay, Wisconsin, to found a school, The Clearing, which is still maintained on his principles by the Wisconsin Farm Bureau Federation. He died October 1, 1951.

When a young man in Europe, Jens Jensen had experienced both the formality of the French garden and the freedom of the English landscape park, but there is no evidence that he thought seriously of landscape architecture as a career until a few years after his arrival in Chicago. The prairie landscape around that city made a profound impression on him. In old age he recalled that on his first train ride into the city, the crabapple and the hawthorn, natives of the area, affected him strongly by their beauty; in time their branches came to symbolize the horizontal line of the prairie itself. He was also struck by the richness of the color at every season of the year, but especially in the autumn. Every weekend he botanized in the country, coming to know well all the plants indigenous to the region.

In 1888 he planted, in a corner of Washington Park, what he called his "American Garden." It consisted mostly of perennial wildflowers, stock he had gathered himself with a team and wagon. Nurserymen were unable to supply the plants since there had never before been any demand. To Jensen's delight the transplantings flourished, and the garden was exceedingly popular with the public, which recognized the wildflowers as old friends. Over the next few years Jensen gradually developed the theory of the prairie garden, a form specifically adapted to the Midwest. Probably the most important aspects of his doctrine were his insistence on the use of native plant materials and his rejection of imported varieties. There was nothing new about these ideas; they were part of the teaching of the elder Olmsted, whose work Jensen undoubtedly encountered at the World's Fair of 1893. What *was* new was the consistency and skill with which Jensen applied them. They were concepts much needed at that time in Chicago. The city was full of newly affluent people who yearned to demonstrate their wealth in ostentatious gardens containing rare and exotic plants. To these individuals Jensen turned a deaf ear. He would, he declared bluntly to Wilhelm Miller, a writer for *Country Life in America*, "do nothing for show," and his practice bore out the truth of his claim.

Jensen was a great regional artist. So devoted was he to mid-America that he was actually reluctant to undertake a seaside estate for Edsel Ford on the coast of Maine for fear that he would be out of sympathy with the site. As it ultimately developed, the job was a great success, but Jensen was always happiest when working in his beloved Midwest.

Unlike Wright, with whom he is usually compared, Jensen never felt the necessity of world travel. Except for a single trip back to Denmark in 1929, he never returned to Europe, and it does not seem to have occurred to him to visit the Orient. Insofar as can be determined, all of his executed works are within the boundaries of the continental United States, and most of them are concentrated in Illinois and Michigan. Clearly he was not troubled by the rootlessness which characterizes so many twentieth-century artists. On the contrary, his writings are filled with songs of praise to mid-America, and he was obviously quite content to work there. Like Wright he displayed, particularly at the end of his life, a pronounced dislike of city life and a bias in favor of rural living. This feeling is quite understandable when it is recalled that Jensen witnessed the progressive deterioration of an urban environment which he himself had struggled desperately hard to humanize. The wonder is that he stayed in Chicago so long and did not move to northern Wisconsin until 1935.

Even more than with the architecture of Louis Sullivan and Frank Lloyd Wright, Jensen's design concepts grew directly out of the soil and owed nothing whatever to any Eastern or European precedent. Aside from the landscape itself, the chief influence acting upon Jensen during his formative years was music. In speaking of one of the earliest prairie gardens, the Rubens estate at Glencoe, Illinois, he remarked that many things had gone into it. Particularly important were Schubert's "Unfinished Symphony" and a deepening knowledge of the native flora of Illinois. The "water feature" on the estate was essentially an attempt to recreate an Illinois water system in miniature—spring, brook, cascade, river, and lake. Japanese iris and geraniums were used as stopgaps until wild iris and prairie phlox could be established. Jens Jensen was a thoroughly original artist who drew his basic inspiration from the region which he had made his own.

Small works such as the Rubens garden were the prelude for

Jensen's first major undertaking, a tremendous remodeling job for the West Park System of Chicago. In 1906 conditions were especially favorable for this effort: The city was undergoing a civic renaissance remarkable in the history of American urbanism. At the new University of Chicago, on the Midway, the distinguished faculty assembled by Pres. William Rainey Harper was rapidly putting Chicago on the intellectual map; among its luminaries at this period were A. A. Michelson, John Dewey, and Thorstein Veblen. In the field of literature, Harriet Monroe was publishing the first verses of Carl Sandburg, Edgar Lee Masters, and Vachel Lindsay in *Poetry* magazine. Theodore Dreiser was working on his Chicago novels, built around the career of the traction magnate, Charles Yerkes. In architecture, while Louis Sullivan had already done his last great building for Chicago, a number of excellent firms were working in his tradition, and the famous Burnham plan was being formulated under the aegis of the Commercial Club. Out in Oak Park, Frank Lloyd Wright was in the midst of his magnificent series of prairie houses, which changed the entire concept of American residential building. In politics the forces of righteousness appeared to have at least a fair chance of cleaning up the city; Lincoln Steffens, the well-known muckraker, reported that Chicago was at least half-free of graft and corruption—much further along the road to good government than most other American municipalities. It is not surprising, then, to find Jensen coming back into public service as general superintendent and landscape architect for the West Chicago Park System.

Jens Jensen was closely connected with many aspects of this revival of Chicago's civic consciousness. As a member of the Cliffdweller's Club he was well acquainted with the city's cultural elite. Carl Sandburg and Vachel Lindsay were good friends, and he knew the poetry of both men well. The sculptor, Lorado Taft, was likewise an intimate, and Jensen more than once showed his interest in the possibilities of sculpture in the landscape garden by staging exhibitions in the city parks.

More important still were Jensen's connections with the business leaders of Chicago, who at this time were striving mightily to improve the physical fabric of their city. Jensen shared with these men an enormous willingness to serve on boards and commissions of all kinds and to agitate unceasingly for every variety of worthwhile civic

project. Thus he took the lead in the struggle to set aside the lands now known as Cook County Forest Preserve, still the largest wilderness area contiguous to any major American city. Convinced that America's finest recreational lands were being misused, he devoted an unconscionable amount of time and energy to the cause of conservation. In all these activities he came into close contact with men like Ogden Armour and Charley Wacker, for both of whom he later did private estates. A sociologist would say that he had ready access to the power structure of Chicago. It could be added that Jensen was a public figure in the best sense of the term: a person who devoted a substantial portion of time to work in the city's behalf.

Part of Jensen's appeal lay in his personality, unquestionably one of the most persuasive in Chicago. Well over six feet in height with a ruddy complexion and flashing blue eyes, he automatically brought to mind the image of his Viking ancestors. In later years he was distinguished by a superb head of white hair and bristling white mustachios. Like many men of his day, he knew how to dramatize himself through his dress and enjoyed doing so; he was always immaculately clothed in rough tweeds, which contrasted beautifully with the richly colored silken ascot scarves made for him by Mrs. Jensen. The scarves were drawn through a silver ring, cast in the form of a Danish sea wolf.

All witnesses agree that he was really eloquent when speaking for a cause in which he believed, and while he dearly loved to hold the center of the stage, he could on occasion be an excellent listener. In general his conversation was much more pungent than his writings. To a wealthy client who wanted to build a French chateau on his estate in Lake Forest he growled, "You are an American. Why do you want to be a stuffed shirt?" Concerning a fountain which adorned a public park in Marquette, Michigan, he remarked to a group of local businessmen that it was "like a diamond stickpin in the necktie of a dirty bartender." For newspapermen, what Jens Jensen had to say was ordinarily excellent copy. After 1920 the deterioration of municipal politics in Chicago caused him to retire from work on the city's behalf and to concentrate on the establishment of state park systems. In this field his influence, not only in Illinois, but in other midwestern states as well, was far-reaching.

What, then, was Jens Jensen's reaction to the Chicago architecture of his day? We may begin by stating that he was a devoted admirer of Louis Sullivan and all he stood for. Jensen responded immediately to Sullivan's theories that America must have a new architecture, radically different from the outmoded forms of Europe and the East Coast. As Sullivan hated the Beaux Arts eclecticism of McKim, Mead and White, so Jensen scorned the formal French and Italianate gardens of the East. His relationships with the American Society of Landscape Architects were surprisingly like those of Sullivan and Wright with A.I.A. Except for the Olmsteds, he had no regard whatsoever for his eastern colleagues, and again like Sullivan and Wright, he lost no opportunity to make his feelings abundantly clear. He was bound to Sullivan philosophically by their mutual, highly emotional response to nature. Although friendship with Sullivan was difficult, Jensen always felt close to the great defeated leader of the Chicago School. Jensen mourned Sullivan's descent into alcoholism, contributed to his support at the end of his life, and wept when he died.

With Wright, Jensen's relationship was more complex. Here again there was an obvious personal and professional kinship, since both men got their start in Chicago at approximately the same time and stood for approximately the same things in their respective arts. For many years the two were close friends. Jensen's secretary of 1918–1920 recalls that Wright was a frequent visitor at the Jensen office and that there was much correspondence between them. Wright offered Jensen the hospitality of Taliesin and in later years even invited him to lecture to the Taliesin Fellowship. Few artists were so honored. Perhaps even more important was Jensen's vigorous defense of Wright during the 1920s, a difficult period for the great architect in most respects. Although he did not always approve of what Wright was doing, Jensen sensed in him a great creative imagination and therefore spoke up in his behalf at a time when it was not popular to do so.

In some respects the Wrightian imagination was very much at odds with the ideals for which Jensen himself was striving. Wright's enthusiasm for Japanese culture is well known. Jensen, in contrast, had an abiding distrust for the Japanese character and intensely disliked Japanese landscape gardening. On one occasion he observed, "The Japanese mind distorts and destroys the spirit of plants for its own pleasure. This is clearly an expression of selfishness. . . . The changing of a flower, a tree, or any other life into a different shape than that of its own choosing deprives it of its birthright as a living thing. Such methods have nothing in common with the art of gardening." In a letter to a German editor in 1937, he wrote, rather picturesquely, "Frank Lloyd Wright is a dear friend of mine and a great architect, but Oriental, and here we part. When the last Anglo-Saxon has gone to his forefathers, the soul of Frank Lloyd Wright will halloo over his grave."

In addition to his doubts about Wright's Japanophilia, Jensen had reservations about his friend's arrogance. A man of genuine humility himself, he could not stomach Wright's insistence on total virtue in his own work and complete incompetence in that of his fellow architects. It is not surprising that their one collaboration was a stormy affair, or that they finally broke off their relationship in 1946.

Jensen's attitude toward architecture in general was conditioned by his discovery that architects usually wanted to do their own landscaping. This, he said, was a vast mistake, since the two arts in reality are entirely different in character. In *Art Has Its Roots in the Soil* he wrote:

> What comparison is there between the creating of a building, which fits into a narrow and limited space, and the creating of large pastoral meadows where the horizon is the boundary, ever changing in light and shadow with the clouds above, with the light of early morn, at even when the rays of the setting sun cast their reflection upon the earth, in the silvery moonlight, and in the changing colors of spring and summer and fall and winter? Such are the keys to landscaping.

If there is a typical Jensen landscape, it is probably the great meadow in Columbus Park, Chicago (Fig. 7.1). It is beautifully adapted to catch and reflect the rays of the sun at every time of the day, and in addition, it conveys a limitless sense of space in the very heart of a great industrial city.

At the same time that Jensen was fighting for the professional integrity of the landscape architect, he was also pushing the West Park commissioners of Chicago toward an awareness of contemporary architectural design. It is largely due to him that some of the park structures in the city have real architectural interest. Typical of these is the light, airy pavilion structure in Humboldt Park by Hugh Garden (1907); resembling no historic building, it is distinguished by its strong lines and graceful proportions, and exhibits a remarkable integration with the landscape beyond. Cleverly conceived to allow for boat storage underground, this building was published in Hugo Koch's *Gartenkunst im Stadtebau* (1914), a volume which did for Jensen what the Wasmuth publications of 1910 did for Wright. In fact, it is fair to say that Jensen had a larger European reputation than any American artist of his generation except Wright. His work was frequently seen in the pages of *Gartenkunst* and *Gartenschonheit*, and he was also well known in the Scandinavian countries.

Even more characteristic of the kind of structure Jensen wanted for his parks was the boat-landing pavilion designed by John Van Bergen, a Wright disciple, for Columbus Park in 1920. With its long, low, horizontal lines and powerful treatment of the structural elements, the building is a perfect example of the Prairie Style. Unhappily, funds ran out and it was never built.

Fig. 7.1. Columbus Park, Great Meadow. Photo: Chicago Park District.

So strong was the Prairie influence during Jensen's years with the West Parks that it even extended to the lighting fixtures. More than one visitor has noted that these look "Wrightian." In point of fact they are the work of Hugh Garden, a prominent member of the Chicago School and a close personal friend of Jensen. Several of these fixtures adorned the entrance to the famous rose garden at Humboldt Park. This garden, today no longer planted with roses, was an excellent example of Jensen's painstaking attention to detail. For several years he planted it with zinnias to prepare the soil before the roses were ever set out. It was also notable as one of Jensen's few formal works, so conventionalized that it contained no prairie flowers. He did, nonetheless, put hawthorns at the entrance to symbolize the meeting of woods and prairie, and he lowered the garden by two feet in order to place the flowers well below the level of the eye, as they are on the prairie in spring. In the later years of his long and phenomenally productive career Jensen condemned this garden as a bit of youthful folly, but it remains dear to the hearts of many Chicagoans. Hugh Garden, the designer of the fixtures, later helped Jensen with the architecture of his school buildings in northern Wisconsin. He recalls that Jensen was exceptionally easy to work with and adds thoughtfully, "I never in my life appreciated a man more than Jens Jensen."

No study of Jensen's contributions to the Chicago Park System would be complete without some mention of his plan for a Greater West Park System. In 1917 the West Park Commission, alarmed by the burgeoning growth of the city, asked Jensen to undertake a survey with a view to extending the system. He spent the entire winter of 1917–1918 on the job and in the spring of 1918 presented the plan to the Commission. Essentially he proposed a belt of parks following the north and south branches of Chicago River and Des Plaines River to the west and, as connecting elements, a number of wide vehicular parkways, most of them following existing streets. These parkways were to be approximately 150′ wide with a small park running between the two ribbons of traffic. Small service drives were to be provided for the houses which bordered the Parkways.

The qualities of Jensen's plan may be most clearly seen by comparing it with Daniel Burnham's park proposal of 1909. Burnham contemplated only three large parks: one to the south, one to the north, and one due west of his proposed civic center. These three parks were

137

to be connected by a number of diagonal and radial streets which were to serve not only as articulating links for the system but also as "lifelines of the City." The whole scheme is much more arbitrary and geometric than Jensen's. Behind it, in fact, lies the concept of Baron Haussmann's Paris, from which Burnham never quite escaped. Whereas Jensen aimed to bring the out-of-doors within reach of the masses of working people on the West Side, Burnham wanted to satisfy the affluent membership of the Commercial Club. Hence his design stresses axiality and magnificence; Jensen's plan takes much more advantage of the contours of the land. It is one of the tragedies of American municipal history that it was never adopted. Unhappily it was stopped by the decline in Chicago's political life which began with the last election of Carter Harrison, Jr., and culminated in the era of Big Bill Thompson.

Jensen's actual working relationship with the two great leaders of the Chicago School, Sullivan and Wright, is of particular interest to architects. Where Sullivan is concerned, the great example is Jensen's landscaping of the Henry Babson house in Riverside, Illinois (Fig. 7.2). This fine residence (1907), now unhappily destroyed, was located only a few blocks from Frank Lloyd Wright's great Coonley house. Its front, as Hugh Morrison notes, presents "an appearance of comfortable amplitude, dignified privacy, and admirable adaptation to its site." The remarkable feature of this elevation was certainly the large balcony, projecting from the second story and executed entirely in wood. The garden facade reveals the same mastery of composition; historians now agree that much of the actual building design was done by George Grant Elmslie, Sullivan's chief designer for fifteen years. After the completion of the house, Elmslie, with his partner, William Gray Purcell, did various other buildings for the estate and they were to have done the landscaping as well. Their plans, however, were put aside, and Jensen was called in.

Fig. 7.2. Louis Sullivan. Henry Babson House, 1907. Landscaping by Jens Jensen. Photo: Architectural Record.

The result was a landscape scheme where planting accentuated the horizontal lines of the house. Jensen himself wrote that crabapples were intended to frame the view of the house and give an invitation to the prairie, which is not far away. Especially characteristic of Jensen was the water feature, a superbly handled pool which catches the reflection of the house's side portico most attractively. A great number of Jensen's compositions contain such features. Water was one of his favorite materials, and he inevitably used it with consummate skill. He was, in fact a remarkably pure landscape architect. Customarily he worked with plant materials, rocks, water, and space; tricks and gimmicks were anathema to him, and he scorned those who used them. Many of the fine prairie houses of the 1900–1914 period were spoiled by poor settings, but the Babson house was remarkable for its wonderful union of architecture and landscape.

Fig. 7.4. View of the meadow from Harley Clark House. Photo: Gates Priest.

Fig. 7.3. Richard Powers. Harley Clark House, 1925. Landscaping by Jens Jensen. View toward house. Photo: Gates Priest.

In the 1920s Jensen was less fortunate in his collaborators. It is one of the paradoxes of American cultural history that while his patrons were willing to accept extremely original designs in landscape architecture, they demanded exceedingly conventional houses. Moreover, the vital impulse which animated the original Chicago School had failed, and Jensen therefore found himself not infrequently working with architectural nonentities. Hence the landscaping often dominates the total composition during these years. This tendency was abetted by Jensen's own enormous prestige, which usually enabled him to dictate the actual placement of the house on the site. Often clients would consult him before the purchase of land, and sometimes they asked him for advice on the selection of an architect. With the architectural design of the house itself Jensen never interfered; he did demand, and usually obtained, absolute control over its surroundings.

Typical of his work in the twenties is the Harley Clark estate at Evanston (Richard Powers, architect). With its magnificent lacy network of branches overhead, the exterior space created by Jensen has the breathtaking quality of a fine Gothic cathedral (Figs. 7.3 and 7.4). The linear patterns are reminiscent of the vaulting ribs or window tracery of Chartres and Amiens. Jensen is usually described as a naturalistic landscape architect, but a space like this is naturalistic only in a very special sense. Nothing like it occurs in nature, but it does represent a highly idealized and carefully ordered concept of nature. In every respect it is the work of a great artist.

Appropriately enough, Jensen always thought of himself as carrying on the traditions of North European art in the New World. It is significant that he had vast respect for Gothic architecture. It is also important to note that he had very little regard for most of the architects with whom he worked and that on at least two important occasions he went so far as to mention the name of Frank Lloyd Wright to his clients. The twenties were, however, as Lewis Mumford has remarked, "a sere decade" for the great architect, and a Wright-Jensen collaboration did not eventuate until 1936.

In that year, Wright was building a small country house for Mrs. Abby Longyear Roberts, a prominent citizen of Marquette, Michigan, whose daughter and son-in-law were members of the Taliesin Fellowship. Mrs. Roberts, a knowing and enthusiastic gardener, had a hilltop site with a northern orientation. For this site Wright designed a small house with a superb high-ceilinged living room overlooking a wonderful open meadow. She was not, however, satisfied with the relation of the house to the ground on which it stood, and so, at Wright's suggestion, Jensen was called in to do the planting. It speaks volumes for the closeness of the relationship between the two men that Wright would even mention another name; ordinarily he considered that his services were "inclusive," extending not only to landscaping, but also to the design of household furnishings.

In any event, Jensen came over from his school at Ellison Bay, Wisconsin, and worked out the planting which is shown here. The effect of his landscaping was to relate the house much more closely to its site and also to screen it partially with the tall sugar maples which Jensen planted across the front (Fig. 7.5). In addition, he took certain other measures on the estate. These included a change in the entrance road to make the house more easily accessible, the laying out of a charming flower garden for Mrs. Roberts, and the planting of evergreens around an existing pool to make it "more mysterious." Here Jensen wanted to create a water feature where the presence of Scandinavian trolls might be felt, but Mrs. Roberts forcefully replied that while trolls might be all right for Norway or Denmark, only Indian spirits were acceptable in Michigan's Upper Peninsula!

There the matter rested. Neither of these measures bore any direct relation to the house, and their location is indicative of Jensen's feelings about this type of landscape element. Ordinarily he felt that flowers should play no part in the landscaping of the house itself but should be concentrated in another section of the grounds. In this case the form of the garden is a helix, and its contents can be varied according to the owner's wishes. Much the same theory applied to water features; they were usually placed to one side, as at the Babson House. Wright, in contrast, had wanted to place a pool directly in the center of the meadow. Jensen took the meadow as it existed (it was the kind of terrain which he might have created if it had not already been there) and emphasized its edges by planting evergreens along the sides. He also put in massed sumac for color in the fall (Fig. 7.6).

The effect of all these innovations was to infuriate Wright. He demanded to know why Jensen had spoiled the elevation of his house with "those spindly trees." Jensen, with the long perspective of the landscape architect, replied that the trees would not always be spindly.

Furthermore Wright objected to the alteration in the access road and demanded to see Jensen's planting plan. Here it developed that Jensen had simply walked about the estate with Mrs. Roberts dropping sticks in the ground and indicating to here where the different types of plant material should go. This procedure, incidentally, was quite characteristic of Jensen in the late period of his career. In the early period, his office customarily furnished detailed planting plans to clients; but after 1935, Jensen gradually withdrew from practice, literally carrying his office under his hat. Since Mrs. Roberts was in a position to be her own superintendent, their arrangement worked beautifully. It is easy to envision cases where this might not have been so.

The upshot of the entire affair was a decided strain on the relations between Wright and Jensen. Collaboration between two artists with such strong personalities was, after all, bound to be a tricky proposition. As always, Wright fought hard for his ideas, and Jensen, as might have been expected, fought with equal vigor for his concept of the appropriate landscaping. Who contributed most to the total achievement of house-and-landscaping is hard to say; partly because of Jensen's participation and partly because of later additions by the owner, Wright was for many years reluctant to acknowledge the house as his. The most recent listing of his works, *Frank Lloyd Wright: Writings and Buildings* (1960) states that it was "unsupervised" (despite the fact that much of the actual construction was done by the apprentices of the Taliesin Fellowship). It is good to know that the friendship between Wright and Jensen survived the harrowing experience of collaboration. For other reasons a final break between them came after World War II.

In sum, Jens Jensen was a major American artist, one of the most distinguished this country has produced. His design concepts were as original and daring as anything developed by the Chicago School in architecture, and with that school he had an intimate connection. For thirty years he pushed what he understood to be contemporary architecture whenever he could. One result of his efforts was a number of interesting structures in Chicago's West Parks; even more might have been built if funds had been available. It would be too much to say that the architects of the Chicago School turned to Jensen for inspiration; he has no more claim than anyone else to being the first to notice the long, low, horizontal line of the prairie. It would be

more accurate to state that he and they profited from the new spirit of independence which was abroad in the Midwest during the early years of the twentieth century. Perhaps the central tenet of the new movement was a belief that the region had a cultural identity distinct from that of the rest of the nation. Wright, Sullivan, Purcell and Elmslie, Sandburg, Masters, and Jensen, all adhered to this notion, and from it they derived some of the finest works of art America has seen. The achievement of Jens Jensen must, then, be understood in relation to the work of his contemporaries. In his best moments none of them surpassed him.

Fig. 7.5. Frank Lloyd Wright. Longyear Roberts House, 1936. Planting by Jens Jensen. Photo: Ike Wood.

Fig. 7.6. View from the terrace of the Roberts House. Photo: Author.

8

Two Michigan Buildings by John Wellborn Root

Thanks largely to the excellent work of Donald Hoffmann, we can now make a reasonable estimate of the position of John Wellborn Root in late nineteenth-century American architecture. In two fine books, miraculously accomplished in the course of an active journalistic career, Hoffmann achieved a very fair estimate of the contribution of Root to the Chicago School. The scholar who writes on Root after Hoffmann can only aim at supplementing his evaluation in certain ways. That is the object of this essay.[1]

One of the problems with Root is that two of his key Chicago buildings from the early 1880s are known only through old engravings of rather poor quality. These are the Grannis Block of 1880–1881 and the Montauk Block of 1881–1882. In the absence of good photographs of these structures, we can turn to an excellent illustration of the facade of the Morley Brothers Hardware Store in Saginaw, Michigan, which was exactly contemporary with these better known buildings (Fig. 8.1). Though the building is substantially altered today, an excellent photograph of the 1930s gives a good idea of the kind of brick wall with which Root was working in the early stage of his career. Here, as with Adler and Sullivan's Music Hall for Kalamazoo (1882), the small town supplies an example of what has mostly been lost in Chicago.

The Morley Brothers Store was, at the time of its construction, the second largest hardware store, wholesale and retail, in the United States. Its grand opening in 1882 attracted a great deal of attention, both locally and regionally. Metropolitan newspaper reporters were sent to write about the building. Thanks to their reports, we can make an accurate assessment of the building as it was in its early years.[2]

The facade of the Morley Brothers Store is four stories of dark red brick and is 90′ in width. Five brick piers divide it into four identical sections. The first floor is devoted to large display windows. An old engraving shows that the only major alteration between the early 1880s and the 1930s was the provision of a single entrance rather than four separate openings (Fig. 8.2). The windows of the upper three floors are grouped into sets of three between the piers. As it looked in the year 1882, with the recessed windows measuring 10′ high and 5′ across, the facade was a virtual wall of glass. Small bands of terracotta foliage adorn the spandrels between the second and third stories. Four flat arches span each set of three windows at the top of the third story. Other than five terra-cotta flowerlike designs and a row of terra-cotta lintels capping the building, this is the only ornamentation, and it is tightly controlled. Perhaps Root thought of the building as having three sections: a base, a middle, and a top. These three sections are indicated by string courses which occur at the top of the first and third stories. Within each section, whether base, middle, or top,

Fig. 8.1. Burnham and Root. Morley Brothers Hardware Store, Saginaw, Michigan, 1882. Photo taken in 1930s. Courtesy Morley Brothers.

Fig. 8.2. Engraving showing original facade. Undated.

all ornament and window treatment is identical.

The Morley Brothers Store incorporates various features of certain other buildings designed by Root. Its four-story height is approximately that of the Chicago, Burlington, and Quincy General Office Building of 1882–1883, but the railroad headquarters carried more ornament, and its window treatment was quite different (See Fig. 4.8). The Calumet Building of 1882–1884 was also of dark red brick with terra-cotta ornament in the spandrels, but it was nine stories high and the windows were grouped in pairs between the piers. One feature of the Montauk Block (Fig. 8.3) is similar; each window was treated as a separate opening, capped by a brick lintel in the form of a flat arch. Each window in the fourth story of the Morley Brothers Store is treated in the same way. The fenestration of the building in Saginaw is certainly its most striking feature. On the whole it is closer to the Grannis Block (Fig. 8.4) than to any other of Root's early works. Seven stories tall and also of dark red brick with terra-cotta trim, the Grannis Block resembled the Morley Building in several respects, particularly in the grouping of the windows into sets between the piers.

Fig. 8.3. Montauk Block, 64–70 West Monroe, Chicago, 1881–1882 (destroyed). From Commercial and Industrial Chicago, *courtesy Donald Hoffmann.*

Fig. 8.4. Grannis Block, 21–29 North Dearborn, Chicago, 1880–1881 (destroyed). Shown rebuilt as the National Bank of Illinois (also destroyed). From Commercial and Industrial Chicago, *courtesy Donald Hoffmann.*

Root wrote extensively about almost every aspect of architecture. In his theory he drew upon Viollet Le Duc, Ruskin, and Gottfried Semper, but put his case in terms entirely his own. In a paper delivered before the Chicago Architects Sketch Club in 1887 he discussed the elusive problem of "style" not in the sense of Gothic, Romanesque, or Byzantine, but as a quality in and of itself, entirely independent of any historical development. In a somewhat Victorian manner he first names the qualities found in a true gentleman and then applies these qualities to buildings. Root argues that it is not necessary for a structure to have all the attributes he lists, but maintains that any building with true style will have most of them. Does the Morley Brothers Store measure up to his qualifications?

144

One of the first qualities he mentions is sympathy. It is, he says, needed in considering the purpose of a building, the individual wishes of the owner, and the particular environment in which the building is to stand. Many brilliant features, he notes, "have been . . . the outgrowth of what at first seemed in a client an idiotic whim, and many most successful buildings are so because they reveal on the part of the designer a point of view in warm sympathy with their intentions."[3] Intention is the operative word here. Root continued: "I am confident that an architect designs a better grocery store if into his own professional view of the problem he will admit in all possible fullness the grocer's view."[4] He then cautions against sympathy without that other gentlemanly quality, discretion. Sympathy is necessary, but it should be used in conjunction with discretion.

Other attributes of a gentleman are knowledge and repose. Knowledge in a building, of course, reflects the learning of the architect. Root believed that this knowledge manifested itself in style. To know not only the architectural styles of the past but also to know their causes was vitally important. An architect who never tires of learning, even of seemingly unrelated fields, will be a better architect for his effort, however remotely it is shown in his designs.

Repose, said Root, is so basic a quality as to be almost overlooked. He points out that large things in the natural world move slowly and are soberly colored. Only small things fly, flutter, and are rainbow hued. Since buildings are large objects created by human beings, we should look to nature as a guide.

In similar fashion Root went on to argue for self-containment, modesty, and a tight control of ornament. He excused historical styles which were "exuberant" with the explanation that exuberance is a result of the essential character of a culture, not something that is copied centuries later. He did not like designs which shouted for attention, and modesty meant great thought in the derivations of an ornamental scheme. "Ideally," he said, "the creator of any design ought to be able to assign a valid reason for every feature in it."[5] Thus he moved toward a theory of organic functionalism. Root believed that while every valid work of art might express several ideas, one idea must be dominant, and every subordinate idea must be governed by it. Similarly, all details of a building must underline and enhance the master idea. He summed up: "There is no reason why every smallest ornament of the building should not tend toward a predetermined result, and buildings constructed and decorated to be as homogeneous in expression and absolute in type as the organic creations of nature."[6] This is at least as well put as anything by Sullivan or Wright.

Let us put the building to the test. In the elevation there is nothing to suggest frivolity or division of purpose. This basically small building is kept simple. It looks exactly like what it is: a container for hardware. While there is ornament, it is extremely quiet. The flattened brick arches and terra-cotta foliage enhance rather than detract from the basic outlines of the building. It is modest, reposeful, and self-contained. And it is sympathetic to its environment. Since it faced east, it received ample fenestration to admit the morning light. The back of the building was approximately 100 yards from the Saginaw River. Goods were delivered by barge and easily conveyed into the storage space at the rear.

The Root building was thus made to join an already existing Morley Store which faced west on the next parallel street. The juncture can be seen in the different encasement of the basement piers in the two sections of the building and in the brick of the interior walls. An existing brick wall which appears to have been opened between the two buildings is left roughly broken. In the floors of the store above this is not apparent. The advantage of so joining the two stores was that the older building measured 150' across rather than the 90' width of the Root building and hence afforded much more space for the efficient unloading and storage of goods. This space was greatly needed since the brothers not only sold retail items to individuals but were major suppliers of machinery and logging equipment to the lumber camps of northern Michigan. The entire depth of the store was over 240'.

The interior does not belie the outer structure. Behind each exterior brick pier there is a series of load-bearing columns encased in plaster. These columns have a diameter of 18" and are made of iron. In the basement they rest on large rectangular slabs of stone masonry. Above the first floor the columns change from iron to wood. At grade level there is a 20' height which gives a great sense of spaciousness and the necessary wall space for shelving which was reached by a ladder of the Morley brothers' own design (Fig. 8.5). It was called "the Railroad step ladder," rolled on wheels on an overhead track, and was used widely throughout the United States. It is no wonder that a *Chicago Tribune* reporter, upon touring the new building in 1882, was sufficiently enthused to write:

> In the busy city of East Saginaw is an establishment which conducts business on so large a scale as to be simply wonderful regarded as one of the sights of this section. Messrs. Morley Brothers are the proprietors. Your correspondent was shown through the building by Mr. E. W. Morley of the firm and was astonished at the magnitude of the business.[7]

Remembering Root's belief that a building should express its purpose in every part it seems fair to conclude that the Morley Brothers Store does so. The facade, the first part of the building to confront the customer, is dignified, modest, and not at all forbidding. The large first-floor windows allow ample room for display. Once inside the visitor experienced the feeling of spaciousness that comes from 20′ ceilings and ample dimensions. He confronted walls stacked with shelves and had the impression of an abundance of goods. All these features con-

Fig. 8.5. Interior of Morley Brothers Store. Undated.

tributed to an environment that was attractive to the customer and efficient for the work force. In summary, the building was a splendid demonstration of the validity of the architect's principles of design.

While Root is best known for his commercial structures, a surprising amount of his practice consisted of residential work. Moreover, in his theoretical writings he gave extended consideration to its problems. In one of the fugitive papers, which Harriet Monroe quoted at length in her biography of her brother-in-law, he wrote:

> What sort of town is the house to be in? How wide are the streets it faces? Where do the prevalent winds blow from? How much hot and cold weather has the town? How much rain? Which way is south? How far from the street is the house to stand? Has the town smoky or clear air? What are the native building materials? What is the character of the workmen likely to be employed? Is the occupant of the house a student? a family man? a public man with many friends? one who has many guests? who gives many entertainments? Is he a man fond of display, or one who shirks it and rather prefers the simplicity of solid comfort? These and many other questions will suggest themselves, and being answered will, when added to suggestions obtained from the client, point out very plainly the general solution of the problem.[8]

The considerations in this passage might be amplified from other sections of Root's writings, but they are certainly sufficient to indicate the high seriousness with which he regarded domestic architecture. When the historian reviews the admittedly incomplete list of executed work in Miss Monroe's volume, he is, in fact, struck by the large quantity of residential building accomplished in the all-too-brief career of the firm of Burnham and Root (1875–1891). Most of this, of course, was in Chicago, and the great portion has been torn down or altered out of all recognition. It is therefore a matter of substantial interest to discover a house for Julian M. Case in Marquette, Michigan done in the years 1886–1887 and in mint condition (Figs. 8.6 and 8.7).

Concerning Julian M. Case himself, not much is known, but the few details which do emerge from his obituary in the *Marquette Mining Journal* of June 27, 1890, are tantalizingly suggestive. He was born at or near Lansing about 1845 and came from a family which was active in state politics. His father was at one time auditor general of Michigan. He came to Marquette in 1880, and, said the *Journal*, was "identified with a number of heavy land and mining deals." Further, the paper added that, "His sociable nature and accessibility made him one of the best known residents of this city in other portions of the country."[9]

It is significant that the cablegram which announced his death in London was sent to John M. Longyear, the city's leading capitalist and a man of truly national stature. Case had gone to England in connection with the formation of a company to work the marble quarries of the county, which he believed to be a very valuable property. Longyear was a pallbearer at his funeral, and one is tempted to posit a reasonably close business and personal relationship between the two men. In short, we have a picture of an energetic and hard-driving man whose business interests were undoubtedly centered in the Upper Peninsula but who was well acquainted elsewhere in the United States and even abroad.

Fig. 8.7. Case House, side elevation, 1972. Author's photo.

Fig. 8.6. Julian M. Case House, Marquette, Michigan, 1886–1887. Photo from Marquette in 1900, *ed. Stanley D. Donan (1900).*

Case probably moved in business circles in Chicago, and this experience could easily explain the decision to employ an architect from that city for a dwelling which was to be a demonstration of recently achieved affluence and sophistication. In this connection it is well to note that in the late nineteenth century travel between Chicago and the Upper Great Lakes was facilitated by frequent boat service provided by the Lake Michigan and Lake Superior Transportation Company. The trip required three days, cost less than the comparable journey by rail, and offered some of the customary relaxation of an ocean voyage. It is quite possible that the hard-working Root had something of a holiday on his site inspection visit, which probably occurred in 1886. The completion of the house was announced in a lengthy article in the *Mining Journal* of December 24, 1887. Allowing for the customary construction period, I would propose a design date of 1886.[10]

Marquette itself in the 1880s had a good many of the aspects of a boom town. Over its immense docks poured a steadily increasing volume of iron ore from the Gogebic Range, a traffic which made wealthy men out of many of the town's leading citizens. While its prosperity thus rested on a seemingly solid industrial base, it had also an aristocratic character not often associated with mining. A visitor in 1873 wrote:

> Marquette is not so large as I at first supposed, containing as near as I can learn, about 6000 inhabitants, but it has immense wealth, a good location for business, and with reference to its geographical position and more particularly to its immediate surroundings, it is most beautifully situated. It is as handsome a town as I ever saw—not tame in its outlines but everything about it is bold, strongly in relief, huge and yet sightly.[11]

Some of the same comments could be made today. Many of the town's commercial structures were built of a striking red material called Jacobsville sandstone quarried along the eastern side of the Keweenaw Peninsula and in the Huron Mountains. The frequent employment of this richly colored stone, which has today been all too often masked by hideous plastic fronts, must have given Marquette in its heyday a continuity of appearance not unlike that of certain European towns such as the Cotswold villages or the Italian hill towns. More important for the Root project, however, was the presence of an incredible wealth of fine timber within easy reach. A brochure of 1891 proudly remarked that immediately surrounding Marquette were vast forests of every kind, "Magnificent varieties of beech, curly maple, poplar, oak, and nearly all other kinds of hardwood."[12] The best of this timber sold at around $15 to $18 per thousand board feet. It is no wonder, then, that Root chose to design the Case House in his own highly individual version of the shingle style. The building is closely akin to his few works in the Chicago area in that manner, notably the Lake View Presbyterian Church (Fig. 8.8) and the Jackson Park Pavilion.

Fig. 8.8. Lake View Presbyterian Church, Chicago. 1887–1888. Photo courtesy Donald Hoffmann.

Equally interesting is its resemblance to some of the earliest Oak Park works of Frank Lloyd Wright, especially the Walter Gale House of 1893 (Fig. 8.9), done while he was still working for Adler and Sullivan. While it is unlikely that Wright knew the Case House, he incorporates many of the same elements that Root employed. The immediately apparent common feature is the massing. Both architects employ a large, engaged cylindrical tower capped with a conical roof.

Like Root, Wright uses a tripartite division in the tower and a horizontal banding which ties it to the roof, but where Root stays within a typical shingle style organization, Wright experiments with the connection of masses and corresponding interior spatial relationships. And he begins to develop his own ideas on exterior and interior connections. The placement of the tower and the expansive porch illustrate his emerging ideas (Fig. 8.9).

Fig. 8.9. Frank Lloyd Wright. Walter Gale House, Oak Park, Ill., 1893. Photo: Oak Park Public Library.

Among the additional elements in common are the roof lines, the handling of fenestration, and the use of applied ornament. The Case House employs the characteristic irregular, steeply pitched roof which is firmly within the tradition of the shingle style. While utilizing this same type of roof, Wright pulls the eave line down toward the earth, anticipating his later Prairie style. It is in the fenestration that he breaks most clearly with convention. On the lower level he retains the same kind of window sash as in the Case House, but on the upper story uses a band of windows to enhance the link between interior and exterior. While the Case House is unadorned, the Gale House shows a rather naive adherence to a Sullivanian doctrine of ornament. Wright concentrates his ornament on and around the windows. The comparison makes one realize that Wright was working in these years with a number of diverse influences to crystallize his own revolutionary ideas on domestic architecture. The Case House, on the other hand, is characteristic of the best shingled work of the 1880s.[13]

In that decade Marquette was engaged in developing an aristocratic residential quarter on a high ridge immediately to the north of its business center. Building lots were ample in size, the area was well wooded, and the best sites offered superb views of Presque Isle and Lake Superior. Root oriented the Case House so as to take full advantage of this outlook. By 1900 the district possessed many other examples of what the period called "fine homes," but none of them possessed the architectural distinction of the Case House.

This quality is traceable essentially to Root's exceptional design and the extraordinary interior detailing, which, the *Mining Journal* truthfully remarked, was "like cabinet work, perfect." In an extended analysis the paper went on to say:

> On both the first and second floors the key room is the reception hall, as it would be styled on the first floor, or the sitting hall on the second. The reception hall is one of the largest rooms in the house and is finished in birch that has a polish equalling that on a piano case. The fireplace with its birch mantel reaching the ceiling and containing a handsome beveled glass mirror, is the principal attraction of the room, having wrought iron work on the chandeliers and on the newel light on the stairs. The room has a birch beam ceiling and the floor is one piece of wood. It is lighted by large windows in the front of the house, the recess being shut off

by spindle work in birch and fitted by one of the large window seats so popular in modern houses. The finest stain glass in the city is that over the hall windows . . . the two large stair windows contain many pieces of double plate glass which casts prismatic colors across the floors within and almost dazzle the eye from without when reflecting the sunshine.

On either side of the fireplace an open doorway with a spindle arch and portieres leads to the dining room while a heavy sliding door with one face of birch and the other of oak connects with the front library. This room is finished entirely in oak including an elegant oak mantel and bookcases. The iron work of the fireplaces is Roman in design having inscriptions and relief pictures copied from walls in the excavated cities of the Roman Empire. This is a southeast corner room connecting with it by sliding doors to a second library, also used as a drawing room. This is the most beautiful room in the house. It is irregular in shape, a square projection from the corner of the house to the north east giving the view of a sweep of the lake from above Presque Isle to the harbor side of the lighthouse. In the center of the end wall of this extension is the fireplace and a mantel with its large double plated mirror. The tiles are all hand decorated, the famous Lowe art tiles, as are all the tiles in the house. The room is finished entirely in solid mahogany with a floor of birch. The rich color and finish of the mahogany with which everything else in the room is in perfect accord, [makes] this room a perfect picture of beauty and a surprise to every visitor.[14]

This language is clarified when we consider the plan (Fig. 8.10). Its major feature is Root's development of the great entry hall, which was such a prominent feature of the domestic architecture of the 1880s in both England and the United States. From this hall the visitor proceeds to the parlor, sitting room, and dining room, all of which have splendid views of Lake Superior. Particularly effective is Root's treatment of the spindled staircase with its brilliant leaded glass windows (Figs. 8.11 and 8.12). Local legend has it that these windows came directly from one of the Paris expositions of the 1880s. The firm of Healy and Millet in Chicago did, in fact, exhibit at the 1889 fair, and these windows might have been installed after the house was built. Given the quality of the glass, such an installation does not seem impossible.[15] The entire interior is in an amazing state of preservation.

Even the original radiator cases have been maintained (Fig. 8.13).

What the newspaper account does not make sufficiently clear is the clever way in which the entire house is adapted to both social program and environmental considerations. The chambers of the entire first floor are linked by a series of sliding doors. When these are drawn back, we are confronted with a single magnificent space, beautifully arranged for the parties with which the little aristocracy of Marquette perforce entertained itself during the long, cold winters.[16]

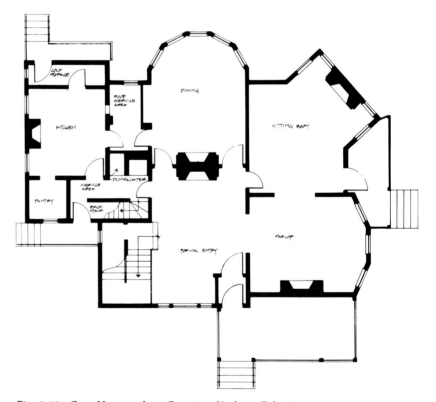

Fig. 8.10. Case House, plan. Courtesy Kathryn Eckert.

Fig. 8.11. Case House, spindled staircase. Author's photos.

Fig. 8.12. Case House, leaded glass window.

Fig. 8.13. Case House, radiator.

The place has, indeed, one of the hardest climates in the Midwest. Temperatures of −30° are not uncommon, and in the summer, a day of 75° weather is hot. While the house possessed a coal-fired hot water system, it was natural for Root to treat the fireplaces very seriously as auxiliaries, and it is not too much to say that they are masterpieces of decorative art. The restrained opulence of the cast silver surround in the dining room fireplace is especially remarkable (Fig. 8.14). The wood carving of course, echoes the floral motifs which Root was fond of executing in terra-cotta on the exterior of his major business buildings (Fig. 8.15). As the photographs indicate, the entire interior is full of bright, shiny, reflecting surfaces, which on a sunny winter day, or in an evening with the fireplace going, must be truly dazzling. These surfaces may be understood as having not only a visual but also an environmental purpose. With the sliding doors closed, the interior would become a series of sealed cubicles, and the mirrors and highly polished tiles would act as conductors for the heat currents generated by the fireplace.

It is also worth noting that the house has a remarkable apparatus of high-Victorian gadgetry. Almost every room was connected with the kitchen by electric bells and speaking tubes, and the refrigerator was built in—a great innovation for the time. Clearly Root paid as much attention to technological and environmental considerations in this small work as he bestowed on them in his large office buildings, and the solutions are worked out with the same architectural finesse that we encounter in the Rookery and the Kansas City Board of Trade. It is no wonder that the *Mining Journal* remarked, "In arrangement [the Case House] seems perfect. Every room is intended for use, the tastes of each member of the family have been consulted, and there are a hundred little conveniences on every floor, which at once attracted the visitor's notice and admiration, yet cannot clearly be described on paper."[17] In an idiom in which he is not particularly well known, the Julian M. Case House is clear evidence of the architectural stature of John Wellborn Root.

Fig. 8.14. *Case House, dining room fireplace.*

Fig. 8.15. *Case house, detail of wood carving.*

George Caleb Bingham and the Election Series
A Reinterpretation

It may seem unusual to include an essay on the political pictures of George Caleb Bingham in a book on environmental design in the Midwest, but I think that the action is defensible. Painting has, at any rate, been a part of my own environment ever since I can remember, though I did not become conscious of Bingham until I became involved with the American Culture program at the University of Michigan during the early 1960s. My colleague, Prof. David Huntington, was a Bingham enthusiast, and he brought the painter to my attention. I am grateful to Professor Huntington for his critical reading of this work, as I am to Professor Shaw Livermore for helping me to understand the intricacies of Whig politics during the 1850s. The essay is, in fact, an attempt to work out a *political* iconography for the paintings in contradistinction to the *religious* iconography so commonly employed by art historians. I am not sure that the idea would ever have occurred to me if I had not lived through the frightening political upheavals of the 1960s. Indeed, that decade seemed really dreadful to me until I immersed myself in the complications of the 1850s. I am happy here to acknowledge the priority of professors James Westervelt and Barbara Groseclose in developing an interpretation of Bingham's Election Series, which I have endeavored to enrich and extend.

In rereading the piece I am also struck by the influence my

research in St. Joseph, Missouri, had on the article. Although that corner of the state is far distant from the Bingham country, it is very southern in its outlook, and the weeks I passed there made me realize that Missouri was both a midwestern and a southern state. Indeed, nothing could have been more southern than the front porch of the Hotel Robidoux, with its assortment of rocking chairs. The incumbents of these chairs, with their cigars and their black string ties, might have been sent over by Central Casting. Elsewhere I have referred to the southern background of the St. Joseph wholesale merchants.

Finally, I have allowed myself a somewhat discursive approach in this piece and have said something about the Dutch impact on still life and marine painting in pre–Civil War America. All I can say in defense of this treatment is that this problem seemed to me to tie in closely with the Dutch models for the Election Series, as did the whole question of influence and affinity.

The Election Series

Between 1851 and 1855 George Caleb Bingham painted three major pictures on political themes. These works of art were immensely appealing in their day, and they have remained familiar to students of

American culture ever since. Because they are "popular" and at the same time first-class paintings they have attracted the attention of numerous historians and critics. While there have been some excellent attempts at interpretation since 1970, the full meaning of the Election Series has yet to be disclosed. This essay is an attempt to do just that. My intention is to set these works in their total artistic and historical context. The nature of Bingham's achievement will then be clear. In order of execution the pictures are:

1. *The County Election*. Probably painted at St. Louis and Columbia, Mo.; begun by mid-August 1851 and completed by February 1852 (Fig. 9.1).
2. *Stump Speaking* or *The County Caucus*. Painted in Philadelphia; begun before November 7, 1853, and completed by early February 1854 (Fig. 9.2).
3. *The Verdict of the People* or *Announcement of the Result of the Election*. Painted in Philadelphia; begun by late May 1854 and finished by June 1855 (Fig. 9.3).

Fig. 9.2. George Caleb Bingham. Stump Speaking *or* The County Caucus, *1853–1854. Oil on canvas, 48½" × 58". The Boatmen's National Bank of St. Louis.*

Fig. 9.1. George Caleb Bingham. The County Election, *1851–1852. Oil on canvas, 35⁷⁄₁₆" × 48¾". City Art Museum, St. Louis. Bingham painted two versions of this subject. The other is in the collection of the Boatmen's National Bank, St. Louis.*

Fig. 9.3. George Caleb Bingham. The Verdict of the People *or* Announcement of the Election Returns, *1854–1855. Oil on canvas, 46" × 65". The Boatmen's National Bank of St. Louis.*

These paintings are at the very center of Bingham's mature artistic endeavor. With the great river scenes of the decade 1846–1856, they constitute the body of work which entitles him to rank among the most important artists in our history. They have, in fact, achieved the peculiar status which is awarded to only a very few artistic undertakings. Like Gilbert Stuart's *Portraits of Washington* and Daniel Chester French's *Minuteman*, they seem to be at one and the same time serious works of art and icons of democratic virtue. There are, however, certain important differences from these other works; all, it may be noted, are loaded with political content. The Stuart *Washingtons* are portraits of a man who stands for a class: The Founding Fathers. The *Minuteman* is a depiction of a type similarly enshrined in American mythology: The yeoman farmer who, like Cincinnatus, left his plow to fight in the revolutionary armies. The three pictures of Bingham are even more ambitious. They show the entire process of American democracy as it existed in Missouri in the early 1850s. Though not painted in this exact order, they show the solicitation of votes, the election itself, and the announcement of the results. That the artist himself saw them as a major effort, and that they were so accepted by his contemporary audience, is clear from many comments. That they continue to be regarded as among Bingham's finest works is evident from the writings of numerous modern critics. Obviously these are pictures with a message. What was Bingham trying to convey and have we understood him correctly?

Briefly, the critics of the 1850s, and the critics of the twentieth century, with few exceptions, regarded the pictures as celebrations of Jacksonian democracy. In a letter sent to the American Art Union early in 1852 concerning *The County Election*, Maj. James Rollins, who was Bingham's friend and patron, wrote:

> It is preeminently a *National* painting, for it presents just such a scene, as you would meet with on the Aroostock in Maine, or in the City of New York, or on the Rio Grande in Texas on an election day. He has left nothing *out*, the courtier, the politician, the labourer, the sturdy farmer, the bully at the poles [*sic*], the beer seller, the *bruised* pugilist, and even the boys playing mumble the peg are all distinctly recognized in the group. The painting is composed of perhaps *fifty* characters. As a mere work, a delineation of character, it is superb. But this is not the point of view in

which its excellence is to be regarded. The elective franchise is the very corner stone, upon which rests our governmental superstructure and as illustrative of our fine institutions, the power and influence which the ballot box exerts over our happiness as a people, the subject of this painting was most happily chosen, and executed with wonderful skill by its gifted author. . . . From its character and its style of execution, it would arrest the attention of every class of our population; it would be admired alike by an exquisite connoisseur in the arts, the most enlightened statesman, and the most ignorant voter, and such a picture *engraved* would be equally sought after, to decorate the walls of a palace and those of a log cabin.[1]

This was the reaction of a man prominent in Whig politics in Missouri and certainly familiar with election scenes like the one portrayed. It was echoed in many quarters. Bingham exhibited the second version of the painting in Louisville, Kentucky, in the late spring of 1853 and was able to write to Rollins from Lexington that "while my picture remained in Louisville, the press was profuse in its commendations, and without a dissenting voice, it was pronounced superior to anything of its kind which had yet been seen in America."[2] In truth, Bingham had good reason to be satisfied with the public reception of his work. *The County Election* was engraved by Sartain of Philadelphia, a leading American firm, and the reproduction was extremely popular. To this day it is a fairly frequent illustration in textbooks on American history.

By 1853 Bingham was, in fact, so successful that the next picture, *Stump Speaking* attracted the attention not only of Sartain but also of Leon Goupil in New York. The Goupil firm ultimately purchased the copyright on terms extremely favorable to the artist. Bingham was to retain possession of the picture unless it sold at the price of two thousand dollars, a considerable sum at that time. While in the East it was exhibited at the Washington Art Association and the Pennsylvania Academy of the Fine Arts. Bingham thought sufficiently well of the series that he attempted, unsuccessfully, to persuade the Library Committee of Congress to purchase the picture along with the first version of *The County Election* and *The Verdict of the People*. The last painting of the group was equally admired. One reporter wrote that it was:

at once suggestive and illustrative of a scene all have witnessed, with a truthfulness that cannot fail to excite our administration . . . the genius of the artist has transferred to canvas a *principle* in our government—the exercise of the elective franchise—and submission by the people to the will of the majority, is *colored* true to the requirements of the constitution, and the instincts of our people.[3]

The evidence clearly indicates that in Bingham's own day the Election Series was both a critical and a popular success.

The twentieth-century revival of interest in Bingham has, in general, continued this evaluation. Fern Rusk in the first modern biography, *George Caleb Bingham: The Missouri Artist* (1917) rated the paintings at the top of Bingham's work. So did artist Albert Christ-Janer, when in 1940 he stated that Bingham "on canvas and in life, gave every indication of his sustained interest in politics," adding that his feelings were "always firm and usually heated."[4]

In 1967 Maurice Bloch, Bingham's best biographer, declared that the Election subjects were the artist's culminating achievement as a figure painter, but made no attempt to relate the pictures to the politics of the 1850s.[5] Almost every art historian who has written about them has held that they are suffused with geniality and good humor. So acute a critic as the late Joshua Taylor remarked, "Even in depicting political harangues and county elections—he was himself active in politics—Bingham proceeded with a genial equanimity."[6] More recently Marshall Davidson wrote:

> There is little apparent foreboding in any of Bingham's pictures. Some of the characters he portrayed are grim of mien, but there is nowhere a specific allusion to the divisive problems that were shaking the very foundations of the Union. Here everything is politics as usual, a combination of bazaar and sporting event, in which fierce local pride and interest operating through a well established party machinery hoped to support the national interest.[7]

My contention is that the message of the Election Series is much more complicated than politics as usual. The pictures were, among other things, a statement that politics as usual was a poor way of conducting national affairs in a period of impending crisis. In order to understand these paintings we must consider their political iconography, their pictorial design, and their historical sources. They are not icons of Jacksonian democracy. On the contrary, they are expositions of the Whig criticisms of the American political system and meditations on an approaching national disaster.

The Politics of the Age

George Caleb Bingham, the painter, was a political man. He was, in fact, more directly involved with electoral politics than any other artist in American history. In order to understand the great political pictures of his mature years, we must examine his family background and the complicated politics of that period.

Born in Virginia, Bingham came from a solid middle-class farming background. His grandfather was a Methodist minister to a country congregation about eighteen miles west of Charlottesville. He also cultivated grain and tobacco with the help of a number of slaves. In a fragment of autobiography Bingham noted, as did most Southerners, that his grandfather was a kind of indulgent master and never used the lash. His father was the eldest son and oldest child. The painter remembered that he had little education but was a constant reader and had a mind well stocked with historical and political information. His mother, the former Mary Amend, was of German extraction. Her father owned a saw mill at a place called Wier's Cave near the town of Port Republic. Because of a drought on the east side of the Blue Ridge, Henry Vest Bingham had to take a load of grain over the mountains to the Amend Mill. He fell in love with the miller's daughter, married her, and took over the management of the place. There, in 1811, George Caleb Bingham was born. In 1819 his father lost the farm and the money he had acquired from his father-in-law and decided to move west. The family settled in the village of Franklin in Boone County, Missouri, where the father built a tobacco factory, became the owner of a tavern, and purchased a farm of 160 acres in Arrow Rock Township. In a rich agricultural area on the Missouri River, the boy grew up.[8]

For the future politician-painter two aspects of this boyhood were important. The first is the reference to his father's reading in politics and history. The second is the reference to slavery. There is no indication of family party affiliation, but the autobiographical fragment does show a lively family interest in politics. Boone County was a stronghold of Missouri Whiggery. The most plausible explanation for its consistent voting habits is that it was settled largely by Kentuckians from Madison County who were Jeffersonian Republicans when they arrived. Although there is no evidence on the point, it is highly probable that Bingham inherited his politics. Certainly he was exposed to political discussions from an early age. Boone County was one of the sixteen counties in Missouri which went Whig in every presidential election from 1840 through 1852.

This part of Missouri was, in fact, the center of rural Whiggery in the state. In nearby Howard County lived Abiel Leonard, a lawyer and land speculator who was the whig candidate for senator in 1838 and thereafter extremely important in the councils of the party. James A. Rollins, who was to become Bingham's close friend and an important patron, was a Boone County lawyer and landowner. Like Leonard he was a speculator; later he was a successful railroad promoter. Socially well connected, Rollins was a descendant of the fashionable Rodes family of Madison County, Kentucky, and the husband of a local heiress, Mary Hickman of Franklin, Missouri. In 1850 he owned 20 slaves. In 1858 he estimated his worth at one hundred thousand dollars. Besides his slaves and his farm land in Boone County, his evaluation included 4000 acres on the North Missouri Railroad near Centralia, land situated at the crossing of the North Missouri and Hannibal and St. Joseph railroads in Macon County, and 200 mules that he expected to sell to the government at $175 apiece. Although he was himself a slave holder, he undoubtedly spoke for a majority of his fellow Missouri Whigs when he said, "So far as the mere slave interest of the state may be compared to her other great interests, it sinks into utter insignificance."[9]

This remark is extremely important as a clue to the attitude of Missouri Whigs on the slavery question. Missouri had come into the Union as a slave state in the Compromise of 1820. Broadly speaking, the state thought of itself as southern. Bingham at least took this view. In December, 1860, he wrote to Rollins, "If you shall be able to wield sufficient influence with the administration of Lincoln, to secure

me an honorable and lucrative appointment abroad, either in France or Italy, I do not think I would reject it, southerner as I am."[10] He went on to say that he had very little hope of a position even though he was convinced that Lincoln's principles harmonized with those of Henry Clay. He knew that "a mountain of prejudice" placed the state entirely beyond Lincoln's reach. As to slavery, he had grown up with it, objected to it on moral grounds but tolerated it, and unquestionably regarded the right to hold slaves as guaranteed to Missourians under federal law. At the same time he did not regard the slave interest as important within the state, and he was extremely conscious of the divisive effect of the slavery issue in national politics. His political evolution, necessary for an understanding of his pictures, requires us to go back to the presidential campaigns of 1840 and to discuss the nature of Whiggery.

The election of 1840, in which William Henry Harrison triumphed over Martin Van Buren, marked the emergence of the Whig party as a viable national organization. It was also important in other respects. It produced a greater degree of voter participation than any previous political contest in American history, and it saw the Whigs adopt the methods of their opponents, the Jacksonian Democrats. These included parades, mass meetings, and spellbinding oratory. Politics took on a carnival or camp meeting atmosphere—closely akin to religious revivalism. The campaign generated so much excitement that contemporaries termed it "the great commotion."[11] Typical of the new type of political personality who came to the fore in 1840 was John W. Bear, "The Buckeye Blacksmith." As early as 1824 he had been anti-Jackson, but he was not discovered until 1840, when certain prominent Ohio Whigs heard him speak at a local meeting near his home south of Columbus. They immediately recognized his talent, and thereafter he was a frequent speaker at meetings in Kentucky and Pennsylvania. Clearly, violence and drunkenness were common features of the rallies in which he took part.[12]

Bingham was caught up in the excitement of the 1840 election. He painted Tippecanoe banners for the great Whig convention at Rocheport and was himself one of the principal speakers, along with A. W. Doniphan, Abiel Leonard, and James A. Rollins. For the next decade he was actively, though intermittently, involved in Missouri politics. From 1841 to 1844 he was in Washington, D.C., mostly engaged in painting portraits of the leading politicians of the age. Reportedly these included Daniel Webster, Henry Clay, Andrew Jackson, James Buchanan, Martin Van Buren, and John Quincy Adams. In 1844 he returned to Missouri and again painted banners for the large Whig meeting at Booneville in honor of Henry Clay. In 1846 he was a candidate for the state legislature from Saline County, and was elected, only to lose his seat to his opponent, Erasmus D. Sappington, when the latter successfully challenged nine of his votes. It is no wonder that he declared in a letter to Rollins his intentions "to keep out of the mire of politics forever."[13] It is also not surprising that, smarting from the defeat, he returned to the political wars in 1848 and this time beat Sappington for the seat in Howard county. In that year he was sufficiently prominent to be mentioned as a possible Whig candidate for governor. When it became apparent that Rollins was a stronger candidate, Bingham graciously accepted his friend's nomination as the best man "to take the track against the next *donkey* that the locos may put forward for governor."[14]

More important still, while in the legislature, he was the author of the Bingham Resolutions. This set of principles was a response to the Jackson Resolutions, which were passed by the Missouri legislature in 1849. "These [Jackson] resolutions," wrote Professor Mering, "denied Congress the power to interfere with the existence of slavery in the territories and further argued that Northern antislavery aggressions relieved the South from obligations to the long-established principles of the Missouri Compromise."[15] The Bingham Resolutions, introduced in the same session of the legislature, held that Congress *did* have the power to legislate on slavery in the territories, but went on to say that Congress would be unwise to use that power. In retrospect they have the look of desperation which one encounters in many of the political measures of that period. They prefigure both the Kansas-Nebraska bill and the Dred Scott Decision. The problems had started with the Wilmot Proviso of 1846.[16]

Here we should inquire into the nature of the party system in which George Caleb Bingham was so intimately involved. Unwanted by the Founding Fathers, political parties had emerged into American life during the administration of John Adams (1797–1801). Thomas Jefferson, dissatisfied with the directions of Washington's administration, resigned from the cabinet, went into opposition, and formed a party which he called "Democratic Republican," probably better known as the Jeffersonian Republicans. Successful in the presidential election of 1800, this party took over from the Federalists and except for the administration of John Quincy Adams (1825–1829), controlled the executive branch of the national government until the election of Benjamin Harrison in 1840. The Whig party, to which Bingham belonged, came into being in different states at different dates. Eighteen thirty-four is probably the best date for a national emergence. Under Andrew Jackson (1829–1837) and Martin Van Buren (1837–1841) party politics took on a new quality. The electorate was expanded. All sorts of new men (like Bingham), who, in the early days of the republic might never have run for office, began to take part, and political life was transformed.

What were the principles of this Whig party to which Bingham gave his allegiance? Generalizations are always difficult, but we would have to say, with David Potter, that the Whigs were "aristocratic in tone, deferential toward property, tenaciously faithful to Puritan values."[17] Potter goes on to add that they disliked Jefferson for his deism, his Gallicism, and his toleration for revolution. A large number were "narrowly Protestant, suspicious of anything exotic, and intolerant of any deviation from accepted Yankee values."[18] A party of ardent Unionists, their chief ideologue was Henry Clay (who was neither a Yankee nor a Puritan). Clay's "American System," which included internal improvements and a protective tariff, made him attractive to business interests north and south. On slavery he supported a program of gradual, compensated emancipation, and advocated "colonization" of the freedmen in Africa. At the same time he defended slavery where it already existed as a means of controlling race relations, thus enabling the southern wing of the party to go on working with the antislavery Whigs from the north.[19] This lamentably brief summary of Clay's views leaves out the unquestionable magnetism of his personality. For a remarkable range of people, including Bingham, he was the very beau ideal of a statesman. Whigs saw themselves as the party of "all who love law and order and peace and prosperity;" their ideal of progress entailed the substitution of moral suasion "over mere brute force."[20] They deplored the drunkenness and violence which were pervasive elements of political life.

It is not surprising that by the 1840s many American intellectuals were thoroughly disillusioned with the party system. As early as 1831 the perceptive Alexis de Tocqueville had interviewed one of the Livingstons, a member of New York's famous patriarchal family, and heard that politics attracted men of the second rank. And his informants assured him that in the new western states the people generally made very poor selections for public office. In 1838 James Fenimore Cooper, returning from a stay of eight years in Europe, was appalled by his countrymen's conduct of affairs. In *The American Democrat* he wrote an extremely bitter book. In morals, habits, and tastes, he said, "few nations have less liberality to boast of than this."[21]

During the 1840s and 1850s disillusionment with the party system was widespread among intellectuals. Ralph Waldo Emerson, leading spokesman for the New England transcendentalists, began as an anti-institutionalist and arrived at a position of truly radical individualism. By 1856 Walt Whitman, who had been immersed in Democratic politics in Brooklyn a decade earlier, was thoroughly disillusioned. He rejoiced at the collapse of the Whigs and the disorganization of the Democrats. He thought political parties were "played out." With Emerson, Theodore Parker, Moncure Conway, William Lloyd Garrison, and Wendell Phillips, Whitman believed that the individual could find fulfillment outside of any political institution. Charles Eliot Norton, Oliver Wendell Holmes, Sr., and Francis Parkman—Boston Brahmins all—lashed out against the unwashed democracy. They especially disliked abolitionists.[22]

Whether or not Bingham was familiar with any of these writers is unknown, but the evidence is clear that the climate of opinion in which his political pictures were painted was one of great skepticism about the party system. And it should be noted that he had ample opportunity to become acquainted with opinions other than those held in Missouri. From 1849 to 1856 he was frequently in New York and Philadelphia in connection with the engraving of his pictures. He could hardly have escaped the fact that a large body of opinion in those cities, while it was willing to let slavery remain where it already existed, was vigorously against the extension of the "peculiar institution" into the territories.

The background for Bingham's political pictures was, in fact, the breakdown of the second American party system. Here the literature which confronts us is immense. Certainly the question of slavery was of primary importance. After the debate on the Wilmot Proviso, it seemed to become entangled with every other issue. In 1848 the Whigs elected Gen. Zachary Taylor to the presidency, a Mexican War hero and Louisiana plantation owner who was generally expected to be sympathetic to the southern cause. Taylor, however, fell under the political tutelage of William H. Seward, a leader of the northern Free Soil wing of the Whig party, and Southerners began to realize that he would probably not balk at the Wilmot Proviso. From the moment that his first Congress met, on December 3, 1849, a crisis began to develop. The essence of the problem was the potential disappearance of the Union's sectional equilibrium through the admission of free states to be carved out of the immense territory gained through the Mexican cessions. "For this crisis," wrote David Potter, "Zachary Taylor had a straightforward Jacksonian response."[23] He would make no concessions to those who sought to disrupt the Union. His attitude provoked the extremist Southerners into thinking seriously about secession. In the spring of 1850, however, Henry Clay engineered the Great Compromise. This settlement had four important provisions: (1) California came into the Union as a free state; (2) Territorial governments were set up in Utah and New Mexico without mention of slavery; (the doctrine of popular sovereignty was explicitly stated); (3) the domestic slave trade in the District of Columbia was abolished; (4) A new and stringent fugitive slave law was passed. It is entirely possible that, if Taylor had lived, he would have vetoed the legislation, and the Union would have been torn apart a decade earlier. But on July 9, 1850, he died; subsequently Senator Stephen A. Douglas took over the leadership of the compromise forces from Clay, and Millard Fillmore signed the bills into law. To evaluate the compromise today is a difficult matter. Perhaps the best description of what it meant to the nation in 1850 is that of Carl Sandburg:

> And over the country there settled a curious, quiet, bland, enigmatic peace. In many a house men breathed easier and slept better because secession and possibly war had been stood off. The quiet was broken only by the abolitionists, Free Soilers, antislavery men in both of the old parties delivering their shrill or guttural curses on the new Fugitive Slave Law. Lincoln, two years later, in eulogizing Clay would say of this new peace, "The nation has passed its perils, and is free, prosperous and powerful."[24]

In 1851 G. C. Bingham painted the first version of *The County Election*. The breathing space was soon to pass.

What the painter thought of the Compromise of 1850 is not specifically on record, but something can be inferred from documentary evidence. During his term in the legislature Bingham was a member of a Committee on Federal Relations on the Subject of Slavery. This committee produced a ringing declaration in favor of the Southern position. In part it said:

> That our glorious Union is also in danger, it is presumed no one will pretend to deny; and in the opinion of your committee, that most fearful calamity to the American people, is only to be averted, either by a tame surrender on the part of the slaveholding states of their dearest rights—by an unconditional submission to injustice, infamy, and insult unparalleled in history—or by resolutely throwing themselves with an undivided and determined front, upon their sovereign and constitutional rights.[25]

This kind of rhetoric, of course, could be duplicated in a great many state legislative documents of the period. The point here is that Bingham must have been thoroughly aware of the explosive potential of the slavery question. He could scarcely have viewed the conduct of political affairs with equanimity at the time when he was painting his first ambitious political picture.

The early 1850s were thus an exceedingly grim period for the Whig party. It is fair to say that few people were really satisfied with the compromise. The fugitive slave law was anathema to the northern Free Soil wing of the party led by men like William H. Seward of New York. In a famous entry in his *Journal* Ralph Waldo Emerson wrote "I will not obey it." At another level of society John W. Bear wrote:

> That law made every white man in the North a negro catcher for the South, for if one of their slaves ran away and got into one of the Northern states, and his master followed him and called on you to assist him to catch his slave, that law compelled you to help catch him; if you refused to assist him and was [*sic*] worth the price of the negro, you would be compelled to pay for him. To this state of things I most positively demurred, and this law I refused to obey.[26]

While Bingham would scarcely have agreed with these sentiments, he would have been well aware that they were shared by many of his countrymen, as he would have been well aware of the effect of *Uncle Tom's Cabin*, which was published in 1852. It was one of the all-time American best-sellers.

In 1852 Bingham went to the Whig convention in Baltimore. Like most Missouri Whigs he was a strong partisan of Millard Fillmore. The president had been much more amenable to Missouri Whigs on patronage questions than Taylor. He stayed with Fillmore for twenty-four ballots, and then, determined not to sit forever on a hung jury, went over to Gen. Winfield Scott, the eventual nominee.[27] In the actual campaign Scott proved to be unable to deal with the slavery question, and of almost equal importance, unable to capture any of the immigrant vote. He ran on a platform almost identical with that of his opponent, Franklin Pierce, and went down to inglorious defeat, carrying only two free states and two slave states. The Whigs were badly divided in the election, and their national organization did not survive the defeat. The situation must have appeared overwhelmingly bleak to men like Bingham, who had devoted years of his life to the service of the party.

It did, in fact, look bleak to a prominent politician in a neighboring state, whose career up to 1852 offers an interesting parallel with that of Bingham. Like the Missouri painter, Abraham Lincoln had been for many years a loyal Whig party leader in Illinois. He had shaken hands with local politicians all over the state, made innumerable speeches, and participated in the drafting of innumerable party platforms. He had served a few terms in the state legislature and one rather undistinguished term as congressman. An ardent admirer of Henry Clay, he had nonetheless been a Taylor man early on and had been disappointed when Taylor refused to give him a federal appointment. Like a good party man, he worked hard for Scott in Illinois, and when his candidate was so badly defeated, he must have felt that the Whig party was dissolving before his very eyes. In the next two years Lincoln in effect retreated from politics and devoted himself entirely to the practice of law, at the same time undertaking a remarkable program of self-improvement. Eight years later he recalled that for a time he had almost lost interest in politics.[28]

The Kansas-Nebraska bill was introduced into the United States

Senate by Stephen A. Douglas of Illinois on January 4, 1854, at which time Bingham was in Philadelphia supervising the engraving of *The County Election* and finishing up *Stump Speaking*. He completed *The Verdict of the People* at his studio in the same city by late spring of 1855. The passage of this bill was, therefore, the immediate historical setting for both pictures.

What were the provisions of the Kansas-Nebraska bill and why did Senator Douglas propose it? The answer to the first question is simple. It repealed that provision of the Missouri Compromise of 1820 which prohibited slavery north of 36° 30′ (The southern boundary of Missouri), and it substituted popular sovereignty in deciding the question of slavery in the territories of Kansas and Nebraska. The answer to the second question is still not entirely clear. It appears to lie in the politics of a transcontinental railroad, in which Douglas was deeply involved, and in his presidential ambitions. In any case it is clear that he vastly underestimated the potential explosiveness of the slavery issue. A certain moral blindness is evident here.[29] In maneuvering the bill through Congress, Douglas made important concessions to the proslavery senators. Thereafter his name was a byword of reproach, not only to northern Free Soil men like Charles Sumner but also to southern Whigs like Bingham, who clearly foresaw its consequences. During the intense debate on the bill he wrote to Maj. J. S. Rollins:

> The slavery agitation is too convenient or instrumental in the hands of demagogues to be dispensed with. Douglas' infamous Nebraska bill will cause the partially smothered fires to break out with greater violence than ever. Such is the peculiar state of parties at Washington that there is reason to fear that it will pass. . . . Let it be consummated, and a fig for all compromises upon the subject of slavery in the future. Their mere proposition will be scouted as an attempt to swindle, and the force of numbers, in the halls of Congress, will carry the day in defiance of consequences.[30]

In point of fact, Bingham was out of touch with his fellow Whigs in Missouri, who, in March of that year, adopted a series of resolutions pledging all General Assembly candidates in 1854 to support the Kansas-Nebraska principles. When he left the party during the winter, he left it by himself. Fourteen years of political effort for

Missouri Whiggery had come to an end.

Here again the course of Lincoln's career is somewhat parallel. Slavery was personally repugnant to Lincoln. On a trip to New Orleans as a young man he had observed the system at close hand, and he knew its iniquity very well. All the same he understood the manner in which the institution was rooted in the South. At no time prior to his election to the presidency was he in the abolitionist camp. Although the press was clamorous, Illinois was not keenly responsive to the antislavery movement, and Lincoln neither led nor retarded mass movements. Until his election to the presidency his solution to the slavery problem was gradual emancipation and colonization. He was content to leave the institution alone in those states where it existed and to allow it in those territories where the Compromise of 1820 said it could exist. The Kansas-Nebraska bill confronted him with an entirely new state of affairs.

Lincoln delivered his opinions on the bill in an address before the Illinois State Legislature on October 4, 1854. It is generally reckoned to be his first great speech, and it certainly differs from all of his previous utterances in its close reasoning and its literary quality. Opening with a short history of slavery in the United States, Lincoln argued that wherever it existed, it had first been introduced without law. Now it was proposed to *legalize* the spread of slavery into territories which had always been free. Putting his finger on a sensitive nerve, he said; "Inasmuch as you do not object to my taking my hog to Nebraska, therefore I must not object to your taking your slave. Now, I admit that this is perfectly logical, if there is no difference between hogs and men."[31]

From this point he went on to reason that the application of what Douglas had called "the sacred right of self-government" depended on whether a Negro was a person. Thus Lincoln tore the Kansas-Nebraska Bill to shreds, and as Carl Sandburg says, the people of Illinois knew that there was a man in the state who could grapple with Stephen A. Douglas.

So much for Bingham, Lincoln, and the Kansas-Nebraska bill. Finally we must assess the American climate of opinion in the early 1850s, when Bingham painted his political pictures. From all accounts there was a sense of loss over the deaths of Henry Clay, Daniel Webster, and John C. Calhoun within eighteen months of each other.

These three men had dominated the United States Senate for a generation, and there were no comparable leaders in sight. There was certainly a feeling in the air that the nation was undergoing a series of profound social, economic, and technological transformations. Hordes of immigrants, many of them Catholic, had to be absorbed into an aggressively Protestant society which had been traditionally mistrustful of the Church of Rome. The steamboat, the railroad, and a variety of new agricultural implements were altering the face of the land. And every question seemed to become entangled with the impossible problem of slavery. After 1854 those who believed in free soil had to deal with a government in Washington dominated by proslavery Southerners. Thinking men all over the United States were, consciously or unconsciously, beginning to wonder if the republic could endure. Because of the slavery question the settlement of the public lands could not proceed in an orderly fashion. Because of the slavery question a transcontinental railroad could not be built. Violence, disorder, and drunkenness were features of public life. The political system seemed to be unequal to the demands placed upon it. For conservatives it was truly an age of anxiety.

George Caleb Bingham shared these feelings. In June 1856 he was in Louisville awaiting the arrival of his wife and daughter by steamboat from St. Louis. He was following closely the reports of violence from Kansas. "These reports," he wrote, "convince me more strongly than ever that slavery is doomed, and that Providence is determined [sic] to use its brutalized champions, as the instruments of its overthrow."[32] His prophetic intuition was excellent. I suggest that it was reflected in his painting.

Theory, Sources, and Design

The artistic career of George Caleb Bingham before his engagement with subject matter from contemporary politics may be briefly summarized. From a very early age he liked to draw, and about 1827–1828 he encountered an itinerant artist who gave him the idea of pursuing a career in portrait painting. Bingham was active as a portraitist in Columbia and St. Louis from 1834 to 1837. In 1838 he went to Philadelphia to study and may have also visited New York. This contact with a major art center was exceedingly important for him. He went back to Missouri with a wagon load of reproductions, which, he wrote to a correspondent, gave him the same advantages as he would have had in Philadelphia. What he saw in the city, particularly the pictures of William Sidney Mount, moved him to try his hand at genre painting. For the most part, however, during the next few years, he continued to earn his living by painting portraits.

From 1840 to 1841 he moved about a good deal, spending a fair amount of time in Washington painting portraits of contemporary politicians. Although he had been interested in genre ever since his visit to Philadelphia in 1838, he still thought of himself as primarily a portrait painter during these years. We have noted that it was the hard-fought presidential campaign of 1840 which first mobilized his political energies. For the great Whig rally at Rocheport he painted banners, as he did for the convention at Booneville in 1844. A year later he scored a major success when he submitted four pictures to the American Art Union, all of which were purchased. One of these was the famous *Fur Traders Descending the Missouri*, today one of the treasures of the American Wing in the Metropolitan Museum of Art. For the next ten years he poured forth a steady stream of pictures connected with the Missouri River. With the Election Series these paintings constitute his claim to artistic greatness.

Bingham first turned to the complex problem of a political picture with many figures in 1847. In that year he painted the first version of *Stump Speaking* now known only through a daguerreotype of poor quality (Fig. 9.4). It was submitted to the American Art Union at the painter's asking price of four hundred dollars and subsequently awarded to William Duncan, a leading cotton merchant of Savannah, Georgia. Professor Bloch writes that the picture was the most ambitious undertaking by the artist since he had begun to devote himself seriously to genre about two years earlier. In this painting he included about sixty figures as against a previous maximum of eight. Bloch argues that the pictorial design was derived from Raphael's *Death of Ananias* (Fig. 9.5) as expounded in Burnet's *Practical Hints on Composition*:

While the foreground ring of figures not only carries the richest concentration of the subject in terms of variety of postures and expression, the dense row of figures in the background somewhat detracts from the total effect, although it was probably introduced to enforce the structure of the composition. The rigid, heavily populated area, with its evenly arranged figure heights, not only offers no relief to the observer insofar as the play of light and shade distractions is concerned, but creates that sense of "monotony" which at least one critic observed in the picture. As a compositional feature the figures also unfortunately preclude any progression into the landscape in the far distance.[33]

In terms of pictorial design, the painting was, in fact, a failure. Bloch shrewdly observes that five years passed before Bingham again attempted a large figural subject and seven before he undertook to paint another version of *The Stump Orator*.

Fig. 9.5. *Raphael Sanzio.* Death of Ananias. *From an engraving published in Burnet,* Practical Hints on Composition *(1828).*

Fig. 9.4. *George Caleb Bingham.* The Stump Orator, 1847. *From a daguerrotype, dimensions unrecorded.*

As we have noted, these five years were for Bingham a period of intense political and artistic activity. We can be sure of certain facts. In July 1848 he was nominated to represent Howard County, Missouri, in the state legislature, and in August he was elected over E. D. Sappington, who had previously beaten him in a recount by one vote. In January and February 1849 he attended the session of the legislature in Jefferson City. Later that year he was probably in Philadelphia. In November 1850 he was in New York, where he submitted *The Squatters* and *The Wood Boat* to the American Art Union. In late March 1851 he was still in New York, and very probably working on *The County Election*. In June of 1852 he went to Baltimore as a delegate for the eighth district of Missouri to the Whig convention. Later in the month he was in Philadelphia and New York consulting with the engravers for *The County Election*. In September 1853 he was again in New York to visit the exhibition of the Industry of All Nations, and then went on to Philadelphia. By early November he was organizing to paint the second version of *Stump Speaking* in that city. He spent the winter there superintending the engraving by Sartain of *The County Election*. In 1854 he remained in Philadelphia, probably through mid-July, with at least one short side trip to New York. He completed *Stump Speaking* by early February and had begun *The Verdict of the People* by late May. In January 1855 he returned to Philadelphia and completed *The Verdict of the People* there in late spring. In December he attended a Whig meeting in Jefferson City and made a speech in the capital on the first of the month.[34]

There are two important feature in this chronology. Bingham was constantly involved in politics in the most direct fashion possible, and he was often in Philadelphia and New York. It is clear that he had an intimate knowledge of the democratic process as it existed in Missouri in his day and that he was completely familiar with the scenes he portrayed. His three major pictures and the two smaller genre pieces, *Country Politicians* (Fig. 9.6) and *Canvassing for a Vote* (Fig. 9.7), can be taken as accurate transcriptions of reality.

That Bingham was so often in the cities of the eastern seaboard meant that he had ample opportunity to visit print dealers, public institutions, and private collections, like those of Jerome Bonaparte and Robert Gilmor. In Bonaparte's collection, as E. P. Richardson has shrewdly noted, he undoubtedly encountered the art of Rubens, which is reflected in *Boatmen on the Missouri*.[35] When he was in Baltimore for the convention which nominated Gen. Winfield Scott, he may have seen in private homes paintings formerly belonging to Gilmor.

Bingham can be understood as an ambitious and extremely intelligent provincial painter looking for ways of dealing with an old problem: organizing a complex figural composition. The design had to be suited to the theme and the iconography. Late in life he composed a public lecture in which he outlined his artistic credo. In a particularly significant passage he wrote:

> To the beautiful belongs an endless variety. It is seen not only in symmetry and elegance of form, in youth and health, but is often quite as fully apparent in decrepit old age. It is found in the cottage of the peasant as well as in the palace of kings. It is seen in all the relations, domestic and municipal, of a virtuous people, and in all that harmonizes man with his Creator. The ideal of the great artist, therefore, embraces all of the beautiful which

Fig. 9.6. George Caleb Bingham. Country Politicians, 1849. Oil on canvas, 20″ × 24″. De Young Museum, San Francisco.

Fig. 9.7. George Caleb Bingham. Canvassing for a Vote, 1851. Oil on canvas, 25⅛″ × 30³/₁₆″. Nelson-Atkins Museum of Art, Kansas City, Missouri.

presents itself in form and color, whether characterized by elegance and symmetry or by any quality within the wide and diversified domain of the beautiful. Mere symmetry of form finds no place in the works of Rembrandt, Teniers, Ostade, and others of a kindred school. Their men and women fall immeasurably below that order of beauty which characterizes the sculptures of classic Greece. But they address themselves nonetheless to our love of the beautiful, and nonetheless tend to nourish the development and growth of those tastes which prepare us for the enjoyment of that higher life which is to begin when our mortal existence shall end.[36]

This passage suggests not only Bingham's respect for classic order but also his appreciation for Dutch genre painting, to which, I believe, he was to turn for the organizations of his political pictures. This suggestion of a Dutch influence on pre–Civil War American painting is not new. As long ago as 1941 John I. H. Baur showed the connection in terms of still life. Bingham may have been self-educated, but he was quite familiar with the aesthetic controversies of his period. These began in the late eighteenth century.

Sir Joshua Reynolds, in his *Discourses* (1769–1797) developed a hierarchical classification of all art in terms of an ideal value system. At the very top of his hierarchy he put the Italian painters of the High Renaissance, especially Raphael. For them the Classic World had been very close. They expressed nobility of mind, and technically they were without peer. To achieve success in the grand historical style, which, in Sir Joshua's view, was the most significant branch of painting, it was absolutely essential to study the Italians. Thus Benjamin West, a clever young American who succeeded Sir Joshua as president of the Royal Academy, began by doing paintings with titles like "Agrippina with the Ashes of Germanicus" and created a sensation by painting "The Death of Wolfe," a contemporary event, as though the participants in the drama were ancient Romans. At the same time Sir Joshua had to confront the enduring popularity of Dutch art in eighteenth-century England. His solution was to place it on a distinctly lower plane in his hierarchy but to proclaim that the Dutch were worthy of study for their mastery of the technical craft of painting. "The Dutch," he said, "were unequaled in the true use of colors," and added, disparagingly, "it is to the eye only that the works of this school are ad-

dressed." Summing up, he held that "painters should go to the Dutch School to learn the art of painting, as they would to a grammar school to learn the language. They must go to Italy to learn the higher branches of knowledge."[37] At the top of his hierarchy of Dutchmen he placed Rembrandt, who had, after all, done many things that could be interpreted as within the grand historical style, and then, surprisingly, Jan Steen and Teniers the younger. Jan Steen, he thought, might have been a considerable painter, if he had only gone to Italy for study.[38]

Now Sir Joshua's opinions were extremely influential on English and American painting until the decade of the 1840s, but they did not go unchallenged. For example, Alan Cunningham, a prominent poet and critic, noted in 1834 that the Dutch genre masters offended Fuseli and other teachers of the grand style. He added, "we ought to be pleased that artists are found who turn to such themes from matters stern and tragic."[39] Cunningham was expressing a popular attitude. Several art historians have noted that, as a consequence of the dispersion of the great royal collections of Europe during the Napoleonic wars, London became the most important art market in the Western world. It was at this period that many of the most notable collections of Dutch art in England were formed. Sir Robert Peel and the Barings avidly collected Dutch pictures. As any visitor to Apsley House will observe, the Duke of Wellington was part of the trend and had a very good eye indeed. The situation is somehow remindful of the position of Andrew Wyeth in art today. No matter how the New York critics may excoriate him, the public continues to show its approval of his work.

American visitors to London inevitably observed this enthusiasm and in some cases joined the buying spree. Undoubtedly the most important of these travellers was Robert Gilmor, Jr. (1779–1848), son of a wealthy Baltimore merchant. As a boy Gilmor actually spent a year studying in Amsterdam, where he probably acquired a taste for Dutch pictures which lasted all his life. At his death in 1848 his collection, certainly one of the finest in the nation, included one hundred fifty items of the Dutch and Flemish schools. It boasted such names as Berchem, Both, Brill, Cuyp, Hals, De Heem, Hondecoeter, Hobbema, Metsu, Mieris, Ruysdael, Teniers, Van der Meer, and Van de Velde. The question immediately arises: How many of these "old masters" were genuine? The answer would seem to be: Many more than we would have thought a generation ago. Certainly there is nothing un-distinguished about the Dutch drawings from the Gilmor collection which today are part of the Randall bequest at the Fogg Art Museum of Harvard University.[40]

About any important private collection there is, of course, al-ways a problem of accessibility. How available were private collec-tions, like Gilmor's, to young artists like Bingham, who first visited Philadelphia in 1838 and thereafter was frequently in the cities of the eastern seaboard? We do not know very much about this problem, but what we do know is tantalizing. Undoubtedly the most important early Dutch collection in the United States was that of Baron Stier, a Belgian nobleman who escaped to America with his holdings in 1794. They were stored in Philadelphia, then in Annapolis, and finally at Bladensburg, Md., where they were hung in Stier's mansion. The col-lection had many visitors, among them Rembrandt Peale. Historians have long known that the Peale still life school was based on early Dutch and Flemish examples. Here perhaps is the connection. Rem-brandt Peale saw the collection while it was still stored in Annapolis and wrote that when it was displayed in Bladensburg, it was much visited by dignitaries from Washington.[41]

Aside from private collections like those of Baron Stier and Robert Gilmor, Jr., there were several public institutions where as-piring painters might make contact with Dutch art in the cities of the eastern seaboard. Perhaps the most important of these was the Penn-sylvania Academy of the Fine Arts. Its first loan exhibition in 1811 contained two hundred loans from private collections; among the art-ists shown were Steen, Ostade, and Teniers, all of them important for this study. Dutch art must have been popular with the Philadelphians, for it was frequently featured in annual exhibits up to the time of the Civil War. E. P. Richardson has remarked that "Only the ignorant now suppose these were all copies."[42] It is also important to note that the exhibitions included all types of painting then in favor in the United States. There were numerous examples of genre painting, which came into vogue in Jacksonian America, and there were land-scapes, which, may have had a decided effect upon some of the Hud-son River painters and the luminists.[43]

Other important centers for the dissemination of artistic culture were Boston and New York. The Boston Atheaneum held its first exhi-bition in 1827, when 317 works of art were displayed. One hundred and eighty-seven of these were classified as Old Masters, the greater number of them of the Dutch and Flemish school; seapieces by Van de Velde, moonlights by Van der Neer, and landscapes by both the Ruys-daels and Swanevelt were among those on view.[44] After 1827 the Atheaneum acquired a permanent collection of European and Ameri-can paintings. Subsequent catalogues demonstrate that paintings from this collection were lent to exhibitions in other cities. Thus the Apollo Association in New York in 1841 exhibited works by Ruysdael which had been shipped from Boston.

The Apollo Association was the forerunner of the American Art Union, an organization with which Bingham was to be intimately connected. The association held annual exhibitions of pictures, mostly borrowed from private individuals and often including works of the Dutch School. These were usually borrowed from private collections, such as that of Charles de la Forest, consul general of France. A sale catalogue of his collection in 1849 listed eleven Dutch landscape paint-ings. The American Art Union was an organization of artists and art lovers. For a few dollars anyone could purchase a membership which entitled him to a certain number of engravings from the works of the member artists. The original paintings, from which the engravings were made, were distributed by lottery to the members. As we have noted earlier, Bingham made his connection with the Art Union in 1845 when it purchased his first great genre painting *Fur Traders De-scending the Missouri*, which appeared as the frontispiece of its journal. The response to the picture was overwhelmingly favorable and launched him upon the most important phase of his career.[45] The American Academy of Fine Arts, founded in New York in 1802, also held annual exhibitions, but was much less successful. It went out of existence in 1841.

Far more important than regular institutional exhibitions were the commercial galleries and print shops which had existed in the seaboard cities from the 1740s onward. Let us take a typical example: William Bradford, bookseller, advertised in the *Pennsylvania Journal*, December 2, 1742, a list of book titles, followed by:

Also a curious Parcel of fine Pictures, either painted in Glass, Mezzotinto or otherwise, such as the Cartoons of Raphael at

Hampton Court, (probably the small plates by S. Gibelin), the 7 works of Mercy, Sea Pieces, Views of the most Magnificent Buildings in Europe, sets of fine Horses, and a variety of other sorts.

The other sorts included both mythology and genre but are hard to trace: Hogarth, Italian engravings, French engravings after Dutch genre painters like Ostade and Wouwermans, and Dutch graphic works by both seventeenth- and eighteenth-century artists. In colonial times prints in the seaport cities were not rare. They were not limited. They were abundant and usually inexpensive. And this happy condition continued up to the time of the Civil War. It is not surprising that Bingham, after his first visit to Philadelphia, wrote so enthusiastically about the works which he was taking back to Missouri with him.[46]

Prints were, in fact, key items in the education of most American nineteenth-century artists. Here we must remember that for hundreds of years painting had been an art which was taught in the studio. In the workshop of a recognized master an apprentice could learn how to mix paints, how to apply glazes, and presumably, the elements of drawing, painting, and pictorial design. Then, too, he might learn much from the masters' own works or from his collections of work by his predecessors and his contemporaries. Thus, Rubens, who lived like a prince, had a princely collection of works of art, which, along with his own powerful paintings, certainly affected the achievements of his numerous followers. So it had been for centuries. Matters were greatly simplified for the young artist with the development of the various processes of *graphic* reproductions in the seventeenth and eighteenth centuries. By studying etchings or lithographs or engravings he could discover much about the enduring problem of pictorial composition.

Today much of the same process is going on all over the Western world, but the medium of communication is the photograph. In the United States thousands of young art students study the works of Picasso. They may not be able to get to the Museum of Modern Art in New York, but they have access to good photographic reproductions of *Les Demoiselles d'Avignon*, and his other masterpieces in that institution. The photograph, of course, is a less effective lesson than an experience with the original work of art. In the first instance an artist learns by copying. When an artist copies a print, he is working

only with elements of composition, line value, and chiaroscuro. In painting there are problems of color, texture, and brush stroke; solutions to these questions cannot be transmitted in an engraving or a lithograph.

Considering the abundance of the graphic work, it is far more likely that the American artists who studied the Dutch in the pre–Civil War period worked from reproductions rather than from originals. The problem is: Which reproductions? We know only that the print trade in Philadelphia and New York was brisk.[47] We can assume that engravings, etchings, and lithographs were easily available to artists like Bingham. I suggest that he found the model for his major political pictures in a reproduction of a Dutch village festival in which a quack doctor was a central character. If so, his selection of this model was extremely significant in terms of imagery and of pictorial design.

The depiction of the Kermesse, or county fair, was a traditional problem for the artists of the Low Countries. The theme went back into the Middle Ages, and its greatest exponent was, of course, Pieter Breughel. Many canvases showing these events survive. *A Village Fair* (Fig. 9.8) by Joost Cornelis Droochschloot (1586–1666) is an excellent example and a fine illustration of the problems which confronted the artist who attempted this kind of picture. He had to organize a great many figures, and ordinarily he had to do this in a reasonably deep space. Droochschloot did so with a tremendous diagonal running from the group of figures in the right foreground along the village street into the distance on the left. An architectural backdrop was necessary. Droochschloot used the church and the dwellings of the village. Finally he had to show people engaged in all kinds of activity: children playing, lovers flirting, men and women drinking copiously, and others gawking at the travelling medicine man on a platform.

If we exclude the lovers, whose erotic play could not be shown in any nineteenth-century American picture, the program is remarkably similar to what Bingham faced in organizing his political pictures. Perhaps the best literary description of a Kermesse is a passage in John Lothrop Motley's biography of Oldenbarneveldt. Motley, the greatest American student of Dutch history, described a fair at Utrecht just prior to the trial of his hero in 1620:

At that particular moment the mass of the population was comparatively indifferent to the terrible questions pending. It was the Kermess[e], or annual fair, and all the world was keeping holiday in Utrecht. The peddlers and itinerant merchants from all the cities and provinces had brought their wares—jewelry and crockery, ribbons and laces, plows and harrows, carriages and horses, cows and sheep, cheeses and butter-firkins, doublets and petticoats, guns and pistols, everything that could serve the city and countryside for months to come,—and displayed them in temporary booths or on the ground, in every street along every canal. The town was one vast bazaar. The peasant women from the country with their gold and silver tiaras and the year's rent of a comfortable farm in their ear-rings and necklaces, and the sturdy Frisian peasants, many of whom had borne their matchlocks in the great wars which had lasted through their own and their fathers' lifetime, trudged through the city, enjoying the blessings of peace. Bands of music and merry-go-rounds in all the open places and squares; open-air bakeries of pancakes and waffles; theatrical exhibitions, raree-shows, jugglers, and mountebanks at every corner—all these phenomena, which had been at every Kermess[e] for centuries, and were to repeat themselves for centuries afterward, now enlivened the atmosphere of the gray, episcopal city.[48]

Here it is appropriate to stress that the Dutch enjoyed a favorable image in the United States during the years of Bingham's most intense artistic activity. Motley's two volume *Rise of the Dutch Republic* was published in 1856 and was at once tremendously popular. Its author emphasized the parallels between the struggles for freedom of the Dutch Republic and the United States and between the characters of William the Silent and George Washington. Further, Motley saw Roman Catholicism as almost entirely evil. This view was congenial for the most Protestant nation in the Western world. We will never know if Bingham read Motley, but he was a man extremely sensitive to the intellectual currents of his time, and it would have been entirely natural for him to admire Dutch painting on what might be called nonpictorial grounds. Indeed, in Jacksonian America, the Netherlands had an excellent reputation. People with long memories would have recalled the early recognition of American independence and the Dutch loan negotiated by John Adams. The Dutch continued

to be heavy investors in American securities and were generally admired for their commercial acuity. William H. Seward visited the Netherlands in 1834 and found it neat, clean, well-ordered, and prosperous. Moreover the Dutch were successful imperialists. They had held onto their empire and were making it pay, as the English were only learning to do.[49]

Mountebanks and charlatans, then, were *common* figures of Dutch seventeenth-century life, a sufficiently colorful feature so that many artists depicted them. The pictorial possibilities inherent in the subject were evident, and the theme lent itself beautifully to the moralizing which was so common in the genre painting of the day. Hence the list of artists who depicted quack doctors and charlatans is long indeed. It includes minor figures such as Pieter Quast and Gerard Dou, those of middling rank like Jan Van Goyen and Jan Steen, but also Rembrandt. The man most fascinated with quacks was probably Jan Steen. According to Hofstede deGroot, he did three different pictures on the theme.

*Fig. 9.8. Joost Cornelisz Droochsloot. Village Fair, n.d. Panel, 27½"
× 42¼". Detroit Institute of Arts.*

Around the treatment of the quack and the village festival certain conventions developed. The quack was usually shown on some kind of raised platform at the left of the picture (most of Shakespeare's villains enter from the left). Ordinarily he would be garbed in black, the conventional dress of the respectable physician. Frequently he would be offering a flask of his miraculous elixir to the crowd. Sometimes there would be a tooth extraction, as in a drawing in the Louvre, formerly credited to Jan Steen but now generally attributed to the circle of Adrian Van Ostade (Fig. 9.9). In most of these scenes people are shown in varying degrees of intoxication. Frequently a wheelbarrow, the traditional symbol of drunkenness, appears. Often a pocket is being picked, suggesting that monetary loss is an accompaniment of interest in the show. A dog or two is almost inevitable, and occasionally a monkey is present. Sometimes a few musicians will be on the platform. The whole scene, of course, has strong theatrical qualities, and the charlatans are closely related to their contemporaries in the Commedia dell'Arte. The charlatan, or quack, will have a banner on his platform, and perhaps a tiny stage. Finally there will be some kind of architectural backdrop. It may be a church, a dwelling house, or a tavern. Thus the scene is anchored in reality. If much seventeenth-century Dutch genre painting dealt with lessons on morality—on lechery, the evils of drink, etc.— these pictures are sermons on gullibility. A classic example is Gerard Dou's *Quack Doctor* (Fig. 9.10).

Since this version of the quack doctor/charlatan theme is so characteristic, it is a good example for analysis. Dou used a well-known section of his native Leiden as an architectural setting. The city wall and the Blauwpoort are a backdrop for the scene. The quack is on a platform protected by an umbrella, and in front of him is a table on which is set a flask of his magic elixir. A monkey is also perched on the table. A mixed group is gathered around the quack. Immediately below him is a woman cleaning a baby's soiled bottom—an obvious reference to the quality of his elixir. At right is an older woman listening with open mouth. At left is an older man with a wheelbarrow. Behind the quack a man is leaning out of a window pointing to a poster with a moralizing inscription which tells the buyer to be wary. Other features of the scene are important in the moralizing tone of the artist, notably the gnarled tree, a symbol of the

quack's deadness to the moral life. It is, as Christopher Brown has pointed out, an elaborate and extremely complicated allegory on the nature of deception.[50]

Fig. 9.9 Circle of Adrian Van Ostade. L'Aracheur des Dents. From Henri de Chennevieres, Les Dessins du Louvre *(Paris, 1885).*

Fig. 9.10. Gerard Dou. The Quack Doctor, 1652. Panel, 112 cm × 83 cm. Boymans-Van Beuningen Museum, Rotterdam.

Rembrandt did two drawings on the subject, though he is not known to have used it in a painting or print. The earlier (Fig. 9.11) is probably dated about 1638–1642; it shows the quack on his platform with his back to the viewer. His banner is behind him, and he is holding a bottle of elixir in his hand while he addresses his audience. Seymour Slive rightly observes that, although the figures are only suggested with a few strokes or some wash, the drawing gives the impression of a work complete in itself.[51] In another drawing, formerly in the Staatliches Museum, Berlin, the quack faces outward toward the viewer and the composition is accordingly reversed. It would, of course, have been impossible for Bingham to have seen either of these drawings, and it would have been highly improbable for him to have seen the etching on the charlatan theme by Constantine Daniel Renesse, who was in Rembrandt's studio from 1651 to 1652 (Fig. 9.12). Only three copies of this work are known, and it is extremely unlikely that one would have been in the print shops of Boston, New York, or Philadelphia in the 1830s and 1840s. On the other hand, the visual evidence that Thomas Rowlandson in the eighteenth century knew the etching of Renesse is overwhelming (Fig. 9.13). In fact, Rowlandson comes close to duplicating the Dutch design. In addition to the quack on his platform with his assistant, we have the musician, the wheelbarrow, the tree, and even the same church tower in the distance. Perhaps Rowlandson saw the version of the etching now in the British Museum, or perhaps he saw another print, now lost. There are simply too many coincidences to be explicable in any way except direct personal contact. The Dutch conventions for the portrayal of the quack were evidently very persuasive.[52]

In the eighteenth century, a period in which quack doctors flourished (see Voltaire), the taste for graphic works which portrayed them in the Dutch traditions remained strong. Jan Van Goyen (1599–1656) is an artist primarily known for his landscapes and marine paintings. At the very end of his life, however, he did a fine drawing of a charlatan at a country fair (Fig. 9.14). Here the composition is somewhat simplified in comparison with the works of Renesse and Rowlandson. The figures are grouped more loosely, and the pictorial space is much deeper. Of major importance is the fact that the drawing was engraved by Jan Jacob Bylaert in 1768.[53] The print might easily have been available to Bingham.

Fig. 9.12. *Constantine Daniel Renesse.* The Quack Doctor, *n.d. Etching. British Museum.*

Fig. 9.13. *Thomas Rowlandson.* The Quack Doctor, *n.d. Pen and watercolor drawing, 6¼″ × 10⅛″. National Gallery of Scotland.*

Fig. 9.11. *Rembrandt Van Rijn.* A Quack Addressing a Crowd, *1638–1641. Pen and wash, 188 mm × 164 mm. Victoria and Albert Museum. This drawing was formerly in the collection of Count Antoine Seiler.*

Fig. 9.14. Jan Jacob Bylaert. The Quack Doctor, *1768 [after Jan Van Goyen, 1599–1656]. Engraving (soft ground and aquatint). Metropolitan Museum of Art, New York. Bylaert (1734–1809) was born in Rotterdam and died in Leiden. He did many engravings of works by prominent seventeenth-century artists.*

Fig. 9.15. Jean Jacques Boissieu. Les Musicians Ambulans; *from* Les Petits Charlatans, *1773. Metropolitan Museum of Art, New York.*

As the history of the Van Goyen drawing demonstrated, interest in Dutch seventeenth-century art remained strong during the Age of Reason. Among the Frenchmen who were close students of Dutch art was the Parisian engraver Jean Jacques Boissieu (1736–1810). He is known to have made engravings after Karel du Jardin, Wynants, and Ruysdael, and in 1773 he issued a folio on the picaresque theme of *Les Musicians Ambulans.* One plate has a typical Quack Doctor design, but the platform, on which the musicians are standing, is now located just outside a Roman triumphal arch. Here is the eighteenth-century fondness for ruins (Fig. 9.15). The entire scene

is imbued with melancholy. It lacks the vitality which we find in Renesse, Van Goyen, and Rowlandson, but it might very well have been available in the United States.

Boissieu was seen by the eighteenth century as an heir to the Dutch tradition. When we consider the graphic works of the Dutch masters themselves and engravings done after their paintings, the figures of Adrian Van Ostade, Cornelius Dusart, and Jan Steen emerge as particularly important. Ostade (1610–1685), probably the greatest genre painter of the Haarlem School, was a prolific artist who in 1646 did a series of fifty etchings which included both an intimate "Quack

Doctor" and "The Village Fair" (Figs. 9.16 and 9.17). In the latter work the format is particularly close to the slightly later etching by Renesse. Unlike the Renesse etching, the Ostade version of the theme went through several editions. At the artist's death the contents of his studio were sold. These included copper plates from which the etchings were made. The purchaser is not known, but a new series of etchings was published in Amsterdam between 1710 and 1730. Somewhat later in the century the plates were in the possession of Bernard Picart, and in 1780 the Paris art dealer Basan issued a new edition of the whole series. His widow, Jean, offered still another edition. So a good many copies of the etchings must have been in circulation in the nineteenth century.[54]

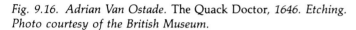

Fig. 9.16. Adrian Van Ostade. The Quack Doctor, *1646. Etching. Photo courtesy of the British Museum.*

Fig. 9.17. Adrian Van Ostade. The Village Fair, *1646. Etching. British Museum.*

Another possibility for a source is Cornelis Dusart (1660–1704), a student and follower of Ostade. His peasant types were similar to those of Ostade, but often he worked in a lighter, more satirical vein, tinged with eroticism. Like Ostade he both painted and etched the village festival theme. His most important graphic work on the subject The "Great Village Fair" (Fig. 9.18) dates from 1685, and it includes all the familiar elements which we have discussed.

Among the Dutch masters of genre the greatest, and the most problematical, is Jan Steen (1626?–1676). Born in Leiden, Steen was never associated with any one Dutch city, but lived at various times in Haarlem, Delft, and The Hague, as well as in his native town. From contemporary accounts and from his pictures themselves, we gather that he was a lover of eating, drinking, and of tavern life generally. His subjects are not the haute bourgeoisie of Hals and Rembrandt, but rather the lower middle class of the country, whom he liked to show at weddings, feasts, and other social gatherings. Among Dutch genre artists of the period he is particularly esteemed for his ability to organize large groups of figures. This is certainly an attribute that would have appealed to Bingham.

Aside from this ability, there is another aspect of Steen which is relevant here. This is his ability to suggest a complex symbolism with a great economy of means. Like Moliere, the contemporary with whom he is often compared, he was something of a moralist. Often the tavern scenes imply that the drinkers and wenchers will come to no good end. This quality is especially evident in the famous *Bad Company* in the Kunsthistorisches Museum in Vienna (sometimes known as *The World's Turned Upside Down* because of its marvelous series of inversions). Quite obviously Steen was fascinated by physicians, both legitimate and fake. There is a large group of paintings with the general theme of *The Physician's Visit*, and in most of these we find that the maiden who is being visited is lovesick; sometimes she is pregnant. The quack doctors are usually sinister characters, usually shown in profile and garbed in black. Most relevant here is the famous version of the theme in the Rijksmuseum at Amsterdam. In this picture the quack holds up for the inspection of an assemblage of yokels a tumor which he has just extracted from a groggy peasant (Fig. 9.19). The scene takes place at a country fair and may be considered a commentary on the gullibility of the public. It contains most of the symbolic language which has become customary in this variety of genre painting. The donkey is an emblem of stupidity. The wheelbarrow is traditionally associated with drunkenness. The audience is a group of peasants who are only casually interested in the agony of the peasant on the platform. The quack himself is the embodiment of the charlatan, whose object is to gull the public. Finally, it is important to note that in seventeenth-century Dutch "to be afflicted with the stone" was an expression conveying an inability to manage one's own affairs: for example, to have trouble with drink or women. Could Bingham have known an engraving of this picture or a copy of it? The somewhat curious answer is that he could have known a pastiche.

Fig. 9.18. Cornelis Dusart. The Great Village Fair, *1688. Etching, 274 mm × 328 mm. Rijksmuseum, Amsterdam. This etching exists in several states.*

In 1833 and 1834 the London publishers John Major and George William Nicol brought out two volumes entitled *The Cabinet Gallery of Pictures Selected from the Splendid Collections of Art, Public and Private, Which Adorn Great Britain*. The well-known poet and critic Allan Cunningham, a major authority of the day, contributed biographical and critical notes. In 1836 the plates for these volumes were bought up by George Virtue, the great remainder publisher, and another edition appeared in that year. Among the pictures which Cunningham discussed was *A Mountebank*, a work then in the possession of a Mr. Charles Heusch, Esq., of Bedford Square (Fig. 9.20). He attributed the work to Jan Steen, and indeed it has

Fig. 9.19. Jan Steen. The Quack Doctor, 1656. Panel, 37.5 cm × 52 cm. Rijksmuseum, Amsterdam.

ing. It must have been in England as early as 1798. In that year the antiquary Matthew Pilkington commented on "A capital picture of Jan Steen's painting is a mountebank attended by a number of spectators in which the countenances are wonderfully striking, as being full of humor and uncommon variety."[55] Pilkington also mentions the fiddler on the platform. The remarkable picture by Steen, which was the rough model for this pastiche was at this time in the collection of the Stadhouder William V and is at present in the Rijksmuseum. By itself this pastiche is insignificant. What is important is that it is part of the tradition of the *Quack Doctor*, with which, I contend, Bingham came in contact in the late 1840s and early 1850s.

Fig. 9.20. Andrew Duncan. A Mountebank; for the Virtue edition of The Cabinet Gallery, 1836. British Museum. Duncan (1795–?) was a London artist who did numerous engravings of the old masters.

features which show familiarity with the "charlatan" pictures now in the Rijksmuseum. The mountebank and the woman pushing her drunken husband in a wheelbarrow are recognizably Steen's figures. On the other hand, the man on the horse might have come from the print after Van Goyen by J. J. Bylaert. The woman carrying the jug on her head is the kind of peasant figure who occurs in any number of eighteenth-century works. The ruins at the far left are also a customary eighteenth-century backdrop. Theoretically the picture might have been a "lost" Steen, but it is very much more likely to have been a pastiche. And as a pastiche it is a clever job—exactly the kind of complex organization of figures for which Bingham must have been look-

Allan Cunningham's text for *The Cabinet Gallery* is significant as a statement of the English climate of opinion concerning Dutch painting in the 1830s. Cunningham, who clearly aspired to be a taste-maker, restates and amends the position of Joshua Reynolds. As we have noted, Reynolds believed that the Dutch addressed themselves only to the eye. They had no concern with the mind.[56] Cunningham showed considerably more understanding. His volumes included sympathetic discussions of pictures by Rembrandt, Mieris, Bol, Cuyp, and Ruysdael, as well as Steen, and he generally argued that the public could be grateful for the richness of Dutch genre painting. He also noted that in Dutch pictures there was no idleness and that everyone was at work and moving, an attitude very much in tune with the Protestant ethic.[57]

In his discussion of the Steen pastiche Cunningham begins by mentioning Sir Joshua's well-known opinion of Steen: that he had a sense of design comparable to that of Raphael, that he had the greatest skill in composition and the management of light and shade, and that he showed great truth in the expression and character of his figures. So a leading authority thought well of the painter. Cunningham goes on to describe the picture in language which shows a fine appreciation of its qualities. He notes that the scene is full of character and drama and that it is comparable to certain paintings by Hogarth and the contemporary work of David Wilkie. Here it is important to note that Wilkie was seen in the Regency period as the legitimate heir of the Dutch genre tradition and as noted earlier, that there was a great vogue among the English aristocracy of the day for collecting Dutch pictures. In short, there was an ample weight of critical opinion which legitimized the use of Dutch models by any painter who wanted to do so. In fact, it can be argued that it would have been logical for any painter in the first half of the nineteenth century to turn to the Dutch for inspiration in the treatment of genre subjects. It has been shown that Gustave Courbet drew much of the composition for *The Burial at Ornans* from a group portrait by van der Helst.[58]

Let us now turn to the political pictures of George Caleb Bingham. With a background of politics and travel, and with a rapidly growing reputation, he set to work on *The County Election* at his studio in Columbia, Missouri, in May 1851. What were the models for his pictorial design? On this point there has been much speculation. Arthur Pope was the first modern writer to point out that Bingham must have learned a great deal from engravings after Renaissance and Baroque masters. He saw in Bingham's pictures a consistent use of compositional schemes acquired from earlier sources. In *The County Election* he observed that an architectural screen at one side was used as a frame for the main action. The remainder of the picture was left open for background, as with the painters of the seventeenth century such as Poussin and Claude. Maurice Bloch, however, holds that, for his general arrangement and descriptive details, Bingham turned to an engraving in reverse of Hogarth's *Canvassing for Votes* and possibly also to David Wilkie's *Chelsea Pensioners Receiving the News of The Battle of Waterloo*, painted in 1822 and much engraved thereafter (Figs. 9.21 and 9.22).

Fig. 9.21. William Hogarth. Canvassing for Votes, 1757. *Engraving. Sixth State. Courtesy Yale University.*

Fig. 9.22. *Sir David Wilkie*. Chelsea Pensioners Receiving the News of Waterloo, *n.d. Oil on canvas, 36½" × 60½". Courtesy Apsley House, London.*

The basic compositional device of *The County Election* is a series of interlocking pyramids. Now this scheme was not at all new. It is common among Renaissance masters; Bingham had used a very large number of pyramids in his river pictures, as he had used figures based on antique statues such as the *Apollo Belvedere*. But the pyramids in the political pictures have a distinction not found in any Raphaelesque models: *They have active figures at the top.* Here it is the clerk who is accepting the paper ballot from the voter. In *Stump Speaking* it is the politician, with his arm flung forward, pleading for votes. In *The Election Returns* it is the crier announcing the results to the crowd. These three figures are in no way Raphaelesque. And the pictorial design itself is not derived from a Renaissance model. Raphael, it is sometimes said, is a master of great designs in which nothing happens. *The School of Athens* is perhaps the best known example.

In the Bingham pictures a great deal is happening. The whole unruly process of a Missouri election is going on. And Missouri, as Page Smith has written "displayed a remarkable capacity for resisting civilizing influences. It remained for decades the model of a raw, crude frontier state."[60] He adds that the frontier was as surely in Missouri in the 1840s as it had been in western Pennsylvania at the turn of the century, and as it would be in Dodge City and Leadville a generation later. Americans were engaged in "a war against a wild and intractable continent, against hunger and disease, against Indians, against a chaotic economy."[61] Small wonder, then, that they were a violent people, a nation given to mob violence, personal violence, and violent crime. And small wonder that the restrained and ordered pictorial design of the high Renaissance was not a suitable framework for portraying the conduct of their political affairs. It should, in fact, be pointed out that Bingham had tried a Raphaelesque design in an early (1847) version of *Stump Speaking* and found it deficient. There was no reason to believe that, five years later, it would work any better in solving the complex problem which he had set for himself.

That some kind of forceful organizing scheme was required is clear if one studies the charming but primitive *Election Scene, State House, Philadelphia* of 1815 by John Lewis Krimmel (Fig. 9.23). It was a popular painting and probably known to Bingham. And he may very well have known both Wilkie's *Waterloo Dispatch* and Hogarth's

I should like to argue that the Dutch tradition is a more plausible source and that Bingham probably encountered it in the New York shop of Goupil during the winter of 1850–1851. I want to stress that it does not matter whether the contact was with etchings by Ostade or Dusart, a pastiche after Steen, or a mezzotint by Bylaert after Van Goyen. What matters is that the Dutch had worked out a convention, or idiom, for the depiction of this kind of scene and that it was beautifully adapted to the purposes of Bingham. Bloch himself has pointed out that the figure of the clerk shaping his quill at the upper right of the picture has a startling resemblance to a figure in an engraving after a painting by Frans Van Mieris. I am simply suggesting that the entire picture is more "Dutch" than had previously been realized.[59]

Election Series, but these would not have presented him with organizing concepts as strong as those in the *Quack Doctor* tradition. It is not surprising that late in life he specifically mentioned Rembrandt, Teniers, and Ostade.

An additional argument in favor of a Dutch derivation for the political pictures lies in the character of the actors in the political process. These personages are rough, hard-featured, and weather-beaten. They bring to mind a recent description of the people from whom Abraham Lincoln came. Lincoln's friends and neighbors, say William and Bruce Catton, were rough-mannered, generous, patriotic and narrowly provincial, superstitious and ignorant, yet often eager for education, hard-drinking and boisterously violent—yet God-fearing, democratic, and gregarious. They were individualists. Their humor was bawdy. Their liquor was hard. Their religion was deeply emotional.[62] If one studies the political paintings at any length, he will feel that he is looking at a crowd of men (there is only one group of women) with exactly these characteristics. And if one looks at any quantity of seventeenth-century Dutch peasant pictures, he will feel that he is seeing a world with very much these same characteristics. That world is a rough place. About the farmers, innkeepers, and merry families of Ostade and Steen one could use almost the same adjectives which were used to describe Lincoln's neighbors. There is, to be sure, this difference: The people in a Dutch genre picture do not enter into the political process. *That* was controlled by the "grande bourgeoisie" of Hals and Rembrandt, and, interestingly, it could be as violent as it was in mid-nineteenth-century America. A mob tore the great political leader Jan De Witt to pieces in the streets of Rotterdam. Life in the seventeenth-century Netherlands was rarely as tranquil as a landscape by Cuyp or Ruysdael.

An additional similarity between Bingham and Steen is in their common use of a gallery of types. It is well known that Bingham constructed his paintings with extreme care from a large series of magnificent charcoal drawings. The models for these were, generally speaking, his friends, neighbors, and in all probability, the boatmen he observed on the river. Thus a number of personages whom he recorded in his work on the lost *Stump Orator* appear in later canvases. In the same way Jan Steen has a cast of characters who populate his *Merry Company* pictures: a variety of jovial tipplers and their wives

Fig. 9.23. John Lewis Krimmel. Election Scene, State House, Philadelphia, 1815. Oil on canvas, 16⅜" × 25⅝". The Henry Francis duPont Winterthur Museum of Art.

or mistresses, musicians, and often lurking in the background, the sinister charlatan. One would very much like to have a reproduction of Steen's *The Holy Roman Emperor Toasting his Subjects* which appeared in the Pennsylvania Academy Exhibitions in 1853. Was it a lost work of that master? Was it another pastiche? Bingham could have seen it, and it might have been influential.

With *Stump Speaking* of 1853–1854, the resemblance to the Dutch quack doctor tradition is strongest. The basic pyramid has been moved to the viewer's left with the agitated speaker at the apex. We are fortunate in having Bingham's own description of the painting written at a time when it was well under way:

The gathering of the sovereigns is much larger than I had counted upon. A new head is continually popping up and demanding a place in the crowd, and as I am a thorough democrat, it gives me pleasure to accommodate them all. The consequence of this impertinence on one side and indulgence on the other, is, that instead of the select company which my plan at first embraced, I have an audience that would be no discredit to the most populous precinct of Buncomb.

I have located the assemblage in the vicinity of a mill, (Kit Bullards perhaps) the cider barrel being already appropriated in the Election, I have placed in lieu thereof, but in the background, a water mellon waggon [sic] over which a *darkie*, of course presides. This waggon [sic] and the group in and around, looming up in shadow, and relieved by the clear sky beyond, forms quite a conspicious [sic] feature in the composition, without detracting in the slightest degree from the interest inspired by the principal group in front. In my orator I have endeavored to personify a wiry politician, grown gray in the pursuit of office and the service of his party. His influence upon the crowd is quite manifest, but I have placed behind him a shrewd clear headed opponent, who is busy taking notes, and who will, when his turn comes, make sophisms fly like cobwebs before the housekeepers broom.[63]

Bloch is undoubtedly correct in claiming that the artist had originally conceived the picture in fairly simple terms and that it grew "as Bingham was swept along by his seemingly ever increasing delight with its dramatic possibilities."[64] What he fails to note is that it is the very structure of the pictorial framework, deriving from the Dutch convention, which makes possible the inclusion of so many figures in various poses. It was a framework which accommodated both liberty and order, qualities which were at the very center of Bingham's iconographical scheme. Bloch has noted the advance in the artist's control "over the varying technical problems involved in the painting of a multiple figure subject of this kind."[65] Bingham, of course, nowhere states that this advance came from a study of Dutch "charlatan" engravings—but neither did he state that he had been looking at a print of *The Death of Ananias* before painting *The County Election*.

The last of the series, *The Verdict of the People*, is the most complex and probably the finest. The pyramid is again at the left of the picture. It is braced by a negro pushing a wheelbarrow in the direction of a figure, probably a drunk, who bears a startling re-

semblance to the *Dying Gaul* of antiquity. The site is the steps of a public building with classical columns, perhaps a courthouse. At the foot of the major pyramid is a small group of men tallying the results. One of these resembles the note taker in *The County Election* and may be Bingham himself. At the upper right a few well dressed ladies, the only women in the Election Series, are watching the spectacle.

It seems not to have been generally noticed that the entire setting is much more urban than in the other pictures. It might be St. Louis, which, in the 1840s, had a population of about seventy thousand people. The deep space is taken up with a crowded street lined with more neoclassic buildings. Overhead flies an American flag, an obvious symbol of nationalism. The inscription on the banner hanging from the balcony is an additional clue. The first two lines read "Freedom for" and the last word ends in "as". Barbara Groseclose has pointed out, that in all probability the slogan would be "Freedom for Kansas," the great issue of 1854, which had come into being because of the Kansas-Nebraska bill, a measure which played a major role in the destruction of the Whig party.[66] Like the Dutch genre painters of the seventeenth century, Bingham often incorporated a comment, frequently ironic, into such inscriptions. Thus the young man in *The Country Politicians* (Fig. 9.6) is gazing at an announcement of "Mabie's Circus." Politics, said Bingham, and the circus, are intimately related.

Bloch has noted that this canvas is very close in design to William Sydney Mount's *Long Story*, of 1838, but has not commented on the inscription. As in the first two pictures, the most remarkable aspect of Bingham's pictorial design in *The Verdict of the People* is its ability to accommodate a large number of figures in a variety of attitudes: serious political workers, drunks, celebrants of all kinds, and children of various ages and descriptions. It is a pageant—like a Dutch Kermesse. And as a pageant it is immensely more sophisticated in meaning and design than Leutze's contemporary *Washington Crossing the Delaware*.

If such a painting is to hold together visually, it must, as the Dutch artists realized long ago, present a balance between *liberty* and *order*. The participants must be shown listening to and accepting *or* rejecting the performance of the charlatan/mountebank/quack doctor/dentist. The design must, by its very nature, accommodate polar

179

opposites. This is the classic problem of American political history. It is perhaps most elegantly stated in *The Federalist Papers* and as I have tried to show, it was very much in the minds of thinking persons in Bingham's day. By the early 1850s when these pictures were painted, the system, which had been so nicely designed by the Founding Fathers, was falling apart. All kinds of people were conscious of what was happening, none more so that the southern Whigs, who had to watch their party dissolving during the debates on the Kansas-Nebraska bill. The complex and superbly ordered structure of the Election Series can, then, be understood as a cry for orderly process in the political life of the country from a perceptive observer who saw that process disappearing. It is no wonder that the pyramids are flying apart at the top.

Imagery and Precedent

I have contended that the historical context and the formal design of the Election Series were more complex than the critics of Bingham's day and those of the twentieth century have generally admitted. These pictures are not glorifications of Jacksonian democracy. They are meditations on the weaknesses of the American political system by a man who knew its defects extremely well. If this contention is correct, the symbolic content of the paintings should be in consonance with the tension between liberty and order in the formal design. In fact it is very much in keeping.

We should first note that in the 1850s not all writers saw the paintings as celebrations of the democratic process. Marshall Davidson noted that at least one angry reporter said that Bingham's *County Election* was a slanderous commentary on the democratic process. This writer remarked that in some small precincts such disgraceful proceedings might occur but that they were a discredit to the national image. He found fault with the entire theory of judges, clerks, and voters, who were a disgrace to any self-respecting community. And he singled out the tipplers for special reproach.[67] This gentleman, however, was in a distinct minority. Most of the critics seem to have accepted the depiction simply as truthful. It was democracy "warts and all," and they were proud of it. The popularity of the engravings for the American Art Union certainly argues for a wide acceptance.

In our own day the election series has attracted much thoughtful consideration. In 1970 James Westervelt pointed out that *The County Election* was susceptible to an unflattering interpretation. More recently Barbara S. Groseclose has convincingly connected the Election Series to the intricacies of Missouri politics in the 1840s, citing Bingham's involvement in the complicated Bentonite and anti-Bentonite factionalism in the state. She is unquestionably correct in her argument that each picture has a reference to a specific episode or place as with Kit Bullard's cider mills in *Stump Speaking*. Professor Groseclose is also correct in connecting the pictures to the Compromise of 1850, the Kansas-Nebraska bill, and Missouri's tragic involvement in the fighting along the Kansas border prior to the outbreak of the Civil War. And she has seen that the three large paintings, and the two smaller works which accompany them, can be taken as a series of digs at both parties. I go farther than she does in believing that the pictorial structure of the works and their iconography are, in fact, visual evidence of Bingham's perceptions of the weaknesses in the entire American political system. In this respect I am extending a line of analysis which has already been staked out.[68]

Page Smith is another historian who has noticed that behind Bingham's great canvases, one senses "the profound ambivalence of the artist."[69] Most certainly Bingham was ambivalent toward politics. On the one hand he relished the drama of the political spectacle. He was a good speaker himself, evidently enjoyed campaigning, and was at least quite open to the possibility of running for governor of Missouri in 1848. On the other hand, he hated the griminess of his recount against Sappington, and his analysis of the Kansas-Nebraska bill filled him with foreboding for the future of the Union. It is precisely this ambivalence which led him to create a series of political pictures uncommonly rich in symbols. The employment of these devices was undoubtedly both conscious and unconscious. They have a basis in actuality and in imagination, and this is what gives them their power.

Architecture is among Bingham's most powerful means of communication. It functions as pictorial structure and as symbol. *The County Election* takes place on the steps of a classically designed public building, probably a courthouse. Since the 1830s and 1840s were the heyday of the Classic Revival in mid-America, there would have been many such structures in the Missouri which Bingham knew.

The building anchors the scene in reality. But it is also an evocation of the period of the Founding Fathers, when public affairs had been managed, in the Whig view, with intelligence and sobriety. Hamilton, Madison, and Jay had, after all, signed their contributions to *The Federalist Papers* as "Publius," and the veterans of Washington's army organized themselves as the Society of the Cincinnati. By the early 1850s the Whigs were looking back on the late eighteenth century as a golden age of republican virtue. Of course they looked at it as through an enchanted glass, ignoring the intrigues in Washington's cabinet. These did not matter. The conduct of affairs in the 1790s looked good alongside of the politicking which went into the Fugitive Slave Law and, a bit later, the Kansas-Nebraska bill. With Bingham the architecture is an extremely incongruous setting for a rowdy and drunken political process featuring a hard-bitten cast of characters. Are these, the painter seems to say, the descendants of the voters who elected Washington, Adams, and Jefferson?

Barbara Groseclose properly points out that the battered figure at the right, probably a victim of violence, and the political worker hauling a drunk to the polls, are mockeries of the inscription on the banner. The same is true of the figure tossing a coin. He is placed under the voter giving his oath. There are two possible explanations of this juxtaposition, neither of them flattering to the democratic process: Voting is equated with the chance flip of a coin, or even more devastating, money may have purchased the vote. The scene underneath the columns and portico is thus charged with an ironic meaning.

The trees in the deep space at the left of the picture are essential verticals to complete the design. But they are also, in all probability, Lombardy poplars, a species which the painter would have identified with Italy and the classic world: another symbolic evocation of order in a picture of a disorderly process. And what of the horseman, galloping off in the distance? Is he meant to connect this scene with some episode in the republican past? He remains enigmatic. Finally there is the inscription on the banner. It reads "The Will of the People: the Supreme Law of the Land." This could well be another irony. The whole picture could then be interpreted as a Whig (or Ciceronian) lament. O Tempera! O Mores! Such a "county election" as this hardly bodes well for the future of the republic.[70]

With *Stump Speaking* the most important symbolism is certainly the transformation of the charlatan (or quack) into the politician at the apex of the pyramid. This, of course, was something which would have been known only to the painter himself—a private joke—but it is perfectly in keeping with the interpretation of the earlier painting. Bingham's own comment on the speaker is suggestive. He is "a wiry politician, grown gray in the pursuit of office and the service of the party." This is not flattering language. Note should also be taken of the barn, which is the architectural backdrop for the scene. It is very much a Low Country structure, particularly close to the example in Ostade's etching of *The Village Fair*. There were plenty of such barns built by the German settlers around Booneville, so the type would have been familiar to Bingham. But it may also be a reference to the source he had used. Finally, there is the pervasive boredom which afflicts so many of the listeners, with the notable exception of the gentleman in the white suit and the top hat, who bears such a startling resemblance to Abraham Lincoln. He could be a representative Whig. Bingham may be saying that if politics becomes boring, we are lost. Hence *The Gathering of the Sovereigns* could be an ironic title.

In *The Election Returns* the political process is once more taking place on the portico of a classically designed building. The street which recedes into the background of the picture also features three buildings designed in the style of the Classic Revival. As in *The County Election*, at an important moment in the electoral process most of the people in the picture are enjoying a kind of carnival rather than attending to serious business. A man with a wheelbarrow, a traditional symbol of drunkenness, has come to haul away one of the participants. Another is cutting himself a piece of watermelon. He is oblivious to the announcement from the platform. A few individuals are paying close attention to the proceedings. The most attentive is the tally-keeper at the base of the pyramid in the center of the painting. Like the note taker in *Stump Speaking* this may be Bingham himself.

In reviewing the entire Election Series we should note that the pre–Civil War period was, for all American artists, an age of symbols. Emerson's "Flower in the Crannied Wall" is a familiar example in the field of literature, and the fiction of Nathaniel Hawthorne is extraordinarily rich in symbols to such an extent that novels like *The Scarlet Letter* and *The House of Seven Gables* reach the level of allegory. And

181

the symbolic content of Herman Melville's *Moby Dick* is so rich as to be inexhaustible.

Critics have been uncovering the complexities of this literature since the time of the Second World War. (In my mind F. O. Matthiessen's *American Renaissance* of 1941 is a landmark.) Only in the last two decades or so have the art historians approached the work of the painters with an intensity equal to that of their literary brethren. The results have been impressive. Professor David Huntington has convincingly demonstrated that Frederick Church dealt with the grand American theme of manifest destiny and more recently that his painting also had connections with the liberal Calvinism of Horace Bushnell. Professor Barbara Novak has connected the luminist treatment of light with Emersonian transcendentalism. In the Maine paintings of Fitzhugh Lane and Martin Heade, and in various other painters of the Luminist School, we have a pictorial manifestation of the Emersonian oversoul. So it is developing that American painting at midcentury *did* have an iconography, and it is not surprising to find that the Election Series is extremely rich in this regard.[71]

In turning to Dutch art, with its strong tradition of symbolic representation and its powerful convention for the depiction of charlatans, Bingham was doing nothing very unusual. Many of his contemporaries were thinking along similar lines. As long ago as 1940, John I. H. Baur noted that there were strong resemblances between the painting of Raphaelle Peale and the works of the early Dutch Still Life School. In the kind of comparison that can be made almost at random, let us study briefly a still life *Fruits and Flowers* by an unknown Flemish painter of the early seventeenth century (Fig. 9.24), and *Still Life with Oranges* by Raphaelle Peale (Fig. 9.25) of about 1818. In both fruit is mixed with leaves which overflow the containers. In both it is arranged with studied carelessness. In both the edge of the table forms the conventional dark band across the bottom of the picture. In both the general illumination is dark and there is pronounced modeling of form. The setting is a table against a bare wall with a suitable shading from light to dark, reminiscent of the natural lighting of Dutch interiors. The shape of the bowl in the American picture may actually be a delicate tribute to a Dutch source. It is hard to avoid the conclusion that Peale saw something like this still life in the Stier collection or perhaps in the house of Robert Gilmor, Jr. Samuel Green, a

later student of the Dutch-American connection, correctly pointed out that painters like Peale generally simplified the elaborate Dutch compositions into an elegant formula of purity and unpretentiousness in the objects, combined with simplicity of design and clarity of color. The American Still Life School thereby achieved the same kind of transformation of a European convention that we find in Bingham's conversion of a seventeenth-century charlatan into a Missouri politician.[72]

Fig. 9.24. Unknown Flemish painter (School of Jacobvan Hasdonck, active 1615–1638). Fruits and Flowers. Oil on panel, 19″ × 25″. The Fine Arts Museum of San Francisco.

oped the specialty of marine painting as never before in European history. As in still life and genre, the Dutch excelled, and as in these other fields, they created a certain number of conventions. Of these the most important for the pre–Civil War American painters were, as Barbara Novak has noted, the open lateral edge and the straight horizon line. The Dutch used these conventions in depictions of ships and harbors, which became a favorite luminist theme. They are well seen in Jan Van de Capelle, *Shipping off the Coast* (after 1651) (Fig. 9.26). We find a similar approach in Fitzhugh Lane's *Salem Harbor* (1853) (Fig. 9.27). This is not to say that there are not great differences between the two pictures. To mention only the most obvious, Lane's picture is much more dependent on a strict geometric spatial construction than Van de Capelle's. And the treatment of light is entirely different with Lane; it is much more the major theme of the picture. Still, it is not surprising to learn that Lane knew the Dutch tradition. As Professor Novak observes, Dutch art was appreciated by artists and by many people who were not very vocal.[73]

Fig. 9.25. Raphaelle Peale. Still Life with Oranges, *ca. 1818. Oil on panel, 18⅝" × 22¹⁵⁄₁₆". Toledo Museum of Art.*

Fig. 9.26. Jan Van de Cappelle. Shipping off the Coast, *after 1651. Oil on canvas, 28¼" × 33⅛". Gift of Edwin Drummond Libby, Toledo Museum of Art.*

In marine painting, another field in which the Dutch excelled and which rapidly became important for Americans, there is also a close relationship. Here we can note another similarity between the seventeenth-century Dutchman and the nineteenth-century American: a fascination with the maritime frontier. For the citizen of the Dutch Republic maritime trade was the path to economic success, political security, and personal and national prestige. Marine painting was therefore called upon to make a very special kind of statement about the place of the sea in Dutch culture. A long line of painters, including Jan Van de Capelle, Simon de Vlieger, and Esaias Van de Velde devel-

Fig. 9.27. Fitzhugh Lane. Salem Harbor, 1853. Oil on canvas, 26" × 42". Karolik Collection, Museum of Fine Arts, Boston.

The attraction Dutch marine painting held for Lane and the other luminists can be understood if we conceive of the United States before the Civil War as having two frontiers. The western frontier has received more attention from historians. For people living along the Atlantic Coast, especially in New England, the maritime frontier was equally important. A career as a ship captain was the ambition of thousands of young men all along the seaboard. And it must be noted that the one industrial object in the design of which Americans were universally admitted to excel was the clipper chip. Samuel Eliot Morison conveyed what these magnificent vessels meant to New Englanders in a marvelous lyric passage:

A summer day with a sea-turn in the wind. The Grand Banks fog, rolling in wave after wave, is dissolved by the perfumed breath of New England hayfields into a gentle haze, that turns the State House dome to old gold, films brick walls with a soft patina, and sifts blue shadows among the foliage of the Common elms. Out of the mist in Massachusetts Bay comes riding a clipper ship, with the effortless speed of an albatross. Her proud commander keeps skysails and studdingsails set past Boston light. After the long voyage she is in the pink of condition. Paint-work is spotless, decks holystoned cream-white, shrouds freshly tarred, ratlines square. Viewed through a powerful glass, her seizings, flemish-eyes, splices, and apointings are the perfection of the old-time art of rigging. The chafing-gear has just been removed, leaving spars and shrouds immaculate. The boys touched up her skysail poles with white paint, as she crossed the Bay. Boom-ending her studdingsails and hauling a few points on the wind to shoot the Narrows, between Georges and Gallups and Lovells Islands, she pays off again through President Road, and comes boming up the stream, a sight so beautiful that even the lounging soldiers at the Castle, persistent baiters of passing crews, are dumb with wonder and admiration.

Colored pennants on Telegraph Hill have announced her coming to all who know the code. Topliff's News Room breaks into a buzz of conversation, comparing records and guessing at freight money; owners and agents walk briskly down State Street; countingroom clerks hang out of windows to watch her strike skysails and royals; the crimps and hussies of Ann Street foregather, to offer Jack a few days' scabrous pleasure before selling him to a new master. By the time the ship has reached the inner harbor, thousands of critical eyes are watching her every movement, quick to note if in any respect the mate has failed to make sailor-men out of her crew of broken Argonauts, beach-combers, Kanakas, and Lascars.

The "old man" stalks the quarterdeck in top hat and frock coat, with the proper air of detachment; but the first mate is as busy as the devil in a gale of wind. Off India Wharf the ship rounds into the wind with a graceful curve, crew leaping into the rigging to full topgallant sails as if shot upward by the blast of profanity from the mate's bull-like throat. With backed topsails her way is checked, and the cable rattles out of the chain lockers for the first time since Shanghai, sails are clewed up. Yards are braced to a perfect parallel, and running gear neatly coiled down. A warp is passed from capstan to stringer, and all hands on the capstan-bars walk her up to the wharf with the closing chantey of a deep sea voyage.[74]

Aside from the superb poetry of these lines, the most significant feature of the passage is the attention called to the meaning of the ship for the entire community. It is not too much to conceive of Boston Harbor, surrounded by low hills as a theatre in which a drama is played out. It is a drama fundamental to the welfare of the city. The centerpiece is not a building, but a ship. In an earlier passage Morison wrote that for the seafaring New Englander the *Flying Cloud* was Rheims, the *Sovereign of the Seas* the Parthenon, and the *Lightning* Amiens. The comparison is not far fetched. And if we conceive of the pre–Civil War period as a golden age of sail, the reason that people desired ship pictures is perfectly clear. They wanted images of the instruments which had brought them prosperity and fame. It is thus not surprising that the United States produced an important school of marine painting. It would, indeed, have been surprising if it had not. And it is not surprising that the painters looked hard at seascapes from the Netherlands, a country with a magnificent tradition in this field of art.

In genre painting (and the Election Series might be so classified) the relationship is likewise strong but more difficult to elucidate. We know that Washington Allston counselled William Sidney Mount, greatest genre painter of the age, to study the Dutch "little masters." We know that examples of prints, and perhaps originals, by Ostade, Metsu, Dou, and a variety of others were undoubtedly available to Mount, who, like Bingham, was interested in politics (he was active in the Democratic party on Long Island), and that he made visits to New York, Philadelphia, and Baltimore. We can be sure that he had access to the same print shops as Bingham. We know that Mount often came close to the moralizing and social comment of the Dutch seventeenth-century genre painters.

Thus a picture like *Walking the Line* (1835) (Fig. 9.28) seems somehow to relate to pictures on similar themes by men like Adrian van Ostade, whose *Villagers Merrymaking at an Inn* of 1652 (Fig. 9.29) is typical of hundreds of Dutch seventeenth-century works. Both pictures show dimly lit tavern interiors and have an overall brownish

tonality. Both pictures show people in various stages of intoxication, and there is a good deal of merriment in both. One of Ostade's dancing figures might have served as a model for Mount's drunkard who must walk the line. Both pictures are seemingly casual in their pictorial design, but in fact are very carefully organized. In both paintings a foreground area composes neatly into a still life. We sense that there is something very "Dutch" about *Walking the Line* and have the same feeling about many other pictures by Mount, particularly the early work.[75] There is an affinity but we are unable to say exactly what it is. The problem of the relationship between Dutch seventeenth-century art and American painting in the years 1830–1860 provides us with an excellent opportunity to clarify the concepts of "affinity" and "influence" and to understand the role of each in Bingham's political series.[76]

Fig. 9.28. William Sidney Mount. Walking the Line, 1835. Oil on canvas, 22¼″ × 27⅜″. William Owen and Erna Sawyer Goodman Collection, The Art Institute of Chicago.

Fig. 9.29. Adrian van Ostade. Villagers Merrymaking at an Inn, *1652. Oil on panel, 16¾" × 21⅞". Toledo Museum of Art.*

Webster defines affinity as "sympathy, especially as marked by community of interest." The history of art and architecture is filled with examples of affinity. An artist, or a group of artists, removed in time and space, face similar problems. Very often this feeling is shared by other individuals in the culture. Thus, the artists were not the only people in pre–Civil War America who admired the Dutch. As we have seen, their respect for Dutch culture was shared by politicians like Seward and literary men like Motley. Painting was the art in which the Dutch were generally admitted to have excelled. In their explorations of marine painting, still life, and genre, the Dutch had developed

certain valuable conventions. There is a great distance in space and time, but we recognize a spiritual kinship.

"Influence" is something more precise. Webster defines it as "the power of persons or things to affect others seen only in its effects." One whole branch of the history of art is built on this concept, and its meaning is clear enough. An artist sees a picture, a graphic work, or perhaps a photograph, likes something about it, appropriates that something, and uses it for his own purposes, which may or may not resemble those of its creator. Thus Courbet's *Burial at Ornans* has very little resemblance in imagery or purpose to the *Group Portrait* of Van der Helst, but the composition of the older picture obviously pleased Courbet and he used it as a basis for his own pictorial design. In the same way Frank Lloyd Wright looked on traditional Japanese architecture, which he knew through prints and in an actual building at the Chicago Fair of 1893, and found it good. Although the houses he was building for midwestern clients around the turn of the century have nothing in common with houses of the Edo period in terms of building technology or program, there is an undeniable Japanese influence. Art historians who specialize in tracing influence are in reality answering the question: Where does art come from? The traditional Germanic answer is: Art comes from other art. This answer is all very well as far as it goes, but it is insufficient to deal with the problem of affinity, which, for the artist, generally comes before influence.

Affinity, I want to suggest, has its roots in social, economic, and perhaps political conditions. Confronted by a particular set of conditions, an artist, or a group of artists will, consciously or subconsciously, search the past to discover an artist, or a group of artists, who faced a similar situation. And then they may attack their own problems in a similar manner. Thus the German expressionists were confronted by the socially, politically, and spiritually oppressive Wilhelmian empire. They reacted by seeking, within their own tradition, a group of artists whose qualities seemed to reflect attitudes similar to their own. They found such a group in Altdorfer, Schongauer, and Grunewald, who had lived through the strange world of late medieval Catholicism. The spiritual foundations of that world were crumbling, and this was a feeling that the twentieth-century expressionists knew only too well. It is no wonder that they felt an affinity.

Consider for a moment, then, the cultural situations of painters in the generation of Bingham and the reasons they had for finding an affinity with seventeenth-century Dutch art. In contemporary terms, both the seventeenth-century Netherlands and nineteenth-century America were modernizing societies. That is to say, they were societies in which technology was advancing rapidly and its applications were widespread. In these conditions there is a great need for skilled and orderly labor. As we have noted earlier, both nations were Protestant trading republics, and the Dutch had an excellent reputation in American eyes. The American republic had a policy of continental expansionism. The Dutch republic had expanded overseas. For both nations a maritime frontier was of enormous importance, and marine painting was called upon to make statements of basic significance.

Perhaps most important of all, much of Dutch seventeenth-century painting, and particularly genre painting, was a response to a demand for an acceptable art by a new bourgeoisie which had replaced a feudal aristocracy. This new painting was "Tot Lering en Vermaak"—for entertainment and instruction. In the United States a new bourgeoisie replaced the old Federalist governing class gradually in the 1820s and 1830s. And, like their predecessors in the seventeenth-century Netherlands, they wanted an art which would represent them and dignify their activities. Hence the popularity of genre painting, a specialty with both Mount and Bingham. There was a real basis for both influence and affinity. I have argued that the conventions developed by the Dutch for their charlatan paintings were an actual influence on Bingham.

It remains to consider the place of the Election Series in Bingham's total oeuvre. The pictures are at the center of his work, and they are the most ambitious canvases he ever attempted. Into them went all the thought and feeling he possessed. They are unique, and their very uniqueness means that they differ in certain important respects from other very fine work by Bingham. His great period began in 1845 with *Fur Traders Descending the Missouri*. Until 1856, when he went abroad, he was extremely successful with pictures on river themes, and critics have generally ranked those works as close to the Election Series in quality. There is no reason to dispute this conventional wisdom. The river pictures are magnificent and there is nothing Dutch about them. The skies could never be anywhere except the western United States. The compositions are often derived from

Renaissance prototypes. The flatboatmen frequently are posed with reference to bits of antique statuary.

Bingham was, in fact, an extremely knowledgeable artist who moved in several different directions. His portraits owe something to Thomas Sully and perhaps to Chester Harding. In his landscapes he sought, without a great deal of success, to emulate Thomas Cole and Frederick Church. His great achievements were in the Election Series and the river pictures, subjects which grew directly out of his own life experience. It might be argued that Bingham was an excellent painter when he dealt with politics or stayed close to the river. In his later work, after his return from Dusseldorf, he was never again so strong. He may well belong to that category of artists, like Nathaniel Hawthorne, who were "broken" by the Civil War.

There is, in fact, a wonderful analogy to Bingham's work in the writings of Mark Twain, whose best work dealt with life on the great western rivers during his boyhood in the 1840s and 1850s. This is the same time period shown in the great river pictures of Bingham.

Central to Twain's literary achievements is *Huck Finn*. It used to be thought that this book was an idyll of the writer's boyhood on the Mississippi before the Civil War. Today the novel is seen in a very different light. Huck's drunken father is really a sinister and terrifying personage. The feud between the Grangerfords and the Shepherdsons is a ghastly business. The commentary on slavery is bitter, and the tone of the whole book is distinctly anti-institutional. It ends with Huck pondering an escape from "civilization." The literature on *Huck Finn* is by now immense, and I have no desire to review it here. But it is clear that Twain wrote a book which, like Bingham's Election Series, can be taken on several levels whether he intended to do so or not—and there is controversy on this point, too.

In literature the problem of the symbolic interpretation of the work of art is clear in the correspondence between Ernest Hemingway and Bernard Berenson in regard to *The Old Man and The Sea*. Hemingway obviously thought a great deal of Berenson and valued his opinions highly. On September 13 1952, he wrote:

> Is it all right to talk about Moby Dick as though we were talking? It always seemed to me two things: journalism (good) and forced rhetorical epic. Thought you could take the ocean, not as

some malignant force, but as the ocean: la puta mar that we have loved and that has clapped us all and poxed us too. We always call her la puta mar and I suppose you can't love a whore but you can be very fond of her and know her well and keep on going around with her.

Then there is the other secret. There isn't any symbolysm [sic]. The sea is the sea. The old man is an old man. The boy is a boy and the fish is a fish. The sharks are all sharks no better and no worse. All the symbolism that people say is shit. What goes beyond is what you see beyond when you know. A writer should know too much.

Hemingway went on to ask Berenson for a few sentences which might be used in a publisher's release. Berenson responded:

An idyll of the sea as sea, as un-Byronic and un-Melvillian as Homer himself, and communicated in a prose as calm and compelling as Homer's verse. No real artist symbolizes or allegorizes—and Hemingway is a real artist—but every real work of art exhales symbols and allegories. So does this short but not small masterpiece.[77]

This exchange throws light on the problem of the Election Series. In Berenson's terms Bingham was a real artist, and it is unlikely that he set out to symbolize or allegorize in these pictures. But precisely because he was so intimately involved in the political turmoil of the 1850s, he could not avoid doing so. To understand the paintings as simple celebrations of American democracy is a vast oversimplification. Bingham knew so much about the tensions which threatened that democracy that he unavoidably selected a pictorial design and an iconographical tradition which were in consonance with his subject. The Election Series is indeed a high point of American painting, and, along with Stuart's *Washington* and French's *Minuteman* it ought to be illustrated in all the textbooks. But it is not an icon of democratic virtue. It is a foreshadowing of the Civil War.

One of the pleasures of scholarship is the acknowledgement of the debts which have been incurred during the process of investigation. In this work my first obligation is to the Netherlands America Commission for Educational Exchange, which awarded me a Senior Fulbright Research Fellowship to the Netherlands in 1981. In that country I enjoyed the hospitality of the Art Historical Institute of the University of Utrecht, and I wish particularly to mention the help I received from Professor Eddie DeJongh. Professor Pieter Singelenberg of the University of Nijmegen was also extremely encouraging. The staff of the print room at the Rijksmuseum in Amsterdam was invariably helpful; they will find several illustrations of their holdings in this book.

My obligation to the H. H. Rackham Graduate School of the University of Michigan is twofold. A Rackham grant made possible a visit to London, where I was able to study the vitally important resources of the print room at the British Museum, the Victoria and Albert, and the Courtauld Institute. A Rackham summer fellowship allowed me the necessary time to prepare the manuscript. A scholar who has this kind of support is indeed fortunate.

The curators of American and European painting in several American museums aided me in this endeavor. I want especially to mention those of the Detroit Art Institute, the Toledo Museum of Art, the Art Institute of Chicago, the De Young Art Museum of San Francisco, and the Boston Museum of Fine Arts. The staffs of all these institutions, and of the print room at the Metropolitan Museum of Art in New York were always both courteous and knowledgeable. Librarians at Michigan and Yale likewise played a vital role in this study.

I also wish to thank the Clark Art Institute of Williamstown, Massachusetts; the Art Department of Tufts University; and the J. B. Speed Art Museum for opportunities to present my material in lecture form and thereby to refine it. Members of the staff of these institutions made numerous excellent suggestions, as did Professor John Coolidge of Harvard University and Professor Will Morgan, of the University of Louisville.

Afterword

As I review these essays, particularly the series on warehouses, I am conscious that the reader may well feel burdened with an excessive amount of detail on the clients. In reply to this charge I can only say that it is almost an inevitable criticism of any writer who sees buildings as the joint production of architects, clients, and craftsmen. In an excellent book on *Architecture, Men, Women, and Money* (1985), Roger Kennedy has recently observed:

> I have imagined myself standing before each work and trying to answer such questions as these: How was the client (individual or community) able to pay for it? Were the building funds acquired in ways that led the client to choose its form for disguise or for celebration? What was the use to which the house was put in the economy? Was it for example, a folly? A reliquary? A rallying-point? A prospectus? A unit of production? Was it just what it seems to be, a shell built around a person or family? Was it a monument to accomplishment or a proclamation of intention?[1]

If one asks these questions about the mid-American warehouses, the answers are reasonably clear. They were built out of the profits of business expansion. There was, as Grace Flandrau noted in St. Paul, nothing dishonorable about the jobbing trade. It was seen as a necessary element in the settlement of the West. The buildings were not follies, reliquaries, or rallying points. They were large containers of goods which had to serve also as proclamations of the success of their builders and as ornaments to the city. In this sense they were, indeed, monuments to accomplishment.

The problem is that this conclusion can only emerge if one studies the careers of the merchants in some depth. Obviously they were a civic-minded lot. It is important that Daniel Noyes was president of the St. Paul Y.M.C.A. and presided over the Winter Carnival. It is important that James McCord was a figure of immense authority among the merchants of St. Joseph. It is important that James H. Ashdown was mayor of Winnipeg. On the corporate side it is important that Oscar Eckerman worked for a company which discovered that he could provide the buildings they needed on tight budgets with a new method of construction. Hence the emphasis on a mass of details which attempt to convey character.

With a few exceptions, notably the Galts and Frederick W. Stobart in Winnipeg, the wholesalers did not have much formal education. Rather, they generally began their careers in somebody else's country store. They rose to positions which enabled them to finance large buildings by virtue of business ability, energy, and integrity. They were in the right place at the right time, and they made the most of their opportunities. Several branched out into manufacturing. Most probably had investments outside their own businesses. They were alert and energetic individuals. While it is an opinion that cannot be supported by any evidence, I would hazard a guess that they would have been at home in the age of the leveraged buy out.

They left almost nothing on record as to their own views about their building activities. Even more than in my book on the early clients of Frank Lloyd Wright and Howard Van Doren Shaw, I felt I was dealing with a series of strong personalities about whom I would have liked to know more. With Wright and Shaw I had the benefit of interviews with a few surviving clients or family and friends who had clear recollections. The great wholesalers have been gone for at least two generations. These studies raise as many questions as they answer. Is there a collection of Ashdown papers with the family in Winnipeg? Ashdown is worthy of a biography, and it ought to include a chapter on his buildings.

It is clear, then, that the jobber wanted first of all a structure which was fire resistant and which would comfortably handle the storage and distribution of his goods. Secondly, it should be a credit to his family and his city. Parallel statements can be made for buildings erected by companies such as Deere, Bemis Bag, and Fairbanks Morse. It was the task of the architect to design an edifice which filled these requirements. Fortunately, I am inclined to think, after H. H. Richardson's Marshall Field Wholesale Store of 1885, everyone in the profession, and some people outside it, had an idea of how a Great Warehouse was arranged and what it ought to look like. Of course there were those who took their cues from Sullivan and Root but the Richardson prototype was most persuasive. So the architects were happily employed and the wholesalers got what they wanted: useful buildings which still have the power to move us today.

So much for a warehouse summary. Finally I should like to record my gratitude to a few individuals who have, perhaps unwittingly, supplied the intellectual background for this work. The first is Lewis Mumford. In 1943 I wrote the second undergraduate honors thesis done on Lewis Mumford in an American university. I have admired him ever since. Mumford, more than any writer of his generation, stressed that environmental design was rooted in the social fabric. Having derived this insight from Ruskin, he carried it much farther and set a wonderful example for the scholars of my generation.

To Lewis Mumford I owe my general approach to the problem of client relationships and patronage. It may be that from Mumford I also derived my interest in the comments of writers, especially novelists, on buildings.

My second obligation is to James Fitch. He is best known as a preservationist, but his writings are a conclusive demonstration that buildings, landscapes, and city plans are not merely designs which may or may not be effective but are also exercises in structural and environmental control. A building may be an extremely beautiful object, but if it fails to deal with problems of structure and climate, it fails as architecture. In my view every architectural historian should ponder Fitch's juxtaposition of the Farnsworth house with and without fly screens in his epochal *American Architecture: The Environmental Forces Which Shape It* (1973). It pleased me greatly that Fitch approved of my environmental analysis of the Case house in Marquette, Michigan.

Alan Gowans is the third individual to whom these essays are indebted. Gowans has analyzed the social function of the visual arts, and in so doing has shown that the traditional methodology of the art historian has to be radically overhauled. Buildings, paintings, and sculptures, he has argued, need to be understood in terms of their social function. They are, among other things, symbols. Of course the approach to architecture and the other visual arts has been articulated elsewhere, notably by the great medievalists, but it is Gowans who has put the case most forcefully in our day. The essay on G. C. Bingham's Election Series would not have been done without his stimulus. And to my students, who have been my teachers, I owe most of all.

Notes

Chapter 1

1. Howard Mumford Jones, *The Age of Energy* (New York, 1970), 65.

2. Graham Hutton, *Midwest at Noon* (Chicago, 1946), 109.

3. Brand Whitlock, *Forty Years of It* (New York, 1914), 66.

4. Henry B. Fuller, *The Cliff-Dwellers* (New York, 1893; Ridgewood, N. J., 1968), 95–96.

5. Robert Herrick, *The Common Lot* (New York, 1904), 400.

6. James L. Woodress, *Booth Tarkington: Gentleman from Indiana* (Philadelphia and New York, 1954), 181.

7. Booth Tarkington, *The Turmoil* (New York, 1914), 4.

8. Sinclair Lewis, *Babbitt* (New York, 1922), 1.

9. Mark Schorer, ed., Sinclair Lewis, "A Minnesota Diary," *Esquire* 50 (October 1958):160–62. Recently Mordecai Richler has written that Winnipeg is a city ". . . utterly without charm," and observed that "the West has yet to develop a distinctive style of architecture." *Home, Sweet Home* (New York, 1985), 76. The literary men need to be educated.

10. Patricia Hampl, *A Romantic Education* (Boston, 1981), 50.

11. Ibid., 220.

12. Carl Jonas, *Riley McCullough* (New York, 1962), 188.

13. Glenn Porter and Harold C. Livesay, *Merchants and Manufacturers: Studies in the Changing Structure of Nineteenth Century Marketing* (Baltimore and London, 1971), 163. See also James Vance, *The Merchants' World: The Geography of Wholesaling* (Englewood Cliffs, N.J., 1970).

14. Russell Sturgis, "The Warehouse and the Factory in Architecture," *The Architectural Record* 15 (1904):1–2.

15. U.S.Congress, House of Representatives, *Report of the Secretary of the Treasury on the Warehousing System*. Executive Document, No. 32, 30th Cong., 2d sess., 1849. Information on Hartley is conveniently available in Quentin Hughes, *Seaport: The Architecture and Townscape of Liverpool* (London, 1964).

16. Theodore O. Sande, "The Textile Factory in Pre–Civil War Rhode Island," *Old Time New England* 66 (1975):19–20.

17. Frank E. Kidder, *The Architect's and Builder's Pocketbook* (New York, 1885), 375.

18. James Marston Fitch, *Architecture and the Aesthetics of Plenty* (New York, 1961), 8.

19. Max Sklovsky, as quoted in Edith Sklovsky Covich, *Max* (Chicago, 1974), 63.

20. Professor James O'Gorman has published the definitive article, "The Marshall Field Wholesale Store: Materials toward a Monograph," *Journal of the Society of Architectural Historians*, 37, no. 3 (October 1978):175–194. On Root see Donald Hoffman, *The Architecture of John Wellborn Root* (Baltimore, 1973).

21. The present system is well described in an article in the *New York Times* of 25 July 1976 entitled, "Life Under the Sign of the Deer." It describes the Deere implement dealership of Butler, Missouri.

22. Certificate of inspection by Green, Blankstein, and Russell, Registered Architects, Winnipeg, 17 Oct. 1945. Letter to the author from Robert Bolt, chief architect, Deere & Company, 24 May 1977.

23. Material on the garment industry in Winnipeg comes from *Winnipeg 1874–1974: Progress and Prospects* (Winnipeg, 1974); Jane Jacobs has written

eloquently on the disruption of the urban fabric in *The Death and Life of Great American Cities* (New York, 1961).

24. *The New York Times*, 11 Sept. 1987. Real Estate section.

25. Ibid.

26. *U.S. News and World Report*, 7 Sept. 1987, 20–27.

Chapter 2

1. *Missouri: A Guide to the Show-Me State* (New York, 1937), 1.

2. Ibid.

3. The literature on Harvey Ellis is by now both extensive and controversial. An entire issue of *The Prairie School Review* (1st and 2d quarters, 1968) was devoted to him; it reprinted the contributions by Claude Bragdon and Hugh Garden, who knew Ellis in his declining years, and featured a long article by Roger Kennedy, who has spent much time trying to track Ellis down. In 1973 the Museum of the University of Rochester held an Ellis show and produced a sizeable catalogue which emphasized the work of Ellis in Rochester.

Dr. Eileen Manning Michaels of St. Paul continues to try to untangle Ellis's activities in the Twin Cities. My own inclination is to accept her contention that there was something like an "Ellis school" in the Midwest during the 1880s and 1890s.

4. This account of Edmond Eckel is based on the following sources: *The Western Architect*, 8 (Sept. 1911); a number of written anecdotes preserved in the offices of Eckel and Aldrich in St. Joseph; interview with Edmond J. Eckel, *St. Joseph Gazette*, 17 May 1931; interviews with Mrs. George Eckel, 19 June 1973.

5. *St. Joseph Times Dispatch*, 24 Sept. 1903.

6. I have dated the building by means of the St. Joseph city directories. The first directory to show the firm in a location on South Third Street is that of 1883.

7. *The Western Architect* 17 (September 1911): 79. The quotation is from an extended account of the work of Edmond Eckel.

8. *Historical and Descriptive Review of St. Joseph* (New York, 1889), 94.

9. Ibid.

10. Ibid., 82.

11. Ibid.

12. Chris L. Rutt, *History of St. Joseph and Buchanan County* (1894), credits the building to Eckel and Mann, so the attribution is clear. No signed drawings have ever been discovered, but they probably exist in the archives of Brunner and Brunner. George Eckel's comment on the weakness of Ellis as a structural designer occurs in a letter to Eileen Manning, quoted in her master's thesis (University of Minnesota, 1955).

13. I have been privileged to examine the original drawings for the bank through the courtesy of Otto Brunner of the firm of Brunner and Brunner, successors to Eckel and Aldrich.

Chapter 3

1. *Minnesota: A State Guide* (New York, 1938), 42–52. The passage from Twain, *Life on the Mississippi*, is quoted on p. 156.

2. Mildred Hartsough, *The Twin Cities as a Metropolitan Market* (Minneapolis, 1925), 113–43. Although more than fifty years old, this study is still valuable for its insights into the economic development of Minneapolis and St. Paul.

3. Theodore C. Blegen, *Minnesota: A History of the State* (Minneapolis, 1963), 282. As late as the 1930s this writer's boyhood was filled with the legend of Jim Hill, who, said my stepfather, let a man know that he was fired by changing the lock on his office door!

4. Albro J. Martin, *James J. Hill and the Opening of the Northwest* (New York, 1976). The book gives an excellent account of the rise of Hill and his impact on St. Paul.

5. Joseph Gilpin Pyle, *The Life of James J. Hill* (New York, 1936), 2:309.

6. Grace Flandrau, *Being Respectable* (New York, 1923), 49–50.

7. William Watts Folwell, *A History of Minnesota* (St. Paul, 1926), 3:480.

8. Ibid., app. 12, 3:479–89.

9. Montgomery Schuyler, "Glimpses of Western Architecture: St. Paul and Minneapolis," in *American Architecture and Other Writings*, eds. Ralph Coe and William Jordy (Cambridge, Mass., 1961), (originally printed in the *Architectural Record*). In 1936 a writer for *Fortune* magazine visited the city and found its downtown cramped, hilly, and stagnant. See "Revolt in the Northwest," *Fortune* 8 (1936):118.

10. For the Lowertown story the best single source is Weiming Lu, *A Report of the Lowertown Redevelopment Corporation* (St. Paul, 1986). On the economic side, see James B. McComb Associates, *Economic Impact of the Lowertown Redevelopment Program* (St. Paul, 1985). Figures are generally dull, but we might mention that in 1985 projects completed and under construction in Lowertown generated approximately $3,900,000 in property taxes. In contrast the figure for 1978 was $852,000. Projects already committed will add another $569,000 in tax revenue by 1990; see *Economic Impact*, 4.

11. For information on the Gotzian Block, and for much else in this chapter, I am indebted to the indefatigable research of Mr. James Sazevich of St. Paul. The city is fortunate to possess an individual so conscious of its architectural heritage.

12. On Daniel Noyes, see the biographical note in C. C. Andrews, *History of St. Paul, Minnesota* (Syracuse, 1890), indexed but unpaged.

13. H. F. Koeper, *Historic St. Paul* (St. Paul, 1964), 64. This little book is the first survey of historic architecture in St. Paul. It has the errors inevitable in a pioneering work but remains invaluable.

14. Murray Wolf, "Discovering Ameritas: Atlanta Firm Tests St. Paul Market," *Minnesota Real Estate Journal*, 30 March 1897, 6.

15. *St. Paul Pioneer Press*, 19 Feb. 1890.

16. Ibid.

17. Henry F. Withey and Elsie Rathburn Withey, *Biographical Dictionary of American Architects (Deceased)*, (Los Angeles, 1956), 326. For illustration of Johnston's work, see *The Western Architect* 3 (December 1904). This is almost a Clarence H. Johnston issue. There is also a discussion in Koeper, *Historic St. Paul*, of Johnston's excellent Laurel Terrace.

18. St. Paul Chamber of Commerce, *Report* (St. Paul, 1900).

19. *Wall Street Journal*, 3 June 1987, 33.

20. Donald A. Bluhm, "St. Paul: City on the Rise," *The Milwaukee Journal*, 16 Sept. 1984. This is a very fair account of the city's development.

Chapter 4

1. Rudyard Kipling, quotation in *A Nebraska Roundup* (Lincoln, 1957), 152.

2. My account of the founding of Omaha is based on *A Comprehensive Program for Historic Preservation in Omaha* (Omaha, 1980), 9–18. This excellent document may be supplemented by *Omaha City Architecture* (Omaha, 1977) and Dorothy Meyer, *Nebraska: A Bicentennial History* (New York, 1977), 53–56.

3. Probably the most objective account of Lincoln's selection process is in Grenville M. Dodge, *How We Built the Union Pacific* (New York, 1910). I have followed it here.

4. J. Sterling Morton, "Speech Delivered at the First Territorial Fair," in *J. Sterling Morton*, ed. James C. Olson (Lincoln, 1942), 52.

5. *Nebraska: A Guide to the Cornhusker State* (New York, 1942), 225.

6. John Gunther, *Inside U.S.A.* (New York, 1947), 255.

7. A fuller account of Durant and his chicanery can be found in Winslow Ames, *Pioneering the Union Pacific* (New York, 1969).

8. Frank M. Blish, *Omaha World Herald*, 1 Jan. 1903.

9. For original research on the Smith Building, and for much other work in Omaha, I am indebted to Ms. Fran Duffy, my research assistant in Omaha.

10. Wright and Wilhelmy, *Centennial Brochure* (Omaha, 1971).

11. Donald Hoffmann, *The Architecture of John Wellborn Root* (Baltimore, 1973), 31–32.

12. *Pen and Ink Sketches of Omaha* (Omaha, 1892).

13. Information on the history of the building is from the nomination to the National Register of Historic Places, 11 Jan. 85. For his kindness in providing me with this material, as well as much else in this essay, I am indebted to Mr. Lynn Meyer of the City Planning Office in Omaha.

14. William C. Edgar, *Judson Moss Bemis, Pioneer* (Minneapolis, 1926), 259.

15. Judith Timberg, "Significance of the Fairbanks-Morse Building to Omaha: History and Architecture" (Unpublished paper, Office of the City Planner,

Omaha, 1980), 14.

16. National Register Nomination, Jobbers Canyon Historic District (Omaha, Nebraska, 1986), Item 8, 7.

Chapter 5

1. W. L. Morton, *Manitoba: A History* (Toronto, 1967), 90. This book has a well-deserved reputation as a classic.

2. The original map is 31½″ × 40½″ in size. The scale is not given in the original but has been computed to be 1″ = 44′ 7″. It was registered by W. G. Fonseca, Lithographer, Ottawa, and a copy is in the Public Archives of Canada.

3. In his excellent *Winnipeg: A Social History of Industrial Growth* (Toronto, 1972) Alan F. Artibise has identified the commercial elite and studied its involvement in politics. Winnipeg is fortunate to have such a historian. I have relied on his work heavily.

4. Grant Hildebrand, *Albert Kahn: Architect to Industry* (Cambridge, Mass., 1974), 86, 218.

5. Charles H. Wheeler to the Hon. James A. Smart, 21 June 1890, Public Archives of Manitoba.

6. *Winnipeg Tribune*, 9 Jan. 1919.

7. F. H. Scholfield, *The Story of Manitoba* 2 vols. (Winnipeg, 1913). Russell's office ledgers are preserved at the Provincial Archives of Manitoba. They show a large number of entries relating to work at Ashdown's warehouse on Bannatyne Street in the years 1899–1910. On the basis of these entries I believe that Russell was Ashdown's architect. Cadham was probably the master builder. Also preserved is Russell's copy of Trautwine's *Civil Engineer's Pocket Book*, which was a favorite with Louis Sullivan.

8. Rupert Brooke, *Letters from America* (London, 1931), 103.

9. *Report of the City of Winnipeg Historical Buildings Committee* (Winnipeg, 1982), 19. This report is mostly the work of Mr. Giles Bugilaiskis of the City of Winnipeg Department of Environmental Planning. I am enormously grateful to him, and to Mr. Steve Barber, formerly of Winnipeg, for sharing the wealth of their knowledge of the warehouse district with me.

10. *The Commercial*, 22 (1903), 202.

11. *Report of the City of Winnipeg Historical Buildings Committee* (Winnipeg, 1984), 23.

12. Ibid.

13. The Bemis Building is discussed in the *Winnipeg Telegram*, 27 Oct. 1906 and the *Manitoba Free Press*, 6 Dec. 1906. For Oscar Eckerman, see Leonard K. Eaton, "Oscar Eckerman: Architect to Deere and Company, 1897–1942," *RACAR–Canadian Art Review* (Saskatoon), no. 11 (1977), 89–99 (reprinted in this volume).

14. For material on Ransome and early concrete construction in the United States, see Carl Condit, *American Building Art: The Nineteenth Century* (New

York, 1960), 231–40.

15. My inspection occurred in Feb. 1977. I am grateful to the management for prints of the original drawings, from which Robert Daverman made the drawings for this article.

16. Andrew Malcolm, *The Canadians* (New York, 1985), 292.

Chapter 6

1. For a comprehensive history of this company, see Wayne G. Broehl, *John Deere's Company: A History of Deere and Company and Its Times* (New York, 1984). It is somewhat astonishing that this work, of 870 pages, can find no space for any mention of Eckerman and that Sklovsky plays only a minor role.

2. Material on Eckerman is scarce. His obituary in the *Moline Times Dispatch*, 3 Mar. 1950, gives a few details. Information on his education at the Chicago Art Institute comes from a letter to the author from Janice Harvey, Assistant Recorder, 7 Oct. 1974. There is no record of his activities in the period 1894–1896.

3. Reyner P. Banham, *A Concrete Atlantis* (Cambridge, Mass., 1986), 62.

4. Professor David Billington has clarified the flat slab problem in Chapter 6 of his excellent *Robert Maillart's Bridges: The Art of Engineering* (Princeton, 1979). Billington compares Maillart's tests of 1908 with those of the American engineer Walter Lord in 1910. (The latter were carried out in the Minneapolis warehouse of Deere and Webber.) Maillart arrived at a theory which correctly explained the slab by concentrating on its overall behavior, whereas Lord erred by measuring only local effects. It was, as Billington says, an interesting case of not seeing the forest for the trees.

5. Mete A. Sozen and Chester P. Siess, "Investigation of Multiple-Panel Reinforced Concrete Floor Slabs," *Journal of the American Concrete Institute*, 33 (August 1963):999.

6. *The Book of Chicagoans* (Chicago, 1917), 409–10.

7. Letter from Nathan Lesser to the author, 24 Feb. 1974, and personal conversation, 10 July 1974. The overhead conveyor is illustrated in Edith Covich's, *Max*, 79.

8. Letter from Nathan Lesser.

9. Colin Rowe, "Chicago Frame: Chicago's Place in the Modern Movement," *Architectural Review* 120 (November 1956): 285–89.

10. For recent information on the Spokane warehouse I am indebted to Professor Grant Hildebrand of the University of Washington in a letter of 14 Oct. 1974.

Chapter 8

1. Hoffmann has published two major works on Root. He edited a selection of the architect's writings with accompanying photographs, *The Meanings of Architecture* (New York, 1967) and produced a definitive biography, *The Architecture of John Wellborn Root* (Baltimore, 1973).

2. Centennial pamphlet, Morley Brothers.

3. Donald Hoffmann, *The Meanings of Architecture: Buildings and Writings by John Wellborn Root* (New York, 1967), 164.

4. Ibid.

5. Ibid., 17.

6. Ibid., 19.

7. Centennial pamphlet, Morley Brothers.

8. Harriet Monroe, *John Wellborn Root: A Study of His Life and Work* (1896; reprint, Chicago: Prairie School Press, 1966), 70.

9. *Marquette Mining Journal*, 27 June 1890. The funeral notice appeared on July 12, 1890. Case left a wife and four children whom I have been unable to trace.

10. No drawings for the house exist in the Root collection of the Burnham library. It is, however, listed in Miss Monroe's compendium of 1896, and the architects are also mentioned in the newspaper article just cited. There should, then, be no hesitancy in attribution.

11. G. W. Hayden to E. E. Foote, esq., 5 Feb. 1873. Michigan Historical Collections.

12. *Marquette, Michigan* brochure published by the Citizen's Association (Marquette, 1891), 69.

13. I owe the suggestion of these affiliations to a generous letter of Mr. Donald Hoffmann, 10 Aug. 1972. The analysis is my own.

14. *Marquette Mining Journal*, 24 Dec. 1887.

15. James D. Kornwolf has given probably the most comprehensive exposition of this theme in his *M. H. Baillie Scott and the Arts and Crafts Movement* (Baltimore, 1971). I have myself devoted some attention to it in *The Architecture of Samuel Maclure* (Exhibition Catalogue, Victoria, B.C., 1971).

16. Since taking possession a few years ago, the present owners of the house, a university professor and his wife, have found themselves impelled to entertain a good deal more than they had done previously.

17. *Marquette Mining Journal*, 24 Dec. 1887.

Chapter 9

1. Major James A. Rollins to Mr. Warner of the American Art Union, 11 Jan. 1852. Quoted in Maurice Bloch, *George Caleb Bingham: The Evolution of an Artist* (Berkeley, 1967).

2. Bloch, *Bingham*, 145.

3. *Missouri Statesman*, 16 May 1856.

4. Albert Christ-Janer, *George Caleb Bingham: Frontier Painter of Missouri* (New York, 1975), 51.

5. Bloch, *Bingham*, 168.

6. Joshua Taylor, *The Fine Arts in America* (Chicago, 1979), 79.

7. Marshall Davidson, "Democracy Delineated," *American Heritage*, October 1980, 12.

8. Bloch, *Bingham*, 9–11.

9. John Vollmer Mering, *The Whig Party in Missouri* (Columbia, Mo., 1967), 67.

10. George C. Bingham to J. S. Rollins, 9 Dec. 1860 in "Letters of George Caleb Bingham," *Missouri Historical Review* 32 (1937–1938):504. The letter is part of a long and valuable series between Bingham and Rollins covering the period 1837–1861.

11. The phrase occurs in Robert G. Gunderson, *The Log Cabin Campaign* (Lexington, Ky., 1957), 160. A fashion for stump-speaking swept the country, and old John Quincy Adams, who had grown up in an age when politics were more restrained, observed in his diary, "The practice of itinerant speechmaking has suddenly broken forth in this country to a fearful extent."

12. John W. Bear, *The Life and Travels of John W. Bear, the Buckeye Blacksmith* (Baltimore, 1873). Bear's autobiography offers a considerable insight into the conditions of political campaigning in the pre–Civil War period. When he spoke at Chestnut Hill, the party organized a force of fifty picked men to protect him, and he was actually mobbed at Reading.

13. Bingham to Rollins, *Missouri Historical Review* 32 (1937–1938):15. Of these only the portraits of Adams and Webster have come to light. The Adams portrait is in the Rollins Collection at Columbia, Missouri, while the Webster portrait is in the Gilcrease Institute of American Art and History at Tulsa, Oklahoma. The committee of the legislature which reviewed the election also threw out five of Sappington's votes. Since Bingham's original majority had been three, he lost by two votes. The legislative records indicate an extraordinarily close review of every contested vote. The grounds for disallowance were age, alienage, and failure to comply with the residence requirement. Bingham acted as his own attorney, and it must have been an exceptionally grueling contest.

14. Bingham to Rollins, 10 March 1848. Quoted in Mering, *Whig Party in Missouri*, 145.

15. Ibid., 244.

16. In the twenty-ninth Congress Congressman David Wilmot of Pennsylvania offered an amendment to an appropriation bill: "That, as an express and fundamental condition to the acquisitions of any territory from the Republic of Mexico . . . neither slavery nor involuntary servitude shall ever exist in any part of said territory, except for crime, whereof the party shall first be duly convicted." From this time onward the slavery question was prominent in almost every aspect of local, state, and national politics. Ultimately it played the major role in the breakdown of the party system which led to the Civil War. For a brilliant discussion of the Proviso, see David M. Potter, *The Impending Crisis 1848–1861*, completed and edited by Don E. Fehrenbacher (New York, 1976). The quotation is taken from *The Congressional Globe*. In a footnote on p. 21, Potter summarizes the extensive literature on the Proviso.

17. Potter, *Impending Crisis*, 244.

18. Ibid.

19. Daniel Howe, *The Political Culture of the American Whigs* (Chicago, 1979), 123–49.

20. Howe, *Political Culture*, 128.

21. James Fenimore Cooper, *The American Democrat* (New York, 1956), 72. Cooper reserved his sharpest strictures for the subject of political parties. That parties were necessary to liberty, he held, was a mistaken opinion. On the contrary, parties encouraged prejudice, were instruments of error, were vicious and corrupt, and had destroyed local independence. Where parties ruled, the people did not rule, but only such a part of them as could manage to get control of the party. Parties misled the public mind as to the rights and duties of a citizen. Many of his comments parallel de Tocqueville's theory of the tyranny of the majority. The United States in Cooper's time did not take criticism easily, and his book raised a storm of protest.

22. George M. Frederickson, *The Inner Civil War* (New York, 1965), 31–32.

23. Potter, *Impending Crisis*, 95.

24. Carl Sandburg, *Abraham Lincoln: The Prairie Years* (New York, 1954), 107.

25. *Journal of the House of Representatives of the State of Missouri* (Jefferson City, 1845), appendix, 222.

26. Bear, *Life and Travels*, 150.

27. Bingham to Rollins, 27 June 1852. *Missouri Historical Review* 32 (1937–1938):24.

28. Albert J. Beveridge, *Abraham Lincoln, 1809–1858*, vol. 2 (Boston, 1928), 164. Beveridge notes that it is an oddity that no records of Lincoln's activities in 1852, when he was Illinois member of the National Whig Committee, are known to exist. The Kansas-Nebraska bill of 1854 called him into action once more. The parallel with Bingham is accurate in the sense that both men had pursued dual careers. Both had reached a certain level of eminence in state politics by 1852. And in the next few years both achieved substantial success, Bingham in art and Lincoln in the law. So far as is known the two men never met, though Bingham produced an uncanny likeness of Lincoln when he painted *Stump Speaking*. By 1856 both men had gone over to the newly formed Republican party, though Bingham declared that in Missouri he might support the American ticket as the surest means of weakening the Democrats. Here the parallel ends. Bingham sailed for Europe in August 1856 and therefore did not vote in the presidential election of that year. Lincoln went on to the White House.

29. The most judicious discussion of the Kansas-Nebraska bill is in Potter, *Impending Crisis*, 145–76. For an important insight into the character of Stephen A. Douglas, I am indebted to Professor Shaw Livermore of the history department

at the University of Michigan.

30. Bingham to Rollins, 1 Feb. 1854, *Missouri Historical Review* 32 (1937–1938):177–78.

31. The quotation is from Carl Sandburg's *Abraham Lincoln: The Prairie Years*, vol. 2 (New York, 1926), 14. Sandburg's analysis is perhaps the best short treatment of the speech. Beveridge, *Abraham Lincoln*, 243–62 is also excellent.

32. Bingham to Rollins, 2 June 1856. *Missouri Historical Review* 32 (1937–1938): 195.

33. Bloch, *Bingham*, 135–36. It is significant that Burnet in his treatise devoted fully two-thirds of his illustrations to the Dutch School. He particularly praised Ostade's *Country Fair*.

34. Ibid., 302–3.

35. E. P. Richardson, *American Art: A Narrative and Critical Catalogue* (San Francisco, 1976), 84. I am indebted to the late Mr. Richardson for his support in preparing this essay.

36. The lecture is entitled "Art, the Ideal of Art, and the Utility of Art," and it is reprinted in Albert Christ Janer, *George Caleb Bingham of Missouri* (New York, 1940), 120–28. Bingham wrote it in 1879 for a University Series of Public Lectures, but because of his illness it was delivered by Major J. S. Rollins.

37. Sir Joshua Reynolds, *Discourses on Art*, ed. R. R. Wark (New Haven 1975), 109–10. Sir Joshua's attitude toward the Dutch recalls Edward Hanslick's famous criticisms of Richard Wagner. No matter what Hanslick wrote, people continued to respond enthusiastically to Wagner's operas.

38. Steen did, in fact, draw on Raphael's *School of Athens* for the composition of his *School for Boys and Girls*, (1670). See Graham Smith, "Steen and Raphael," *The Burlington Magazine*, March 1981, 159–61.

39. Alan Cunningham, *The Cabinet Gallery of Pictures Selected from the Splendid Collections of Art, Public and Private, which Adorn Great Britain, with Biographical and Critical Description*, 2 vols. (London, 1833 and 1834). These volumes were reprinted by the great remainder publishers Virtue & Co. in 1836. Cunningham analyzed pictures by Ferdinand Bol, Teniers, Jacob Ruysdael, Rembrandt, Steen, Ostade, Mieris, and Maes. "Cabinet" simply means "Domestic Scale."

40. Anna Wells Rutledge, "Robert Gilmor, Baltimore Collector," *Journal of the Walters Art Gallery* 12 (1949):19–40.

41. For information on the Stier Collection, see Lois Engelson, "The Influence of Dutch Landscape Painting on the American Landscape Tradition" (M.A. thesis, Columbia University, 1967), 7–9. The collection included Rubens's *Chapeau de Paille* now in the Louvre, as well as other notable works. In 1816, after the overthrow of Napoleon, Stier tried to sell his collection to his son-in-law for $70,000, but the offer was refused. It was returned to Europe and broken up.

42. E. P. Richardson, letter to the author, 10 Nov. 1975.

43. For a cumulative record, see *Exhibition Catalogues of the Pennsylvania Academy of Fine Arts, 1807–1870*, comp. Anna Wells Rutledge (Philadelphia, 1955). A recent treatment of Dutch influence in H. Nichols and B. Clark, "A Taste for the Dutch," *American Art Journal*, Spring 1982, 23–38. Clark concentrates on genre painting.

44. Mabel Munson Swan, *The Athenaeum Gallery, 1827–73: The Boston Athenaeum as an Early Patron of Art* (Boston, 1949), 18, 20.

45. On the Academy and The Art Union, see Bartlett Cowdrey, *American Academy of Fine Arts and American Art Union, 1816–52*, 2 vol. with a history of the American Academy by Theodore Sizer and a foreword by James Flexner (New York, 1953).

46. Bloch, *Bingham*, 37.

47. Nancy Davison, "E. N. Clay: American Political Cartoonist of the Jacksonian Era" (Ph.D. dissertation, University of Michigan, 1980), 43–84.

48. John Lothrop Motley, *The Life and Times of John of Barneveld*, vol. 3 (New York, 1872), 45–46.

49. William H. Seward, *Autobiography*, ed. F. W. Seward (N.Y., 1872), 117–18.

50. Christopher Brown, *Images of a Golden Past: Dutch Genre Painting of the 11th Century* (New York, 1984). Brown generally follows the analysis of L. A. Emmens in *Tot Lering en Vermaak* (Amsterdam, 1976) but notes that not all Dutch genre painting is so allegorical.

51. *The Drawings of Rembrandt*, introduction, commentary, and supplementary material by Seymour Slive, 2 vol. (New York, 1965), vol. 2, Plate 465.

52. Keith Andrews, *English Watercolours and Other Drawings: The Helen Barlow Bequest* (Edinburgh, 1979), illustration 38, no page numbers.

53. The drawing, 173 × 270 mm in black chalk and grey wash, is illustrated in H. Vey, *Sammlung H. Girardet: Hollandische und Vlammische Meistern* (Köln-Rotterdam, 1970), Fig. 82. Bylaert was a Rotterdam engraver who frequently did work of this kind.

54. For the history of the contents of Ostade's studio, see Alfred von Wurzbach, *Nederlandisch Kurnstlerlexikon*, vol. 2 (Vienna and Leipzig, 1910), 273–76. The figures of Ostade's dancing peasants may be a possible source for the dancers in Bingham's *Jolly Flatboatmen in Port*. In my view this is more probable than the suggestion of influence by Steen in Denis O'Neill's "Dutch Influences in American Painting," *Antiques* 104 (1973): 1076–79.

55. Matthew Pilkington, *The Gentleman's and Connoisseur's Dictionary of Painters*, vol. 2 (London, 1798), 635. Pilkington is a fine example of the English antiquary. He was vicar of Donabath and Portrain in the diocese of Dublin and an expert linguist. His dictionary was the first of its kind in English and was read well into the nineteenth century.

56. Sir Joshua Reynolds, *The Works*, ed. Edmond Malone, (New York, 1971), vol. 2, 86. The remark was made in "A Journey to Flanders and Holland in the year 1781."

57. Allan Cunningham, *The Cabinet Gallery of Pictures Selected from the Splendid Collections of Art, Public and Private, which Adorn Great Britain, with Biographical and Critical Description*, vol. 2, (London, 1833 and 1834), 437.

58. Linda Nochlin, "In Detail: Courbet's *A Burial at Ornans*," *Portfolio*, Nov.-Dec. 1980, 33–37. Nochlin notes that Dutch art, from at least the time of the 1848 revolution, was associated with ideals of political liberty, rebellions against oppression, and republican government.

59. Bloch, *Bingham*, 148. Pope also pointed out that Bingham worked in the traditions of the old masters from a highly finished series of drawings. For Wilkie and the Dutch, see Jeremy Maas, *Victorian Painters* (New York, 1969). According to George Beaumont, Wilkie saw a picture by Teniers and at once painted *The Village Politicians*, one of his most popular works.

60. Page Smith, *A People's History of the United States: The Nation Comes of Age* (New York, 1981), 30. Cities like St. Louis were the exceptions to the generalizations.

61. Ibid., 487. Smith is generally good on Bingham but errs when he writes that Bingham was "untroubled by subtle aesthetic consideration," 956.

62. William Catton and Bruce Catton, *Two Roads to Sumter* (New York, 1963), 34–35.

63. Bingham to Rollins, 12 Dec. 1853, *Missouri Historical Review* 32 (1937–1938):171–72.

64. Bloch, *Bingham*, 159.

65. Ibid.

66. Barbara S. Groseclose, "Painting, Politics and George Caleb Bingham," *The American Art Journal* 10 (1978), 14.

67. Davidson, "Democracy Delineated," *American Heritage*, 12 Oct. 1980.

68. Robert F. Westervelt, "The Whig Painter from Missouri," *American Art Journal* 2 (1970):46–53; Barbara A. Groseclose, "Politics, Painting, and George Caleb Bingham, *American Art Journal* 10 (1978):5–19.

69. Smith, *A People's History of the United States*, 954.

70. Parts of this interpretation I owe to Professor Bryan Wolf of Yale University in a colloquium at the University of Michigan, 12 April 1982.

71. David C. Huntington, *The Landscapes of Frederick Edwin Church: Vision of an American Era* (New York, 1966) and Barbara Novak, *American Painting of the Nineteenth Century: Realism, Idealism, and the American Experience* (New York, 1969), 129–31. For a further treatment of the subject, see National Gallery of Art, *American Light: The Luminist Movement 1850–75* (Washington, D.C., 1980). This magnificent catalogue of a major exhibition at the National Gallery of Art is essential for any study of luminism. It contains essays by both Huntington and Novak.

72. John I. H. Baur, "The Peales and the Development of American Still Life," *The Art Quarterly* 3 (1940):80–91; Samuel Green, *American Art and Architecture* (New York, 1971). More recently William H. Girdts has taken up the same theme in *American Still Life Painting (New York, 1971)*. It should be noted that E. P. Richardson proposed a Dutch model in *The Checker Players* by George Caleb Bingham," *Art Quarterly* 15 (1950):252–56 and that Ross Taggart commented on the Dutch quality of Bingham's landscape in *George Caleb Bingham—Sesquicentennial Exhibition* (Kansas City, Mo., 1961), 7.

73. Engelson, "Influence of Dutch Landscape Painting" (M.A. thesis, Columbia University, 1969). Barbara Novak comments on the problem in *Nature and Culture* (New York, 1980), 231–35, and in her contribution to *American Light*. See also the excellent, as yet unpublished, paper by A. G. H. Bachrach, "Early American Marine Painting and its Anglo-Dutch Models," prepared for the Symposium "Politics, Economics and the Arts: The Netherlands and the Foundation of the American Republic," UCLA, 1982.

74. Samuel Eliot Morison, *The Maritime History of Massachusetts* (Boston, 1921), 372–73.

75. Mount painted the picture in 1835 at the house of General Satterlee on Long Island. He used two south windows to divide the two lights. See Alfred Frankenstein, *William Sidney Mount* (New York, 1977), 249.

76. Barbara Novak comments on the problem of affinity vs. influence in *Nature and Culture* (New York, 1980), 231–35. It is also a major theme of the excellent exhibition catalogue, *Primitivism and Modern Art* (Detroit, 1985).

77. Review of *The Letters of Ernest Hemingway*, ed. Carlos Baker (New York, 1982) as reprinted in *The Sunday Times* (London), 27 April 1981, 33.

Afterword

1. Roger Kennedy, *Architecture, Men, Women, and Money* (New York, 1985), 8.

Index

Sacred Sands: The Struggle for Community in the Indiana Dunes (Engel), 132

St. Joseph, Mo., 18–38; National Register buildings, 18; Railroad Station (Eckel), 23

St. Louis, Mo.: as gateway city, 3

St. Paul, Minn., 39–59; in 1887, **43**; Mears Park, **43**; reuse of old buildings, 59

St. Paul Pioneer Press: on Hackett Hardware Store, 52, 53–54

St. Paul Pioneer Press Building (Beman), 34, 42

Salem Harbor (Lane), 183, **184**

Selections from an Architect's Portfolio (Mann): on the Nave-McCord Building, 26; on Tootle, Hosea & Co., 35

Shipping off the Coast (Van de Capelle), 183, **183**

Sklovsky, Max, 120, 125, 128

Smith, Charles Daniel, 31–32

Smith, George H.: Cleveland Arcade, 34

Smith, George W., 66

Steen, Jan, 173–76; *Quack Doctor, The,* 174, **175**

Stevens, J. Walter: Noyes-Cutler Warehouse (St. Paul), 44, 46–49, **47, 48, 49, 50**; Powers Drygoods Company (St. Paul), 45, 50–52, **50, 51, 75**

Still Life with Oranges (Peale), 182, **183**

Stobart, Frederick W., 95

Stump Orator, The (Bingham), 162–63, **163**

Stump Speaking, or *County Caucus, The* (Bingham), 154–55, **154**, 162–64, 177, 178–79, 180, 181

Sullivan, Louis, 3, 4; admiration for Marshall Field store, 13; Carson Pirie Scott store, 5; and Elmslie, 79; Henry Babson house (Riverside, Ill.), 138–39, **138**; influence on Fairbanks—Morse Building, 78, 79; influence on Fairchild Block, 99; influence on Noyes-Cutler Warehouse, 47, **47**; and Jens Jensen, 136, 138–39, **138**; Prudential Guaranty Building, 37; Wainwright Building, 120

Sullivan and Elmslie: Owatonna, 79

Timberg, Judith: on Fairbanks-Morse Building, 79

Tootle, Milton, 33–34

Tootle, Hosea, and Company, St. Joseph (Eckel and Mann), 22, 33–35, **33, 34, 35**

Tripp, C. A.: Bemis Bag Building (Omaha), 76–77, **76**

Turner, Charles A. P.: reinforced concrete construction, 116; the Turner system, 119

Turner, Richard E., 26–27

Turner-Frazer Mercantile Company, St. Joseph (Eckel and Mann), 26–27, **27**

United States Courthouse and Post Office, Omaha, 83

United States National Bank Building, Omaha (Hodgson and Son), 67, 83

Van de Capelle, Jan: *Shipping off the Coast,* 183, **183**

Van Ostade, Adrian: *Quack Doctor, The,* 172–73, **173**; *Village Fair, The,* 172–73, **173**, 181; *Villagers Merrymaking at an Inn,* 185, **186**

Van Ostade, Circle of Adrian: *L'Aracheur des Dents,* 169, **169**

Verdict of the People, The. See Announcement of the Election Returns

Vertical space, use of, 70

Village Fair, The (van Ostade), 172–73, **173**, 181

Village Festival, A (Droochsloot), 167–68, **168**, 181

Villagers Merrymaking at an Inn (Van Ostade), 185, **186**

Voss, Henry: Richardson Wholesale Drug Company (Omaha), 73–75, **73, 74**

Wainwright Building, St. Louis (Sullivan), 120

Walker Warehouse, Chicago (Sullivan), 13, 47, **47**

Walking the Line (Mount), 185, **185**

Walter Gale house, Oak Park, Ill. (Wright), 148–49, **149**

Warehouse, the, 9; architects, 13–15; distribution systems, 120

Warehouse construction: loadbearing capacity, 16; weight of steel required for flat slab, **119**.

Warehouse demolition, preservation, and reuse: Con Agra, Inc., and, 81–83; of Gault Block, 97; of Gotzian Block 45–46; Humana Corp. and, 17, 83; and Lowertown Development Corp., 43; of M. E. Smith Warehouses, 17; of Noyes-Cutler Warehouse, 49; in Omaha, 81–83; of Paxton Hotel, 93; of Powers Drygoods Co., 51; of Richardson Wholesale Drug Building, 74; in St. Paul, 43–44, 59; in the twentieth century, 15–17; in Winnipeg, 110–12

Western Architect: on Eckel, 23; on the Nave-McCord Building, 25

Western Association of Architects, 14, 23

Wheeler, Charles, 89; Galt Brothers Wholesale Grocery (Winnipeg), 90–92, **90, 91**

Whitla, Robert J., 99

Wholesale businessmen: characteristics of, 8, 9; warehouses as symbols of, 9, 19, 21–2

Wholesale Merchants and Peddlers, 1900, **8**

Wilhelmy, John F., 68–69

Wilkie, Sir David: *Chelsea Pensioners Receiving the News,* 176, **177**

Winnipeg, 84–112, **85, 86, 87, 91**; architects, 88–90; in 1884, 86, **86**; in 1912, 87, **87**; Princess Street, **91**; railroads, 85–86; warehouse preservation and reuse, 110–12

Winnipeg Commercial: on F. W. Stobart Building, 94–95

Winnipeg Historic Preservation Committee, 97

Wright, Frank Lloyd, 3, 4; *Frank Lloyd Wright: Writings and Buildings,* 141; and Jens Jensen, 134, 136, 140–41; Larkin Co. (Buffalo), 70; Longyear Roberts house (Marquette, Mich.), 140–41, **141**; Walter Gale house (Oak Park, Ill.), 148–49, **149**

Wright and Wilhelmy Wholesale Hardware, Omaha (Fowler and Beindorff; Latenser), 67–69, **68, 69, 83**